Drawing **from the Model**
Fundamentals of Digital Drawing, 3D Modeling, and Visual Programming in Architectural Design

Frank Melendez

WILEY

For general information about our other products and services, please contact our Customer Care Department within the United States at (800) 762-2974, outside the United States at (317) 572-3993 or fax (317) 572-4002.

Wiley publishes in a variety of print and electronic formats and by print-on-demand. Some material included with standard print versions of this book may not be included in e-books or in print-on-demand. If this book refers to media such as a CD or DVD that is not included in the version you purchased, you may download this material at http://booksupport.wiley.com. For more information about Wiley products, visit www.wiley.com.

Cover image: Courtesy of PATH

Cover design: Wiley

Library of Congress Cataloging-in-Publication Data is available upon request

ISBN: 978-1-119-11562-5
ISBN: 978-1-119-11564-9 (ebk.)
ISBN: 978-1-119-11563-2 (ebk.)

Printed in the United States of America

V1008599_030919

Contents

Part 4: Computational Design

Foreword

As pervasive as Laugier's Primitive Hut myth, the "napkin sketch" occupies a powerful place in architecture's disciplinary and professional narrative. The image, indeed expectation, of the artistic genius sketching out a design, one that is seamlessly realized, with nothing but cocktails, a fountain pen, and a napkin as aids, has simplified the incredible complexities and collaborative systems that have always been required to put a building together. The discipline's embrace of the napkin sketch paradigm has arguably been a force in resisting the integration of new technologies into the teaching of architectural design and visualization. Architecture still likes to think of itself as a creative endeavor, and the transition from the fountain pen to digital tools came to symbolize an abdication of individual authorship. However, the advancements of the technologies and techniques outlined in *Drawing from the Model* reveal the promise to rethink what drawing is, and consequently to embrace the interplay of intention, intuition, iteration, and integration that has always been a part of the design process.

Historically, these first two "i's" (intention and intuition) have been foreground, and reflected by the napkin-sketch scenario. While *Drawing from the Model* does not deny their importance, its focus on the interplay of drawing, model, and technology puts a spotlight on the pedagogical importance of iteration and integration. In this volume, "drawing" and "model" are terms that flow between digital and manual techniques, as intertwined players in a process of discovery and materialization. As such, in considering the role of drawing and modeling as teachers, we need to shift our obsession with physical output and understand how different tools can expand the various possibilities for cognitive and creative input. How can our students move fluidly between tools to sketch; to ideate; to translate between two-dimensional drawing and three-dimensional space and volume; to evaluate; to fabricate; to collaborate with others; to represent in four dimensions; to simulate the real; to foreground the idea over the real? The boundlessness of what drawing can be and what it can do opens up opportunities and expands our notion of architectural creativity.

Digital tools have become an unquestionable part of the design process, and less threatening to the creative territory we architects like to claim as intrinsic. Consequently, we now find ourselves in a post-rendering age, where what drawing and modeling can be is ever-widening. This is the perfect time to acknowledge the many places that we draw from, and the explore the possible routes to get there that *Drawing from the Model* presents us.

Sunil Bald

Sunil Bald is founding partner of studioSUMO and associate dean and professor at the Yale School of Architecture where he teaches design and visualization.

Acknowledgments

This project was initiated while teaching at The Bernard and Anne Spitzer School of Architecture, City College of New York (CCNY). Many faculty, staff, and students have been supportive of this project and have contributed in various ways. I would like to thank the following faculty members for their guidance, suggestions, and critical feedback during this process: Gordon Gebert, Julio Salcedo-Fernandez, Jeremy Edmiston, Marta Gutman, Michael Sorkin, M.T. Chang, and Bradley Horn. This book was supported in part by The Bernard and Anne Spitzer School of Architecture, CCNY. Thank you to the Spitzer family for their support of the school. Thank you to Camille Hall. Thank you to Hannah Deegan for her assistance. Many of the drawings and images in this book are the result of architectural representation and digital design courses that I have coordinated and taught over the past few years at The Bernard and Anne Spitzer School of Architecture, CCNY, as well as courses that I taught at Carnegie Mellon University. I would like to thank my colleagues who have helped to shape these courses and all of the students who have contributed their work.

I would like to thank the following reviewers for their generosity in providing great comments and suggestions: John Eberhart, Susannah Dickinson, Mara Marcu, Bradley Cantrell, Chrisopher Dial, Yichen Lu, and Michael Young.

A special thank you to Sunil Bald for writing the foreword to this book. I'm very grateful for his insight and meaningful contribution to this project.

I would like to express my gratitude and a appreciation to all of the talented architects, artists, and designers who supported and contributed to this book by providing drawings, renderings, photographs, and other images of their exemplary projects and work. Also to all of the foundations and organizations who provided access to resources as well as permission to include images from their collections in this publication.

I would like to thank Robert McNeel and Jody Mills for their support and the various individuals who contribute to the Rhinoceros and Grasshopper software, add-ons, communities, and forums.

Thank you to the editorial and production teams at Wiley, in particular Margaret Cummins, Amy Odum, Kalli Schultea, and Vishnu Narayanan, Amy Handy for her editorial contributions,and Helen Castle for supporting me in initiating this project with Wiley.

This book was written in part during a residency at the MacDowell Colony in Peterborough, New Hampshire. Thank you to the members of the MacDowell Colony for their support of this project and their larger mission of supporting the arts.

Finally, I would like to thank my family for all of their continuous support and encouragement.

Introduction

Architectural drawing is a communicative medium that is based on our ability to translate ideas pertaining to three-dimensional geometry into two-dimensional representations. Since the Italian Renaissance, the primary mode of representing architecture through drawing has been based on parallel and perspective projection techniques. Although other mediums of architectural representation have developed from technological advances such as photography and film, drawing remained the primary communicative medium of architecture. With advances in computing and the invention of computer-aided design (CAD) tools in the 1960s, the production of architectural drawing shifted from hand drafting to computer-aided drafting. Computer-aided design drawings proved to be more accurate, faster to produce, and easier to correct and copy. While this had a big impact on the production of drawings in both academia and practice, the technique of creating drawings by two-dimensional drafting methods remained the same. It wasn't until advances in 3D modeling, beginning in the 1990s, that the role of drawing in architecture was called into question. 3D models provided opportunities to generate and visualize new geometries and forms based on topology. This visual imagery relished the appearance of rendered, seamless surfaces, often output as matrices from animation sequences. Digital models demonstrated the potential for iterative designs based on variable parameters. Animation software introduced temporality to the virtual environment, and the impact of forces and behaviors on geometry and form. As computational technologies continued to evolve, so did the digital tools, techniques, and workflows used to design, model, and draw architecture. Today, 3D models, in tandem with visual-programming tools, offer architects and designers new methods for generating geometry, forms, and systems through the use of scripting and algorithmic processes that continue to impact architectural design and representation.

Drawing from the Model presents design students and professionals with a broad overview of drawing and modeling in architectural representation, beginning with historical analog methods based on descriptive geometry and projection, and transitioning to contemporary digital techniques and workflows based on computational processes and emerging technologies.

Part 1 offers an overview of drawing, modeling, and computing, with descriptions and examples of drawings that range from hand sketching to computational visualizations, and descriptions and examples of models that range from analog material performance studies to digital physics-based simulations. Additional content includes methods that blur the boundaries of physical and digital environments, such as scanning and digital fabrication technologies.

Part 2 provides an overview of digital drawing and 3D modeling tools, techniques, and workflows for creating geometry in Robert McNeel & Associates Rhinoceros® (Rhino 6 for Windows) software. This includes descriptions of vectors, splines, and NURBS (nonuniform rational B-splines) geometry to better understand the mechanics of digital models. Methods for generating various types of surface geometries, such as planes, ruled surfaces, and doubly curved surfaces, are described and depicted through examples of paradigmatic works of architecture.

Part 3 focuses on the use of linework to create architectural drawings. Readers are introduced to conventional architectural drawings, such as plans, sections, elevations, axonometrics, and perspectives, and methods for creating projections within digital modeling environments. This section describes methods for exporting linework to the vector-based software Adobe Illustrator® CC, to apply line weights, line types, color, text, and other graphic qualities to produce and enhance architectural drawings.

Part 4 provides an overview of computational design processes including an introduction to parametric and algorithmic modeling tools through visual programming processes in Grasshopper®, a node-based algorithmic editor for Rhino. Readers will be introduced to scripting procedures for developing various types of incrementally varying patterns, modular assemblies, and emergent forms. Through visual programming add-ons for Grasshopper, such as Ladybug, Kangaroo, and Firefly, environmental data visualizations, physics-based simulations, and physical computing technologies can be explored as novel tools for architectural design and representation. This section introduces the topics of robotics and physical computing platforms as instruments for creating experimental drawings and visualizations by using Arduino microcontrollers to drive drawing machines.

In summary, *Drawing from the Model* presents a comprehensive overview of digital drawing and modeling skill sets that are required in contemporary architectural education. This opens up new possibilities and approaches to teaching and learning architectural drawing in a manner that builds on the history of drawing, while preparing students and future generations of architects for designing architectures that are based in computation, automation, responsive design, and robotics.

Part 1
Architectural Representation and Digital Technologies

Part 1 focuses on the topics of *drawing*, *modeling*, and *computing technologies*, and situates these terms within the context of architectural design and representation. This begins with an overview of architectural drawing based on how we (humans) perceive the forms and spaces that surround us and the use of drawing as a tool for visual expressions based on our observations and imagination. This includes the use of analog and digital tools for creating two-dimensional projections of three-dimensional geometry, and conventional and novel methods of drawing that range from the dexterity of the hand and pencil to the processing of computational algorithms.

This section describes the role of architectural models and their application in various stages of the design process. Architectural representation includes the use of physical models, real materials, to sketch and to create experimental, performative instruments, as well as the use of digital models, and virtual environments, to create geometry, explore topologies, parametrically driven iterations, algorithmic processes, and computational simulations. Additionally, technologies such as virtual, augmented, and mixed reality, and scanning devices, provide new methods for visualizing digital environments and digitizing physical spaces. This ability to navigate back and forth between the real and the virtual is continuing to blur what used to be distinct boundaries between these two worlds, through advances in digital fabrication tools. Digital models can be output directly to various rapid prototyping machines and industrial robots, and realized as physical, material constructs. Conversely, physical elements can be scanned and data can be used to drive digital models. Computing technologies continue to evolve and expand abilities for working fluidly between analog and digital processes, opening up new possibilities that are expanding the role of architectural drawing and representation.

Chapter 1
Architectural Drawing

Chapter 1 provides an overview of the role of drawing in architectural design and various methods that are utilized for creating design drawings through analog and digital techniques. This begins with how we (humans) experience the world; including the perception of our surrounding environment and our ability to form mental images. Architectural drawing is based on our ability to see and imagine physical forms and objects, and to translate three-dimensional geometry into two-dimensional representations through descriptive geometry and projection techniques. This process plays a critical role in architectural design and the construction of buildings.

Various drawing methods provide architects and designers with the ability to visualize, represent, and communicate information through hand sketches, technical drawings, three-dimensional projections, simulations, and visualizations, to name a few. These various historical and contemporary analog and digital techniques can be applied throughout various stages of the architectural design process, expanding the tools that are available to architects and designers. This presents a new paradigm in architectural representation and the education of architectural drawing, which ranges from the development of visual acuity and dexterity that is required for hand sketching and drawing, to the development of coding skills for generating computational simulations and visualizations. In this chapter, the role of architectural drawing is presented as an increasingly expansive field that ranges from analog representations based on visual observation to computational simulations based on input parameters and data.

1.1 Drawing and Perception

"A line is a dot that went for a walk."

—Paul Klee

This well-known definition of a line by the German artist Paul Klee seems simultaneously to express the simplicity and the complexity of the subject and the act of drawing. The analogy comparing a line to a dot going for a walk is fairly straightforward. The tip of a pencil can be placed on a piece of paper to create a dot (point), and moved along a trajectory to create a line. This is something that most children can do instinctively when handed a piece of paper and a pencil. However, we might find ourselves confronted with other questions when drawing a line, such as: What do I want to draw? Where on the page should I start my drawing? Do I want to draw something that I am observing, or something that I am imagining? What am I trying to represent or communicate? When these questions arise, a connection between drawing and thought is established.

The act of drawing has been used throughout human history to express thoughts and communicate information. From prehistoric markings found on the walls of caves to contemporary data visualizations generated by computational processes, humans have utilized various types of tools to make marks—points, lines, curves, shapes, and forms—to create drawings as a method for visualizing a thought or idea, representing an object or place, storytelling, communicating information to others, and for many other reasons and applications.

Klee's drawing titled *In Engelshut* (*In Angel's Care*) at first glance appears to be a very simple, almost childlike illustration of a few closed shapes, depicting various elements of overlapping figures. (See Figure 1.1.) However, the overlapping shapes result in the generation of other figures and blur the reading of any one specific figure. This simultaneity of forms creates a dynamic, multi-dimensional quality in his work.[1] The resulting nonhierarchical juxtaposition of shapes eliminates any singular reading

Figure 1.1. Paul Klee, *In Engelshut (In Angel's Care),* 1931.

of a recognizable form, and creates a visual ambiguity in the drawing, which shifts depending on how the viewer combines the various shapes in their mind. This is due to the human sense of vision and our ability to recognize shapes and edges as a way of mentally processing the objects and forms that we see in the world. Through the elimination of a recognizable pattern this drawing sparks an awareness of this phenomenon, which leaves the work open for interpretation by the viewer. The simultaneous reading of various figural elements and shape combinations creates a visual complexity through the use of a few relatively simple lines and shapes.

Patterns and Light

The human senses of seeing, hearing, smelling, tasting, and touching allow individuals to experience and understand their surroundings. Of the five primary senses, the most effective one for understanding our situational environment is the human sense of sight, which uses light energy to detect formal and spatial information such as shapes, textures, depth, and color. This information varies based on the amount of light that is diffracted as it passes through a medium, or absorbed and reflected by a surface. Eyes receive light of varying intensity and wavelength as an image in the retina, which the brain processes as a spatially related pattern.[2] The human mind and eye process images through pattern matching, comparing a pattern to an image that has been previously stored in the brain.[3] Patterns can be recognized through the visual perception of *edges* and *contours*. For example, in the *Kanizsa Triangle,* the illusion of a triangle is created by the juxtaposition of line segments and major circular sectors, which allow the mind and eye to form visual connections between the geometry. This results in the perception of a solid white triangle, as well as the appearance of depth, with the illusion of the white triangle appearing in the foreground. (See Figure 1.2.)

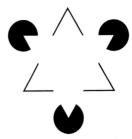

Figure 1.2. Gaetano Kaniska, *Kanizsa Triangle,* 1955. Example of illusory contours. *Courtesy of the author.*

This method, in which the human mind and eye recognize patterns, allows for our ability to recognize three-dimensional forms through two-dimensional representations of their edges. For example, a collection of twelve lines on a two-dimensional, flat surface can be perceived and understood as a three-dimensional form, a box.[4] (See Figure 1.3.) However, the particular arrangement of lines in this example allows for a double visual reading of the box: facing in the upward direction, or facing in the downward direction. A single reading can be achieved by creating hierarchy within the linkwork, such as through the introduction of dashed lines, or by rendering the box to suggest the location of a light source through the use of tone.

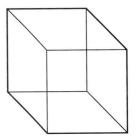

Figure 1.3. A representation of a block form created by a collection of lines. *Courtesy of the author.*

In addition to the detection of contours, the visual reading of shapes, surfaces, and forms can be accentuated through the use of *tone. Tone* is the change in the perception of a color based on the amount of light that strikes a surface. If a light source is located at one end of a surface, the intensity of light that strikes the surfaces varies from one end to the other, lighter on one end and darker on the other. Tonal variations provide the perception of lightness or darkness on a surface to describe the

Figure 1.4. A representation of a sphere created through the use of tonal values. *Courtesy of the author.*

effect of light on a form. For example, a variation in tone that is rendered within a circle changes the perception of a flat, two-dimensional circle into the perception of a round, three-dimensional sphere, and provides an understanding of the light source and the interaction of light with the form. (See Figure 1.4.)

1.2 Drawing from Observation and Imagination

Hand-drawing processes involve the act of creating images of shapes and forms, with linework and tone, using tools such as pencils and pens in mediums such as graphite and ink. This differs from other methods of representation, such as collage, painting, and photography, which utilize other tools and mediums for creating imagery. However, in more recent history, with the invention of the computer and advancements in digital technology, the meanings of the term *drawing* and terms associated with drawing have expanded and can be understood through both analog and digital methods of representations. A *sketch*, for example, which is a quick, rough drawing made by hand, has also been used to describe little computer programs (code), for creating digital two- and three-dimensional graphics.[5] Although the topic of drawing is vast, two common and fundamental methods for hand drawing are drawing from observation and drawing from the imagination. These two methods of drawing, which are referred to in Francis Ching's seminal book on architectural drawing, *Design Drawing*, continue to be fundamental methods for creating visual acuity, improving dexterity, and creative innovation.

Drawing from Observation

Drawing from observation requires an ability to perceive and draw *contours* and *tones*, and the dexterity to control the hand and tool (pencil), to draw the shapes and forms that are being observed. Drawing *contours* allows for the suppression of symbolic abstractions, and instead relies on paying careful attention to experience a subject through the sense of sight.[6] Contours include the edges of a form, where there is a break in the direction of a surface, or where surfaces meet, as well as edges that are created from abrupt changes in the reflection of light on a form or surface, such as the edges of highlights and shadows. Adding tones to the drawing enhances the perception of the form by providing an understanding of its relationship to light. Drawing from observation with contours and tone is a method for enhancing the ability to perceive and understand shapes, surfaces, forms, and light; therefore, it is a technique for expanding our ability to "see." This is a useful skill that provides architects and designers with an acuity for recognizing visual patterns within the surrounding and built environment, representing formal and spatial information, and applying these principles when designing and drawing from the imagination. (See Figure 1.5.)

Figure 1.5. Álvaro Siza, Architect, *Sketch of Machu Pichu.* *Courtesy of Álvaro Siza, Architect.*

Drawing from the Imagination

Architectural design involves creativity and the use of the imagination to invent, problem-solve, and speculate, among many other things, on possible formal and spatial designs. Architecture consists of the design and construction of inhabitable structures. The process of designing architecture involves imagining possible spatial organizations, geometrical relationships, tectonic assemblies, and other complex issues related to designing and fabricating a building. The ability to sketch and draw from the imagination is a useful method for "thinking through an idea," inventing, and solving problems related to these topics.

Architecture is also influenced by many factors outside of design and construction, such as political, social, and economic issues. These factors play a vital role in the design of our built environment. Drawing from the imagination can be a powerful method for expressing architectural ideas that respond to geometry, form, aesthetic, social, economic, political, and other factors, to create visionary images that speculate on possible future architectures, landscapes, urban spaces, and worlds. There are many examples of visionary architectural drawings; some of the most influential are the works of the Italian artist Giovanni Battista Piranesi. In the etchings from his series titled *Carceri d'Invencione (Imaginary Prisons)*, c. 1750, massive forms, structures, cables, and stairways create a dark, ominous, and mysterious atmosphere, conveying a sense of confinement and immensity.[7] (See Figure 1.6.) Some techniques that art critics and historians have described to achieve these effects in the imagery of the prints include a range of tonal contrast, spatial fragmentation, and the experience of observing the spaces in perspective from below.[8] Piranesi's works have influenced the work of many artists, architects, writers, and film makers for centuries.

Figure 1.6. Giovanni Battista Piranesi, *Carceri d'Invencione (Imaginary Prisons)*, Plate XI, The Arch with a Shell Ornament, c. 1750.

The architect Daniel Libeskind has produced a body of work that includes drawings, installations, buildings, and musical performances. His *Micromegas* series of architectural drawings compounds an inventive energy with drawing.[9] (See Figure 1.7.) For Libeskind, architectural drawing is as much a prospective unfolding of future possibilities as it is a recovery of a particular history.[10] The drawings

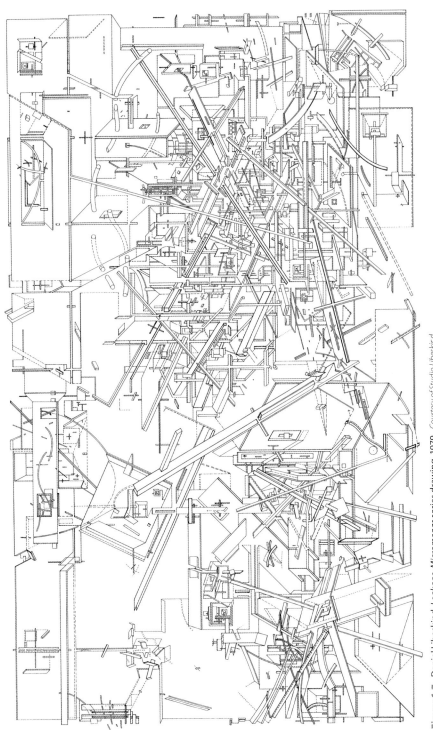

Figure 1.7. Daniel Libeskind, *Leakage, Micromegas series drawing*, 1979. *Courtesy of Studio Libeskir d.*

of Lebbeus Woods often illustrate dystopian architectural conditions as imagery that reflects the political nature of architecture and its ability to influence society.[11] In his drawing *Photon Kite*, from his series *Centricity*, a curvilinear mechanical architecture hovers in the air, defying gravitational forces while maintaining a single connection to its surrounding environment through a tube. (See Figure 1.8.) These drawings and many other examples demonstrate the capacity for architectural drawing to influence, reveal, discover, and invent new scenarios and possibilities for architecture.

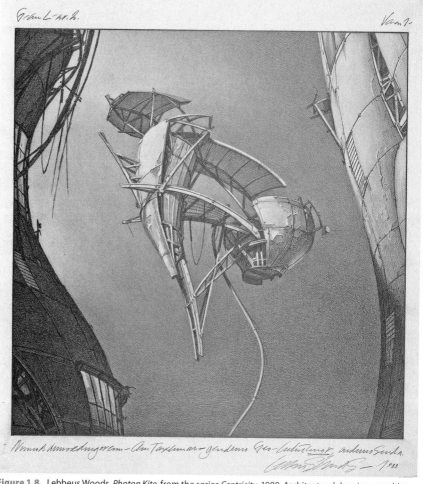

Figure 1.8. Lebbeus Woods, *Photon Kite*, from the series *Centricity*, 1988. Architectural drawing, graphite on paper. *Collection SFMOMA. © Estate of Lebbeus Woods.*

1.3 Drawing and Projection

There are many forms of drawing in architectural design, such as sketches, design drawings, technical drawings, renderings, and other forms of visual imagery. Although architectural drawing plays a critical role in the design and construction of buildings, drawing as a primary method for design and construction did not occur until the Italian Renaissance. Prior to this period, architects communicated information to builders, craftsmen, artisans, and others who labored on site through the use of physical models. The shift to drawing as the primary mode of creating architecture occurred around the mid-fifteenth century when the Florentine polymath Leon Battista Alberti claimed that architecture is an idea, conveyed by the author, notated in drawings, and built by manual workers.[12] During the Renaissance, which started in Italy and spread throughout Western Europe, architectural drawing was advanced through discoveries in descriptive geometry and projection techniques. The role of drawing in architecture took on two functions: the use of drawings as *visualizations* to explore and develop the idea of the building, and the use of drawings as *notational tools* provided to the builders for construction purposes.[13] Alberti also noted the necessity for architecture to convey principles of perfect geometric forms that, as described by Vitruvius, relate to the human body.[14] This inspired artists and architects to seek beauty in the truth of ideal geometric forms through a human-centric vision of the universe, as depicted in Leonardo da Vinci's drawing *The Proportions of the Human Body According to Vitruvius*. (See Figure 1.9.)

Descriptive Geometry

Architectural forms are often depicted and visualized through methods of *descriptive geometry*, the representation of three-dimensional objects on a two-dimensional plane. Descriptive geometry includes *parallel projections* and *perspective projections*. In *parallel projections*, points from a three-dimensional object in space are projected onto a two-dimensional plane, resulting in projection lines that remain parallel to one another. *Points* are geometric figures that have zero dimension. In descriptive geometry, points are projected onto a plane and can be connected with line segments to form a two-dimensional image of a three-dimensional object. As the complexity of the form increases, the number of points needed to create an accurate depiction of the form also increases. Piero della Francesca, the Italian painter of the early Renaissance, produced works that were known for accurately depicting the human figure through descriptive geometry and perspectival techniques. His interest in mathematics and perspectival theories led to the development of texts, including the treatise *De Prospectiva pingendi* (*On Perspective in Painting*), in which he

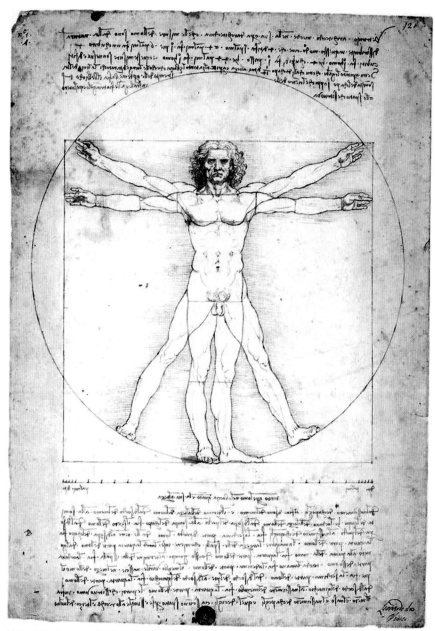

Figure 1.9. Leonardo Da Vinci, *The Proportions of the Human Body According to Vitruvius*, c.1490.

describes methods for designing, positioning, and coloring figures in space. The text focuses on perspective and describes the projection of complex surfaces and volumes that form the human body. In one of his drawings, a series of points are positioned to create various orthographic projections of a human head. (See Figure 1.10.)

Orthographic projections are a type of parallel projection in which the projection lines remain perpendicular to the projection plane. Orthographic projections are abstract representations and provide accurate scale and metric information of forms and spaces. Conventional architectural orthographic projections include plans, sections, elevations, and axonometric drawings.

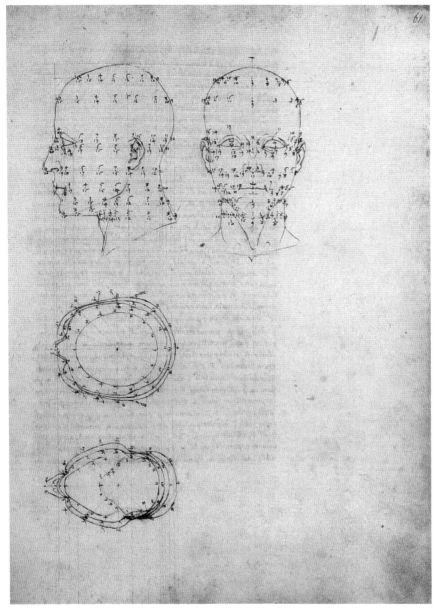

Figure 1.10. Piero della Francesca, *Projection of a Human Head,* from *De Prospective Pingendi,* c. 1474–1482.

In *perspective projections*, three-dimensional objects are represented by projection lines that converge at a vanishing point. Perspective projections convey forms and spaces as experienced through human vision. The Italian architect Filippo Brunelleschi is credited with discovering methods for creating accurate perspective drawings, and Alberti codified the methods for creating perspective drawing in his text *De Pictura (On Painting),* in 1435. This very influential text provided artists and architects with techniques for accurately depicting shapes, forms, and spaces as experienced through the sense of sight. Albrecht Dürer, a painter and theorist of the German Renaissance, depicted perspective projection techniques by illustrating methods for projecting points of an object onto a plane. In the engraving *Man Drawing a Lute*, a string (representing a visual ray) connected from a point on an object to a hook on the wall (representing the eye) traverses a plane with a swinging panel. Points are recorded where the string intersects the plane to form an identical image as perceived by the eye.[15] (See Figure 1.11.)

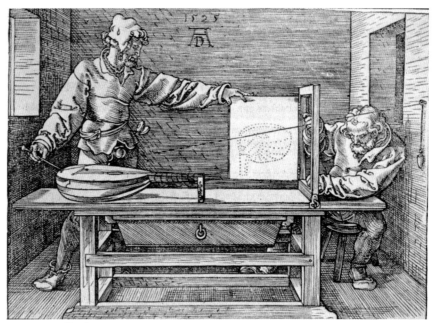

Figure 1.11. Albrecht Dürer, *Man Drawing a Lute*, 1525.

The use of both parallel and perspective projections provided methods for designing and conveying architectural designs through drawing. (See Figure 1.12.) Within digital 3D modeling software, the location of points in space and the projection of points onto a plane are the basis for viewing three-dimensional representations within viewports and on flat screens and monitors, and creating two-dimensional drawings from three-dimensional models.

Figure 1.12. Étienne-Louis Boullée, *Restauration de la Bibliothéque Nationale (Restoration of the National Library)*, 1785–1788.

1.4 Drawing Methods

Architects use many different methods for designing and communicating designs. There are various types of drawings that are often implemented throughout the architectural design process. Some of the most significant architectural drawing types that are used to problem solve, visualize, and communicate information include sketches, design drawings, technical drawings, and simulations.

Sketch Drawings

Sketches are typically drawings that are produced quickly to visually understand or communicate an idea. Sketching, whether by hand or through the use of digital technologies, provides a method for quickly creating visual information to think through an idea and/or communicate an idea to others. The sketch of the Cube I Office Tower in Guadalajara, Mexico, by the Spanish architect Carme Pinós illustrates the formal and spatial arrangement of the tower's floor plan, and visually conveys a conceptual idea of three triangular shapes that overlap to form a central core. The sketch also illustrates the linear inner edges of the triangular shapes, which are merged together through a series of curves that create continuity in the envelope. (See Figure 1.13.)

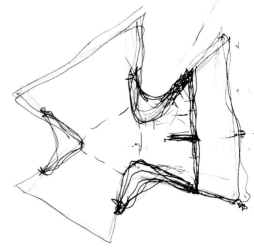

Figure 1.13. Carme Pinós, Cube I Office Tower, Guadalajara, Mexico, 2002–2005. Sketch drawing. *Courtesy of Estudio Carme Pinós.*

The sketches of the Guggenheim Museum Bilbao by the architect Frank O. Gehry indicate the sinuous nature of the building and communicate a sense of hierarchy and organization, through an overlapping and layering of linework that is slightly off center and diminishes in intensity to either side. The sketches also distinguish between various intensities of curved geometries, which represent a range of sinuous forms and surfaces (See Figure 1.14.)

Figure 1.14. Frank O. Gehry, Guggenheim Museum Bilbao. Hand sketch. *Courtesy of Gehry Partners, LLP, Los Angeles.*

Hand-Drafted Drawings

Architectural drawings can be used to represent technical information that is necessary for the construction of a building. Drawings that communicate information related to the design and construction of physical objects, buildings, and environments are known as *technical drawings*. A set of technical drawings and other information, such as schedules, that are used in the design and construction of a building are called *construction documents*. Technical drawings are scaled, and proportionally accurate to the physical reality of the object, architecture, landscape, or urban design project that they represent. Technical drawing requires precision and accuracy that historically had been achieved by *hand drafting*, which is drawing with tools, such as straight edges, triangles, and compasses, that allow for control in drawing geometry and linework that can be measured. Additional tools, such as *French curves*, were developed to aid in drafting curve geometry. These hand-drafting tools provide a means of accurately drawing smooth continuous curves. In the historical process of wooden ship building, ribs and keels, the elements that form the transverse and longitudinal structural framework of boats, were fabricated by drawing long, smooth curves onto timber, which were then cut to shape. In order to draw the curve geometry, a template consisting of long flexible strips of wood or steel, called *splines*, were defined and held into position by weights.[16] (See Figure 1.15.) These tools and techniques served as a method for drawing the curve on large sheets of timber at a scale of 1:1, and eventually on paper. Although most contemporary boat design processes utilize digital methods for the production of technical drawings, the artform of hand-drafting *splines* is a practice that can still be found in use today. Computer-aided design (CAD) systems also use the term *spline*, which is derived from the traditional term, and is the basis of creating curve geometries in digital drafting and modeling environments.

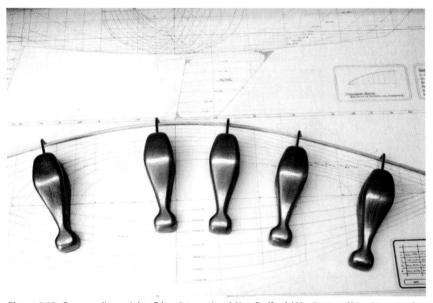

Figure 1.15. Bronze spline weights, Edson International, New Bedford, MA. *Courtesy of Edson International.*

The form of the Trans World Airlines (TWA) Terminal Building is an example of a modern work of architecture that consists of complex curved geometry. Located at John F. Kennedy Airport in New York, it was designed by the Finnish American architect Eero Saarinen and completed in 1962. This concrete and glass building, which has been interpreted as a metaphor for a bird or an airplane in flight, consists of sinuous forms that exhibit compound curvature. The curved Y-shaped concrete columns that blend into the concrete roof were constructed as a cast-in-place concrete structure that required extensive amounts of formwork to be built on site that reflected the curved geometries of the design. (See Figure 1.16.) The construction documents reflect the complexity of the curve geometries that were hand-drafted to accurately depict the sinuous forms and provide the information necessary for constructing the formwork. The hand-drafted technical drawing of the front column illustrates a series of horizontal contours cut at equally spaced intervals. These curves were generated by taking measurements from horizontal datums that intersected with the physical model, and transcribing the measurements of these intersections into a two-dimensional drawing, to draw the curves that describe the sinuous surface. (See Figure 1.17.)

Figure 1.16. Eero Saarinen and Associates, Trans World Airlines Terminal Building, New York, NY. **c.1956.** *Photograph of the curved column and roof. Eero Saarinen collection, 1880–2004 (inclusive), 1938–1962 (bulk). Manuscripts & Archives, Yale University Library. Photo: Richard Knight.*

During this same time period that the TWA Terminal Building was completed, the Spanish and Mexican architect and engineer Félix Candela was completing his project Los Manantiales Restaurant in Xochimilco, Mexico City. This project is a thin-shell, cast-in-place concrete structure, consisting of doubly curved, ruled surfaces. Many of the hand-drafted technical drawings that were produced for the construction of Candela's projects illustrate descriptive geometry and projection techniques that describe *ruled* surface geometries, which are surfaces that can be described with straight lines. Candela's projects reflect his interest in using ruled surfaces in design as a means of constructing complex curved formwork using straight planks of wood. His designs reflect modernist ideals, such as the use of minimal forms, absence of ornament, and reinforced concrete, to create formally expressive, structurally efficient designs that use minimal amounts of material. Using descriptive geometry and projection techniques, the various views of curved *hyperbolic paraboloid* surfaces could be accurately represented. (See Figure 1.18.) This drawing method was used to create the technical drawings for Los Manantiales Restaurant, where plan, section, and elevation views illustrate the rule lines and surface curvature of the architecture. (See Figure 1.19.)

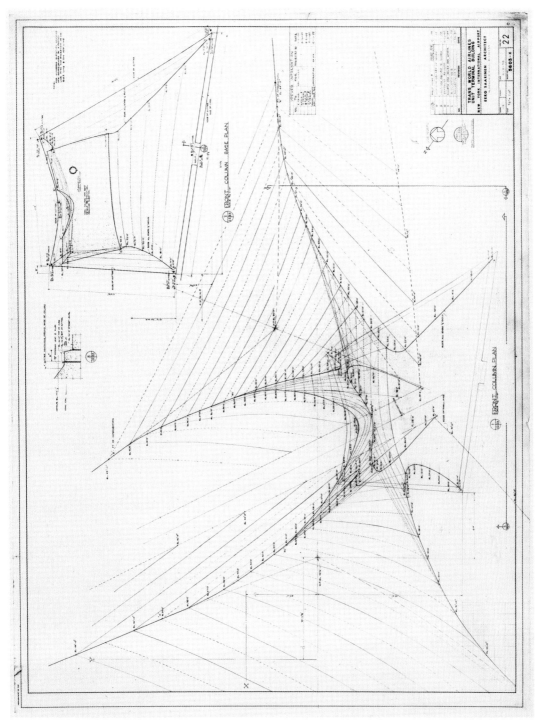

Figure 1.17. Eero Saarinen and Associates, Trans World Airlines Building Terminal, New York, NY. c.1956. As-builts, plan for the curved front column. Eero Saarinen collection, 1880–2004 (inclusive), 1938–1962 (bulk). Manuscripts & Archives, Yale University Library.

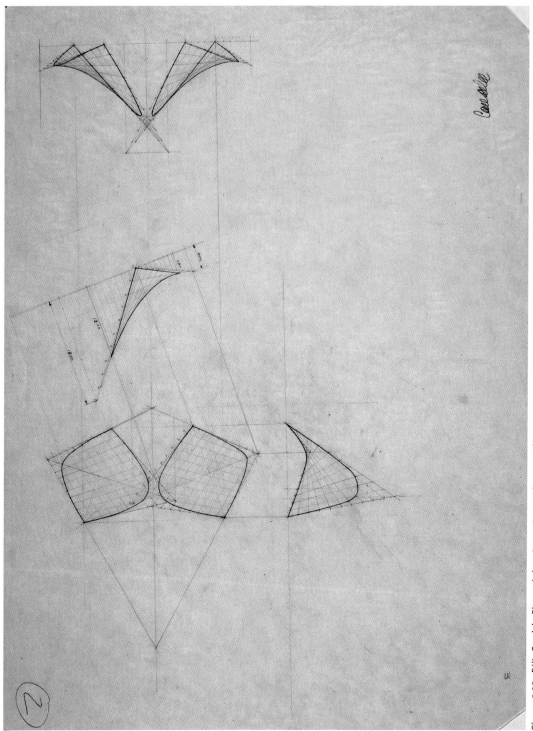

Figure 1.18. Félix Candela, Plan and elevation projection drawings of hyperbolic paraboloid surfaces. © Avery Architectural & Fine Arts Library, Columbia University.

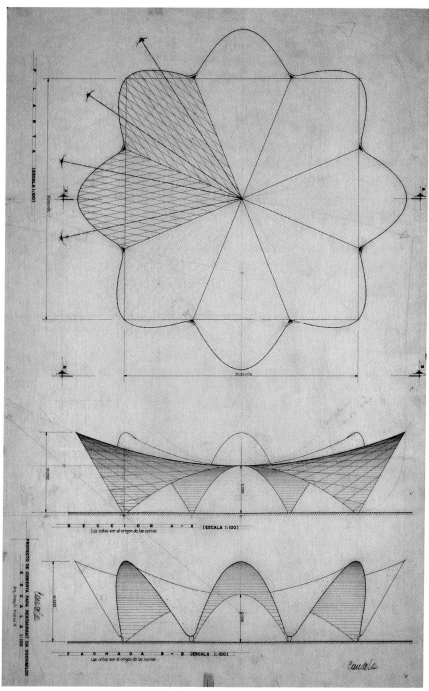

Figure 1.19. Félix Candela, Los Manantiales Restaurant, Xochimilco, Mexico City, Mexico, 1958. Drawing of the roof geometry. *© Avery Architectural & Fine Arts Library, Columbia University.*

Computer-Aided Design (CAD) Drawings

In the 1960s and 1970s, the invention and early advances of computer-aided design (CAD) systems demonstrated the use of digital platforms that could facilitate the process of creating technical drawings. The use of CAD systems eventually led to the replacement of hand drafting with computer-aided drafting. The majority of architectural practices today rely on CAD tools to create design drawings and technical drawings because, among other reasons, CAD tools can generate technical drawings faster, more accurately, and with fewer errors. By the late 1970s and 1980s, CAD systems had advanced and were being used to create geometry and forms through 3D modeling. During the 1990s, advances in CAD led to the ability to create 3D models that were based in topology, offered parametric capabilities, and could generate complex geometry, forms, and surfaces. Coupled with advances in computer-aided manufacturing (CAM) tools, capable of fabricating complex forms, with data that was output directly from the digital model, this opened up new possibilities for the design and construction of architecture. These technological advances led to some of the first built works of architecture that were designed primarily within 3D models. For example, the Yokohama International Passenger Terminal by Farshid Moussavi and Alejandro Zaera-Polo of Foreign Office Architects, designed in the mid-1990s and completed in 2001, was primarily conceived in section, as a series of digitally modeled surfaces that curved and folded to create an architectural topography.[17] The continuous changes in the undulation and folds of the surface topology are visualized in an oblique drawing in which all of the transverse sections are represented. (See Figure 1.20.) This digital drawing demonstrates the ability of 3D models to influence new explorations of architectural representation through conventional projection techniques. Additionally, the ability to create section cuts in the 3D model provided a means for exporting the geometry from the digital model, which could be developed as technical section drawings. (See Figure 1.21.)

CAD drawings also include technical drawings that are produced through building information modeling (BIM) tools. BIM technologies utilize parametric modeling capabilities that link three-dimensional geometries with two-dimensional drawings. This parametric *associativity* between 2D and 3D representations allows for changes made in the 3D model to automatically update the associated 2D technical drawings, and vice versa. The Marqués de Riscal Winery in Elciego, Spain, designed by Gehry Partners, LLP utilizes Gehry Technologies' Digital Project BIM software to create 3D models that are associated with 2D projections. In addition to embedding data, or information, in the 3D model, BIM software is designed to allow for greater consistency and reduced errors between the 3D models and 2D technical drawings. This has become a very useful digital workflow for managing the design and construction of large-scale architectural projects that are complex. (See Figure 1.22.)

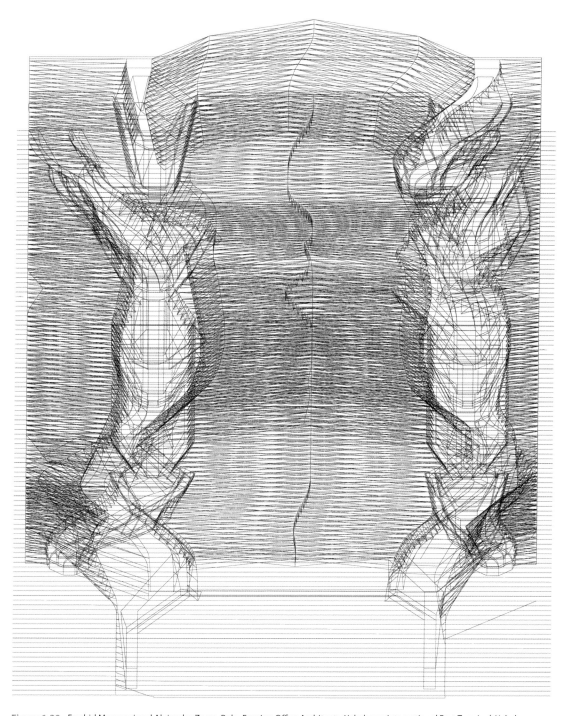

Figure 1.20. Farshid Moussavi and Alejandro Zaera-Polo, Foreign Office Architects, Yokohama International Port Terminal, Yokohama, Japan, 1995–2002. Oblique drawing of the transverse sections. *Courtesy of Farshid Moussavi Architecture.*

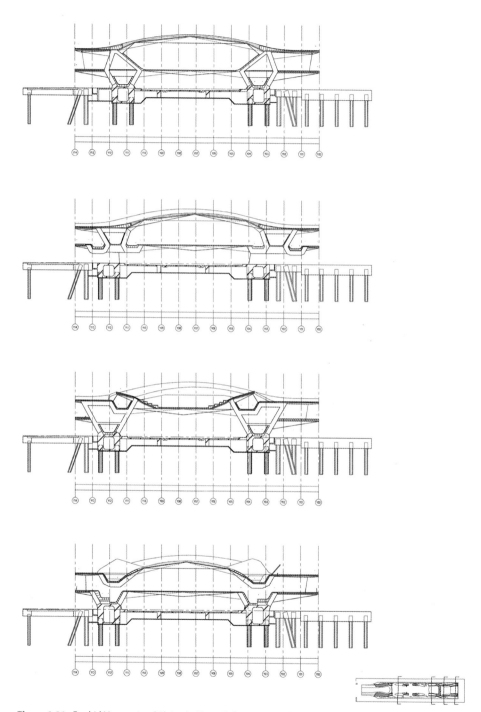

Figure 1.21. Farshid Moussavi and Alejandro Zaera-Polo, Foreign Office Architects, Yokohama International Port Terminal, Yokohama, Japan, 1995–2002. Technical drawings of the transverse sections. *Courtesy of Farshid Moussavi Architecture.*

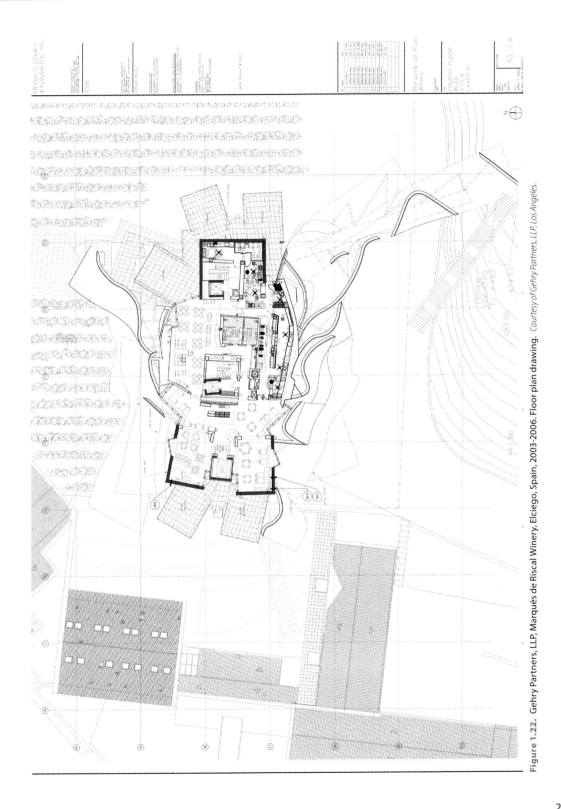

Figure 1.22. Gehry Partners, LLP, Marqués de Riscal Winery, Elciego, Spain, 2003–2006. Floor plan drawing. *Courtesy of Gehry Partners, LLP, Los Angeles.*

Figure 1.23. Young & Ayata, *Symmetry Series*, 2013. Computational drawing.
Courtesy of Young & Ayata, New York.

Computational Drawings

The ubiquitous use and influence of computational tools and algorithms are evident and appear in many facets of contemporary culture. During the 1990s and 2000s, architects explored digital models, parametric design, algorithmic procedures, and simulation methods as tools for generating new architectural forms, modes of fabrication, and performance optimization. In terms of drawing, algorithms—which are essentially a set of instructions—can be utilized to create visual expressions built on rule-based operations. This opens up new possibilities for drawing, because algorithms and computational procedures are capable of generating visualizations of complex information and of processing large amounts of data, which is difficult if not impossible for the human mind to do. The drawings in the *Symmetry Series*, produced by the New York-based architecture firm Young & Ayata, are the result of questioning the role of architectural drawings that are produced through the use of digital computations. The drawings express a discourse that confronts the topics of what is real and what is abstract in representation, and challenges the usefulness of the antiquated categorization of mediums such as drawing, painting, and photography.[18] (See Figure 1.23.)

Computational simulations provide opportunities to simulate various types of forces and behaviors within digital modeling environments. These simulations are often used to evaluate and test geometric forms as a means of optimizing their performance. For example, simulating the effects of wind loads on a building within a digital model provides a means for structural engineers to test and improve the structural design and performance of a building. However, simulations have also been used as generative design tools for exploring emergent geometries and forms that are based on input parameters. These computational processes provide a means for discovery and the visualization of complex forces and behaviors through drawing and modeling. An example of the use of computational simulations as a generative design tool can be seen in the plan drawing for the design of the Kartel-Pendik Masterplan in Istanbul, Turkey, in 2006, by Zaha Hadid Architects. In this project, inputs of circulation within the urban fabric, and computational simulations of bundling curve networks, influenced by Frei Otto's bundling wool-thread models, were used to generate the network of curves for the masterplan.[19] (See Figures 1.24 and 1.25.)

Figure 1.24. Zaha Hadid Architects, Kartal-Pendik Masterplan, Istanbul, Turkey, 2006. Simulation of a wool-thread model used to design the path network. *Courtesy of Zaha Hadid Architects.*

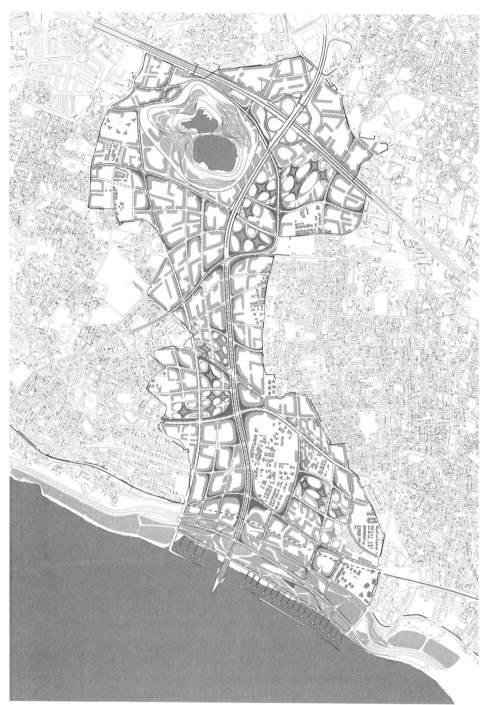

Figure 1.25. Zaha Hadid Architects, Kartal-Pendik Masterplan, Istanbul, Turkey, 2006. Site plan of the street layout and urban fabric. *Courtesy of Zaha Hadid Architects.*

Endnotes

1. Dennis J. Schmidt, *Between Word and Image: Heidegger, Klee, and Gadamar, on Gestures and Genesis* (Indiana: Indiana University Press, 2013.)
2. Simon Bell, *Landscape: Pattern, Perception and Process* (New York: Routledge, 2012).
3. Yehuda E. Kalay, *Architecture's New Media: Principles, Theories, and Methods of Computer-Aided Design* (Cambridge, MA: MIT Press, 2004).
4. Ibid.
5. Casey Reas and Ben Frye, "Environment IDE," https://processing.org/reference/environment/, accessed October 15, 2017.
6. Francis D. K. Ching and Steven P. Juroszek, *Design Drawing* (2nd ed.), (Hoboken, NJ: John Wiley and Sons, 2010).
7. Sergio Roncato, "Piranesi and the Infinite Prisons," in *Spatial Visions* 21 (1–2, February 2007): 3–18, Koninklijke, Brill, NV, Leiden.
8. Ibid.
9. Peter Cook, *Drawing: The Motive Force of Architecture* (2nd ed.), (West Sussex, UK: John Wiley & Sons, 2014).
10. Daniel Libeskind, *Daniel Libeskind: Countersign* (New York: Rizzoli International Publications, 1992; Great Britain: Academy Editions, 1991).
11. Amy Frearson, "Lebbeus Woods: Early Drawings," *Deezen*, November, 2012, https://www.dezeen.com/2012/11/08/lebbeus-woods-early-drawings/.
12. Mario Carpo, "The Art of Drawing," *AD: Drawing Architecture*; Neil Spiller, guest ed.; Helen Castle, general ed. (London: John Wiley & Sons, May 2013).
13. Mario Carpo, *The Alphabet and the Algorithm* (Cambridge, MA: MIT Press, 2011).
14. Robert A. M. Stern with Raymond W. Gastil, *Modern Classicism* (New York: Rizzoli International Publications, 1988).
15. Jeanne Peiffer, "Constructing Perspective in Sixteenth-Century Nuremberg," *Perspectives, Projections, and Design: Technologies of Architectural Representation*, Mario Carpo and Frederique Lemerle, eds. New York and London: Routledge, Taylor and Francis Group, 2008.
16. Alastair Townsend, "On the Spline," *International Journal of Interior Architecture + Spatial Design: Applied Geometries*, Jonathon Anderson and Meg Jackson, September 16, 2014.
17. David Langdon, "AD Classics: Yokohama International Passenger Terminal," www.archdaily.com/554132/ad-classics-yokohama-international-passenger-terminal-foreign-office-architects-foa, accessed October 7, 2014.
18. Young, Michael, "Essay: Drawing, Painting, Photography," *Economy, Issue 14: All Visual*. http://theeconomymagazine.com/ISSUE-14-MICHAEL-YOUNG-ESSAY-DRAWING-PAINTING-PHOTOGRAPHY-SYMMETRY.
19. Patrik Schumacher, "Parametricism: A New Global Style for Architecture and Urban Design," *AD: Digital Cities*, Neil Leach, guest ed.; Helen Castle, general ed., vol. 79 (4, July–August 2009).

Chapter 2
Architectural Models

Chapter 2 provides an overview of the use of three-dimensional models in architectural design. This covers a range of methods for utilizing both physical and digital models in the architectural design process that are based on concepts related to performance, parametric design, simulation, information, and data. Physical models allow individuals to understand architectural geometries through real materials that are tangible. In addition to representations of forms, these models allow for the exploration of form and geometry through studies of material performance, behavior, and phenomenon.

Over the past few decades, advances in computing technologies and the use of digital models in architectural design have opened up new opportunities for architectural drawings and representations, as well as the output of physical artifacts through the use of digital fabrication tools. Digital models can be used to simulate material behaviors, atmospheric flows, environmental phenomena, and other properties to visualize information and data and to aid in the architectural design process. This has extended the limitations experienced with traditional drawing and representation methods, allowing for optimized, data-driven design solutions, advanced understandings of complex systems, and the ability for mass-customized fabrication. The projects presented in this chapter serve as examples of the use of architectural models as design instruments, used to discover geometries and forms, aid in the production of drawings, and create performance-based simulations. The chapter also describes current scanning technologies and digital fabrication tools that are being integrated into design workflows, and that support new approaches to architectural design that allow for an agility and nimbleness in moving back and forth between the physical and the virtual, and between hand craft and digital craft.

2.1 Physical Models

Physical models play an integral role in architectural design processes. Unlike drawings, physical models allow for three-dimensional representations of architectural designs. This allows individuals to view the model from different angles and different proximities, and also creates opportunities to communicate information through material effects, textures, and tactile qualities. The use of physical models in the architectural design process varies from abstract studies of geometry and form to accurate, scaled replicas that represent a final design. This wide range of uses allows physical models to be used in various ways, in various stages of the design process, resulting in different types of models, such as "sketch" models, massing models, working models, and final presentation models. Physical models can also be used to aid in translating three-dimensional geometries into two-dimensional drawings through both analog and digital methods.

Historically, architectural scale models represented the cultural aspects of a place. Physical models discovered in the ancient tombs and pyramids of Egypt were built in accord with religious beliefs. Complete sets of figures and building replicas, made of wood and clay and modeled in fine detail and color, were believed to provide aid to their ruler in the afterlife. In Greek culture, architectural scale models were not made as exact replicas and were built with less attention to scale and detail. Instead, they were used to study specific architectural elements, and were made with enough information to communicate architectural ideas.[1]

This same approach to the use of physical models as a tool to convey ideas can be found in the treatise *De architectura (On Architecture)*, (c. 30 BC), by the Roman author, architect, and engineer Marcus Vitruvius Pollio. In this text, he describes the scale models that were used to demonstrate the mechanics of military devices and structures.[2] Centuries later, architects of the Italian Renaissance evolved their use of physical models to demonstrate architectural ideas and as tools to communicate information to the craftsmen involved in the construction process. The Italian architect and engineer Filippo Brunelleschi used physical models as a design and communication tool for the construction of the dome of the Cattedrale di Santa Maria del Fiore in Florence, Italy (c.1420-46). (See Figure 2.1.) The design and construction of the dome was an engineering feat of its time, as it needed to be built without the use of scaffolding, due to a lack of the amount of timber that would be required, and without flying buttresses to support

Figure 2.1. Cattedrale di Santa Maria del Fiore, Florence, Italy, dome, c.1420-46, Filippo Brunelleschi, wood models.

the structure. During this time period, it was common for construction methods to be examined through the use of large-scale physical models. Brunelleschi devised a large-scale wood and masonry model, which was built by craftsmen, and served as a working model to systematically test construction techniques and sequencing.[3]

Physical models can also be used as design tools. Quintessential examples of the use of physical models to aid in the design process are the catenary models by the Catalonian architect Antoni Gaudí. These innovative models were developed using a system of strings and weights to design the structure and form of the Basilica i Temple Expiatori de la Sagrada Familia, in Barcelona, Spain. (See Figure 2.2.) The project, which Gaudí took over as lead architect in 1883, is still under construction today, with a completion date projected for 2028. Gaudí used his system of strings and weights to determine the ideal curvature of the structural vaults that form the soaring vertical spaces of the cathedral. (See Figure 2.3.) By spacing weights equally on a string, and suspending the string from its endpoints, Gaudí allowed the force of gravity on the suspended strings to determine the ideal catenary curve. The inverted shape of the catenary curves reflected the ideal curvature for carrying structural loads through the vaulted structural system.

Figure 2.2. Antoni Gaudí, Basilica i Temple Expiatori de la Sagrada Familia, Barcelona, Spain. Catenary model. © *Pep Daudé. Temple of the Sagrada Família.*

Figure 2.3. Antoni Gaudí, Basilica i Temple Expiatori de la Sagrada Familia, Barcelona, Spain. Vaulted structural system. © *Pep Daudé. Temple of the Sagrada Família*

The use of physical models as "working" models can be seen in photographs that document the design process of the Trans World Airlines Building Terminal, designed by Eero Saarinen. The large-scale physical models were used in the design process to develop the form and geometry of the concrete building. (See Figure 2.4.) The models were also used in tandem with horizontal, planar templates that intersected the curved forms of the model, essentially creating a series of horizontal contour cuts, which were used to create the two-dimensional drawings that described the curvature of the forms, illustrated in Chapter 1. (See Figure 1.17.)

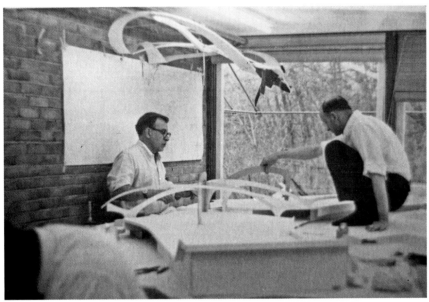

Figure 2.4. Eero Saarinen and Associates, Trans World Airlines Terminal Building, New York, NY., c.1956. Saarinen with TWA model. Eero Saarinen collection, 1880–2004 (inclusive), 1938–1962 (bulk). Manuscripts & Archives, Yale University Library.

Many of the tensile structures by the architect and engineer Frei Otto were designed using form-finding techniques through phyiscal working models that utilized soap film. Otto's innovative technique involved the use of wires and soap film to study minimal surface geometry, which influenced his designs of tensile structures. These "performative" models reflected material efficiencies and beautiful geometric formations that were produced naturally by the material. The direct correlation between the material behavior in the soap film model and the tensile fabric surfaces can be seen in the models and built structure of the Tranzbrunnen (Dance Pavilion), in Cologne, Germany. (See Figures 2.5 and 6.19.)

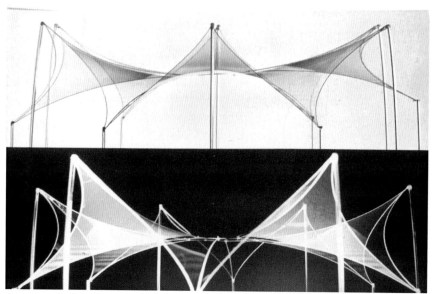

Figure 2.5. Frei Otto, Tranzbrunnen (Dance Pavilion), Cologne, Germany, 1957. Soap film model. Photo: Frei Otto. *Courtesy of Atelier Frei Otto + Partner, Kunstler + Ingenieure.*

The architect Frank O. Gehry is well known for his sculptural works of architecture that comprise twisting and undulating metal forms and surfaces. The use of physical models plays an integral role in the design process at his architectural firm, Gehry Partners, LLP. (See Figure 2.6.) Physical models are used at various stages of the project from beginning to end. The design process typically begins with a hand-sketch by Gehry, which serves as a visual representation of the idea and concept for the project. The sketch is interpreted and explored through multiple iterations of massing models, typically made out of wood blocks, where each block represents a programmatic element of the project. The wood blocks are juxtaposed and assembled in various ways to study alternative possibilities for the programmatic organization of the building or project. The schematic designs integrate curved paper surfaces, which are used to clad and wrap the block massing, and to create new spaces and forms. The paper—a flat sheet material that is pliable and can be bent, folded, and twisted into various curved forms—is used to represent the flat sheets of metal panels that are used in the built project. Theoretically, if the surfaces and forms in the physical model can be made out of flat sheets of paper, then the surfaces and forms of the building can be made out of flat sheets of metal, such as stainless steel and titanium, because they are both *ruled* surfaces. While the design is developed in a rigorous process that explores composition, balance, scale, and materials through physical models, the fabrication and construction of the buildings rely on the use of digital models. This translation from physical to digital models involves the process of "digitizing" the physical models, which will be further explained in the next section.

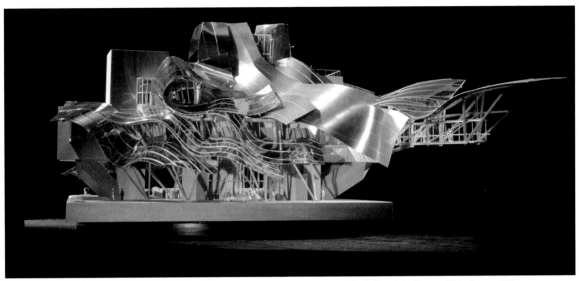

Figure 2.6. Gehry Partners, LLP, Marques de Riscal Winery, Elciego, Spain, 2003-2006. Physical model. *Courtesy of Gehry Partners, LLP.*

Physical models are often used as final presentation models that depict the over-all vision of the architectural proposal. Architectural models range from abstractions of the architectural design, often used to convey or exaggerate the conceptual idea of the project, to accurate and realistic miniature replicas of the architectural proposal, intended to depict what the final project will look like. Architectural models vary in scale and scope. The physical model for the project Humanhattan 2050, by the Denmark based architecture firm BIG-Bjarke Ingles Group, represents their proposed design for future development and flood protection along the edges of Manhattan where the urban fabric of the city meets the surrounding natural bodies of water. (See Figure 2.7.) The large physical model allows for multiple individuals to walk around and simultaneously experience the model and understand the scale and scope of the project. The model incorporates various materials, such as wood, representing existing context, and illuminated acrylic, highlighting the architectural design and development proposal by BIG-Bjarke Ingles Group.

The use of physical models by the San Francisco-based architecture firm Future Cities Lab often serve as prototypes for architectural projects that are dynamic and responsive. (See Figure 2.8.) Their projects, both built and speculative, often incorporate sensors that detect external stimuli as input data—for example, environmental phenomena like light and temperature. This input data is used to drive actuators that create a response, such as a kinetic, mechanical motion. To achieve this, the physical models are embedded with sensors, actuators, and electronics. This use of physical computing and robotic technologies result in "live" physical models that convey the animated qualities of the design. They also serve to represent the same design objectives for larger-scale works of kinetic architecture.

Figure 2.7. BIG-Bjarke Ingles Group, Humanhattan 2050. Design for NYC waterfront. Physical model. Photo: Laurian Ghinitoiu. *Courtesy of BIG-Bjarke Ingles Group.*

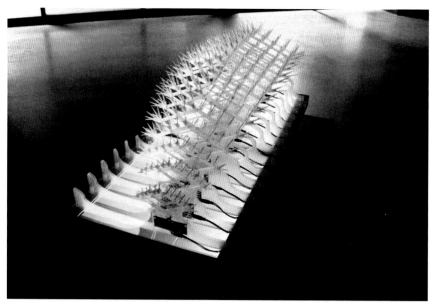

Figure 2.8. Jason Kelly Johnson and Nataly Gattegno, Future Cities Lab, Xerohouse, Phoenix, AZ, 2012. Physical model, demonstrating the kinetic and responsive aspects of the design. *Courtesy of Future Cities Lab.*

2.2 3D Models

With the development of computer-aided design (CAD) tools, the use of the computer to create 3D models transformed architectural design processes and practices. Beginning with the replacement of hand drafting by computer-aided drafting tools in the 1980s, CAD software that allowed for two-dimensional drafting was developed into three-dimensional modeling software, and began to be used in architectural academia and practice. By the 1990s, many CAD software packages utilized calculus-based NURBS (non-uniform rational B-spline) systems, which allowed for the modeling of more fluid curves.

Similar to physical models, 3D models provide a dynamic interaction with the viewer. The viewer can rotate and move around the model to change their view of forms and spaces, as opposed to a static perspective view or rendering that provides one specific view.[4] However, unlike physical models, 3D models are immaterial and are not tangible. They are abstractions of three-dimensional forms and spaces. They are virtual simulations that typically represent geometrical forms through combinations of computational *data structures*, which are arrangements of information in a computer, organized for efficient use.[5] The individual primitive elements that are used to create 3D models are the result of predefined mathematical operations developed by software engineers and designers. Simple to complex geometry can be constructed from primitives such as points, line segments, curves, polygons, surfaces, and solids. There are many different software packages that support 3D modeling, such as Autodesk's AutoCAD, Maya, 3ds Max, Revit, Dessault Systèmes CATIA, Gehry Technologies' Digital Project, Bentley's MicroStation, Bentley's GenerativeComponents, Robert McNeel & Associates' Rhinoceros, and many more.

Computer-Aided Design (CAD) Models

Similar to physical models, 3D models can, and often are, used in various stages of the architectural design process, as "sketch" models, massing models, working models, presentation models, and in various other ways, depending on the objective. However, unlike physical models, 3D models can often be produced faster, and with more accuracy, to describe architectural geometry. 3D models can be used to model intricate geometric elements that may be too difficult or time consuming to create through traditional physical model-making methods. They can also be simultaneously shared, viewed, and updated with the various team members of a project, such as other collaborators within the architecture, engineering, and construction (AEC) industries. This allows architects to design, analyze, and simulate an architectural project within the digital model and provide three-dimensional geometry and data to engineers and contractors for use in the development of their structural designs and fabrication methods. An example of this can be seen in the structural model for the BMW Welt project in Munich, Germany, designed by the Austrian architecture firm

COOP HIMMELB[L]AU. (See Figure 2.9.) In contemporary architectural practices, the digital models typically serve as "master models" that are shared between the various AEC team members that are involved in the project.

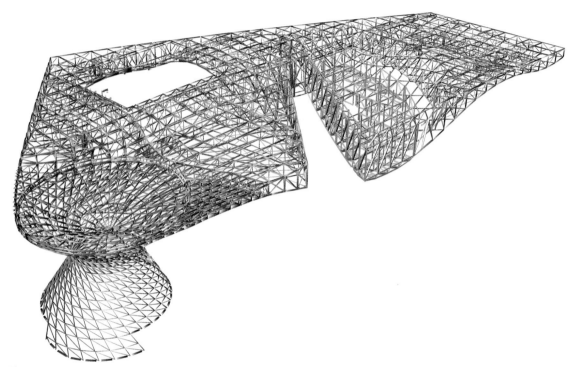

Figure 2.9. COOP HIMMELB[L]AU, BMW Welt, Munich, Germany, 2001–2007. Axonometric view of the structural model. *Courtesy of COOP HIMMELB[L]AU.*

3D models can be used to generate two-dimensional drawings, produce renderings with mapped materials, create animations, store data and building information, simulate real-world forces, form immersive environments, and provide output data for digital fabrication purposes. For these and many other reasons, over the past few decades, 3D models have become one of the primary design tools and preferred methods of working within architectural practice and academia.

3D modeling software supports the ability to create and transform various types of geometry and topology. Topological entities, such as curves and surfaces, are composed of a series of continuous stream of values, not discrete points.[6] These curves and surfaces utilize *spline* geometry, vectors that have a direction. The splines are defined by points and lines, which form the *control points* of curves and surfaces. Moving the control points or changing their weight value modifies the surface topology. Topological surfaces can be continuously distorted by stretching, bending, and twisting, without tearing or ripping.

Within parametric models, the *parameters* that control a surface include control points, as well as numerical values and geometric constraints. By changing the parameters that define the geometry of a 3D model, multiple iterations of the model can be produced that are topologically the same. (See Figure 2.10.) Through the use of parameters, 3D models can be used to quickly generate different versions of a project. This method of working aids designers by allowing multiple iterations of a design to be modeled and evaluated to select the best design solution.

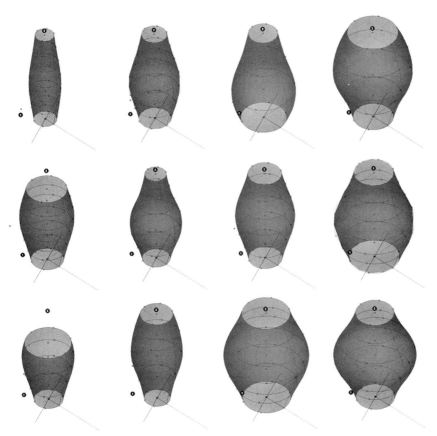

Figure 2.10. Parametric model used to generate multiple formal iterations by modifying variable input parameters. *Courtesy of the author.*

The design of the Embryological House by architect Greg Lynn exploits the use of the parametric and topological aspects of 3D models, and the ability to fabricate them with computer-aided manufacturing (CAM) technologies. The project rethinks the notion of the mass-produced prefabricated house based on modules, as mass-customized houses based on unlimited iterations derived from a basic form, "primitive."[7] The designs are based on a matrix of elements, defined by the architect, which can be combined in various ways, allowing the users to participate in the design process to create their unique customized work of architecture. (See Figure 2.11.) Once the design has been finalized, the architectural components can be output using digital fabrication processes. The ability of CAD/CAM tools to produce complex geometries and unique elements has challenged the historical industrial manufacturing processes of *mass production* to shift toward the contemporary computer-aided manufacturing processes of *mass customization*.[8]

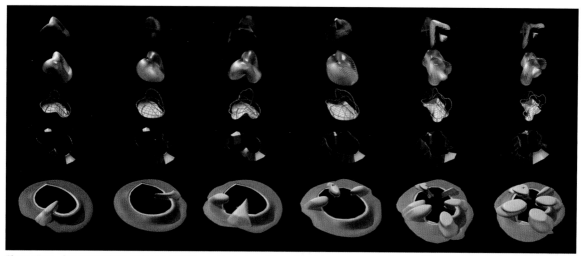

Figure 2.11. Greg Lynn FORM, Embryological House. Rendering of the volumetric components. *Courtesy of Greg Lynn FORM and the Canadian Center for Architecture.*

Simulation Models

The geometry from 3D models can be incorporated within various types of simulation models, to simulate the effects that forces, behaviors, and environmental phenomena might have on an architectural design. Simulation models can be used in many different ways and at various stages of the architectural design process. For example, they can be used to test the structural performance of a building by simulating the effect that various forces, such as gravity and wind loads, have upon the design. In these virtual simulations, the effects of the forces can be visualized to obtain a better understanding of how the design will perform in reality. If certain elements of the design appear to fail or are problematic, the design can be adjusted to meet the necessary criteria. In this scenario, the simulation model allows for the performance of the design to be tested and analyzed prior to construction, which can be useful in avoiding costly mistakes. The structural simulation model of the Sky Reflector Net at Fulton Center, New York, designed by James Carpenter Design Associates, Grimshaw, and Arup illustrates the various deformation attributes of the structural elements through a spectrum of colors. (See Figure 2.12.) In this example, the simulation model is used to test the design and performance of a proposed architectural project. It allows for the visualization and analysis of information that can begin to inform design decisions.

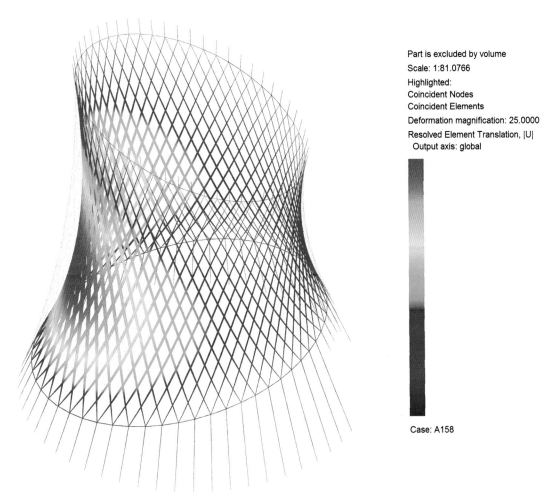

Part is excluded by volume

Scale: 1:81.0766

Highlighted:
Coincident Nodes
Coincident Elements

Deformation magnification: 25.0000

Resolved Element Translation, |U|
  Output axis: global

Case: A158

Figure 2.12. James Carpenter Design Associates, Grimshaw, and Arup, Sky Reflector Net, Fulton Center, New York, 2014. Structural simulation of various forces. *Courtesy of Arup.*

Digital simulation models can also be used to explore emergent and generative design solutions. For example, agent-based simulations that utilize computational algorithms can be used as a method for generating design solutions. These methods support bottom-up approaches to design, which are based on individual systems, their behavior, and their relationship to each other, leading to 'emergent' formations that are greater than the sum of its parts.[9] Agent-based computational simulations utilize particle systems, collections of large numbers of individual particles, each having its own behavior.[10] Similar to large populations that are composed of discrete elements, such as colonies of ants, schools of fish, and flocks of birds, bottom-up systems display a collective intelligence that is more sophisticated than the behavior of its parts.[11] In his article "Swarm Urbanism," the architect Neil Leach describes "swarm intelligence" and bottom-up approaches to design, where individual agents with embedded intelligence respond to one another, resulting in behavioral translations of topology and geometry that can have radically varied outputs.[12] An example of an agent-based simulation model can be seen in a design research project titled "Bio Simulations" by Augmented Architectures based in New York. (See Figure 2.13.) In this research project, *Physarum polycephalum*, also known as slime mold, was grown and observed in order to better understand the growth patterns of the organism, which have been found to have the ability to solve the shortest path problem. These growth patterns were then digitally simulated through the use of computational tools. The geometry and forms of these growth simulations are based on defining the point locations where the growth begins (emitters), and the point locations that the growth is attracted to (attractors). By changing these parameters, multiple iterations and formations of the structure were generated that reflected optimized connections between points. The simulations were produced using an open-source software named *Physarealm,* which adopts a previous stigmergic multi-agent algorithm that is expanded for three dimensions.[13]

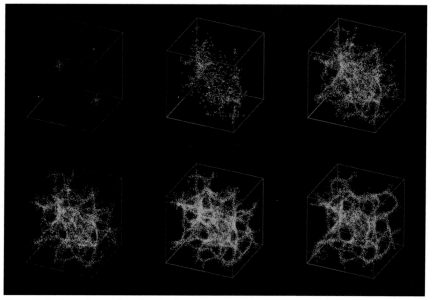

Figure 2.13. Nancy Diniz and Frank Melendez, Augmented Architectures, "Bio Simulations," 2018. Agent-based simulation of Physarum polycephalum growth patterns and formations. *Courtesy of © Augmented Architectures.*

Virtual Reality and Augmented Reality

3D models are typically viewed on screens and monitors as two-dimensional projections. However, they can also be experienced through the use of virtual reality (VR), augmented reality (AR), and mixed reality (MR) environments. Virtual reality (VR) relies on display technologies, including worn and fixed placement, that allows users to experience 3D models with the visual sensation of presence, or *immersion*.[14] This is accomplished through the use of stereoscopic head-mounted displays and semi-immersive projection-based systems such as computer-assisted virtual environments (CAVEs) and domes.[15] The first head-mounted display, titled "The Sword of Damocles," projected wireframe images onto a lens while the user's head was tracked, and was developed by the computer scientist and engineer Ivan Sutherland in 1968. Sutherland's goal was to place humans inside computer-generated graphic simulations. This research turned out to be the origins of cyberspace technology.[16] With current VR systems such as the Oculus Rift, users can wear the head-mounted display (HMD) in order to experience the 3D model as if they are standing inside of it, and can move their head to look around, as one would experience a space in reality. (See Figure 2.14.) Users can also navigate to various locations within the 3D model and use hand-held devices to control virtual hands to select and grab objects within the digital model. The first head-mounted displays date back to the 1960s; however, their affordability for mass use has only become available in recent years.

Figure 2.14. Institute for Advanced Architecture of Catalonia (IaaC), Global Summer School, NYC, *Body Architectures*, 2018. Virtual Reality installation using sensors, point cloud model, and Oculus Rift. *Courtesy of the author.*

Within VR environments, users are unable to see or experience the real-world environment that is around them. On the other hand, augmented reality (AR) and mixed reality (MR) systems combine virtual and real-world environment information and spaces. This technology allows users to have both the immersive experience of a 3D model while maintaining the ability to see and experience the actual space that they are standing in. These systems, such as the Microsoft HoloLens, allow users to wear head-mounted displays and view 3D models and information, which augment actual physical environments and models. (See Figures 2.15 and 2.16.)

Figure 2.15. Mara Marcu and Ming Tang, MMXIII and TYA Design, *Augmented Coral,* 2016. Mixed reality installation using a Microsoft HoloLens.
Courtesy of MMXIII and TYA Design

Figure 2.16. Perkins+Will, Thornton Tomasetti, and the University of Cambridge, River Beech Tower, conceptual design for a timber tower located in Chicago. A composite image demonstrating the use of a Microsoft HoloLens to interact with building models in mixed reality.
Courtesy of Perkins+Will.

Digitizing (Physical) Models

"Digitizing" physical models refers to the translation of analog, physical models into digital, virtual models, typically through the use of scanning technologies. Scanners provide the ability to detect many elements that make up our physical environment, including objects, people, buildings, landscapes, and convert this information into digital values that are used to generate 3D models. This is useful for designing physical models or with physical elements that can be scanned and converted into 3D models. Many of the projects by the architecture firm Gehry Partners, LLP are designed through a combination of analog and digital processes, beginning with hand-crafted physical models of paper and wood, which are then digitized. A digitizing arm is used to locate point coordinates, which are used to create 3D models in Rhino that are used for design development. Similar to the use of a cursor on a screen, the endpoint of the digitizing arm is placed at various point locations on the physical model, and entered to define the control points of lines and curves in the 3D modeling space. (See Figure 2.17.) The curves are edited and refined within the digital model and used as inputs to model the smooth, sinuous surfaces that make up the architecture. These 3D models are further developed as building information models (BIM) in Gehry Technologies' proprietary BIM software, Digital Project, which was designed in collaboration with Dessault Systèmes, developers of the software CATIA, originally a mechanical engineering software used in the design of aircraft. The BIM models are used to aid in the production of technical drawings, construction documents, and in the building fabrication process through the use of CAM technologies.

Figure 2.17. Gehry Partners, LLP, Marques de Riscal Winery, Elciego, Spain, 2003-2006. Digitizing process. *Courtesy of Gehry Partners, LLP.*

Other methods of digitizing physical models or physical environments include photogrammetry and LIDAR scanning. Mobile scanning devices use the camera and sensors of smart phones and tablets to create photogrammetric data, which is turned into a 3D model. (See Figure 2.18.) LIDAR (light detection and ranging) scanners use a laser and a sensor to detect and target physical elements, and converts the scanned data into a *point cloud* model. (See Figure 2.19.) Point cloud models are digital models that consist of many points. In architectural design, LIDAR scanning and the resulting point cloud models are typically used to survey existing structures, landscapes, urban conditions, and environments. These models generally consist of millions of points that provide detailed and accurate information of the existing conditions of built or natural environments.

Figure 2.18. Institute for Advanced Architecture of Catalonia (IaaC), Global Summer School, NYC, *Body Architectures*, 2018. Digital scans from a hand-held device used to create 3D models of individuals for designing customized wearable devices. *Courtesy of the author.*

Figure 2.19. MYND Workshop, *Colorized Point Cloud of Brooklyn Building,* New York. 3D laser scan point cloud model. *Courtesy of MYND Workshop.*

2.3 Digital Fabrication

Along with the advancement of computer-aided design came advances in computer-aided manufacturing. For over three decades CAD/CAM technologies have been used significantly in architectural design, providing new opportunities for the design and fabrication of complex geometries. These technologies have prompted a reevaluation of the modernist machine paradigm, where singular, identical parts can be mass produced, to a digital machine paradigm, where infinite variations of parts can be mass produced.[17] Digital fabrication is the process of using a digital file, typically a digital drawing or 3D model, to control the method in which a machine shapes material. 3D digital models are used to provide machine instructions, which are used to create a physical artifact. In addition to supporting file-to-factory workflows for machining parts directly from the digital model, the digital fabrication process provides design opportunities based on the interactions of the machines with materials. Decisions based on which machine to use, the selected tooling, and assembly techniques have provided designers with opportunities to build with the computer to achieve unprecedented visual, material, and formal results.[18] These tools and techniques have impacted how architects, engineers, and contractors make physical models, prototypes, building envelopes, structures, and other architectural systems. The translation from digital model to physical artifact is achieved through the output of data that provides instructions to the machine, and the machines interaction with materials. Digital fabrication methods incorporate *subtractive* and *additive* processes for shaping and forming materials. Subtractive processes are methods that involve removing material, by cutting and carving solid materials, with machines such as laser cutters, CNC (computer numerically controlled) routers, and water jet cutters. Additive processes involve forming materials, by building up layers of materials, with machines such as 3D printers.

Laser Cutters

Laser cutters shape materials by cutting and etching flat-sheet materials through the use of a high-powered laser and optics, to burn, melt, and vaporize materials at the location in which the laser is pointing. Laser cutters that are used within architecture schools and offices are typically used for model making and prototyping purposes, and can cut flat-sheet materials such as paper, mylar, chipboard, foam core, acrylic, cardboard, particle board, and other materials, usually up to ¼" (0.6cm) thick, depending on the material. Higher-powered, industrial lasers are used in the manufacturing industry to cut stronger materials such as flat sheets of steel for building parts and assemblies. Laser cutters have flat horizontal beds, in which flat-sheet materials are placed, and a track system for moving the laser in the X and Y directions while cutting, and the Z direction to set the laser's height position and distance from the material. Laser cutters utilize vector linework for cutting and engraving, as well as raster images for engraving. Linework from programs such as Adobe Illustrator or Autodesk's AutoCAD can be exported to the laser cutter, along with the specified laser cutter power for cutting and engraving, and the cut speed. These settings, which vary depending on the material and thickness, are exported to create the G-code, the computer-numerical control (CNC) programming language that is used to control the machine.

There are various techniques for creating digitally fabricated artifacts from 3D models. Many of these techniques have been described in seminal books such as Branko Kolarevic's *Manufacturing Material Effects*, and Lisa Iwamoto's *Digital Fabrications: Architectural and Material Techniques*. These techniques open up new possibilities for design through the use of the material and tool as methods for digital craft. The *sectioning* technique can be used to create various sections through the 3D model. This includes *contouring*, in which the digital model is sectioned, at a distance equal to the thickness of the material, to create multiple laser cut profiles that can be stacked and glued to create the physical model. (See Figure 2.20.) Sectioning techniques can also be used to create sections in the 3D digital model, spaced apart at specified distances, in both directions, to create an *interlocking* assembly.

By reducing the power setting of the laser, materials can be etched or engraved. This is useful for labeling all of the cut parts within the digital

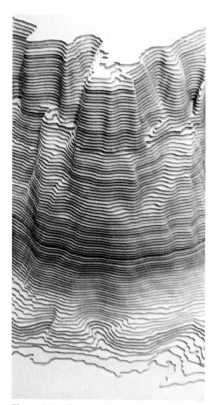

Figure 2.20. Topographic site model, laser-cut foam core sheets stacked to create a physical topographic site model of the landscape. First-year undergraduate architectural design studio. Instructor, Frank Melendez. The Bernard and Anne Spitzer School of Architecture, City College of New York. *Courtesy of the author.*

file, so that each part that is cut within the laser cutter is engraved with the label, which is useful for managing and facilitating the assembly process. Engraving can also be used to create various types of patterns and effects within the material. (See Figure 2.21.)

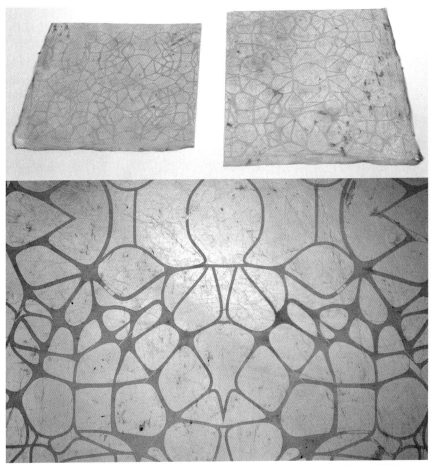

Figure 2.21. Nancy Diniz and Frank Melendez, Augmented Architectures, *Embryonic Spaces,* 2016. Laser-cut patterns engraved into sheets of biomaterials. *Courtesy of © Augmented Architectures.*

CNC Routers

CNC routers shape materials by cutting and removing material, in the form of flat sheets or solid volumes, through the use of a drill bit. Materials can be placed onto the CNC router's horizontal bed and secured in place, using vacuum pressure systems that are integrated into the machines, or with other devices, such as clamps. A track system allows for the movement of the bit in the X, Y, and Z directions, in three-axis machines. The drill bit, which is attached to a spindle with a *collet*, can be set to rotate

at a specified RPM (revolutions per minute), known as the *spindle speed*, and set to move at a specified speed, known as the *feed rate,* in order to cut material. The spindle speed and feed rates can be calculated to cut materials such as foam, wood, metal, and acrylic. (See Figure 2.22.) The movement of the drill bit in the X, Y, and Z directions follows the path of vectors, known as *toolpaths*, which are exported from the CNC router software as *G-code*. The toolpaths are generated from the 3D model using CNC router software packages, such as Rhino CAM. CNC router software has preset options for generating the toolpaths. When cutting flat profiles, the toolpaths can be generated to follow the vector curves from a two-dimensional drawing, and set to cut to the inside, middle, or outside of the lines,

Figure 2.22. CNC milled laminated particle board, showing the rough cut and final cut. *Courtesy of the author.*

based on the drill bit width. When cutting solid volumes, such as an undulating surface, the preset toolpaths can be set to run in one direction, two directions, radially, and other configurations.

Some CAD/CAM software packages, such as Rhino CAM, provide options to create custom toolpaths. In this scenario, the toolpath curves can be designed to cut the materials by following the path of the specified curves. (See Figure 2.23.) This provides

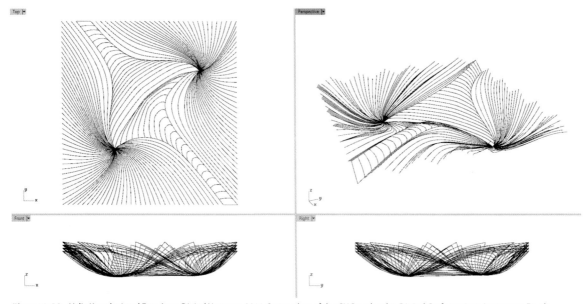

Figure 2.23. Yeliz Karadayi and Esra Aras, *Digital Nouveau*, 2014. Screenshot of the CNC toolpaths, Digital Craft seminar, Instructor, Frank Melendez. Carnegie Mellon University, School of Architecture. *Courtesy of Yeliz Karadayi.*

design opportunities for expressing the material, toolpaths, and the fabrication process, as architectural patterns, textures, and ornament. (See Figure 2.24.) These various factors, such as the material properties, cut speed, drill bit size, drill bit shape (for example, flat or ball end), and toolpaths, all impact the outcome of the formal attributes of the machined objects, opening up design possibilities through the output of information from the digital model, as input information for the fabrication of the physical artifact.

Figure 2.24. Yeliz Karadayi and Esra Aras, *Digital Nouveau,* 2014. Resin cast from the CNC milled mold, Digital Craft seminar, Instructor, Frank Melendez. Carnegie Mellon University, School of Architecture,. *Courtesy of Yeliz Karadayi.*

3D Printers

3D printers create physical objects through an additive process of building up incremental layers of materials. There are many different types of 3D printers and materials that can be used for 3D printing. 3D prints are fabricated from 3D models that are exported as polygon mesh models, typically in .obj or .stl file formats. These models are imported into 3D printing software, which is used to *slice*, or contour, the 3D model into horizontal sections. With plastic printers, these slices are used to define the *toolpaths*, and locations where a heated nozzle, the *extruder*, is used to melt plastic material, the *filament*, which is fed from a spool and deposited as a single layer of plastic. The extruder moves up (or the bed moves down) a specified distance, which establishes the layer thickness, or *resolution*, to deposit the next layer, and repeats this process until the print is complete. (See Figure 2.25).

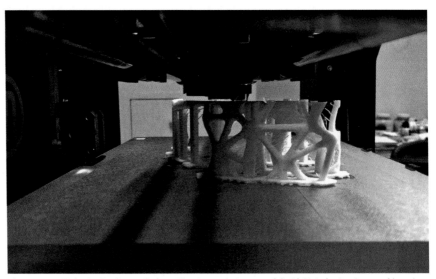

Figure 2.25. MakerBot Replicator desktop 3D printer, printing a model with PLA plastic. *Courtesy of the author.*

Various settings can be established within the 3D printing software prior to exporting the file as the G-code, which runs the machine. These settings include the print resolution, which on average is ~01.mm (100 microns); the *speed* at which the nozzle moves along the tracks in the X, Y, and Z directions; the nozzle *temperature*, which on average is ~230° C, depending on the type of plastic that is being used, ABS or PLA; and additional settings. 3D printing machines range in price and capabilities, from small desktop 3D printers, such as MakerBot that can build parts out of plastic, to larger machines that print at a very high resolution out of composite materials, such as the Object series of printers by Stratysis, that build professional-grade parts and prototypes. 3D printing provides architects and designers with opportunities to create complex three-dimensional forms that would be difficult or impossible to achieve through traditional model-making techniques. (See Figures 2.26 and 2.27.)

Although the most commonly used materials for 3D printers are various types of plastics, resins, and powders, recent advances in 3D printing are providing architects, designers, and artists with technologies that allow for the rapid prototyping and manufacturing of objects out of different materials, including concrete, metal, and glass, and at various scales, including full-scale concrete structures. The Mediated

Figure 2.26. Elena Pérez Guembe and Rosana Rubio-Hernández, *Mille-oeille*, 2008. 3D print of the pavilion's responsive envelope and apertures. *Courtesy of Elena Pérez Guembe and Rosana Rubio-Hernández.*

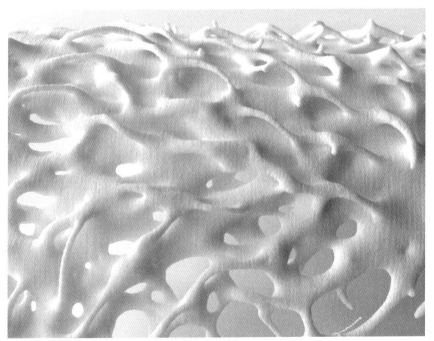

Figure 2.27. Nancy Diniz and Frank Melendez, Augmented Architectures, *Body Architectures*, 2018. 3D printed (nylon) wearable device. *Courtesy of © Augmented Architectures.*

Matter Group at MIT, directed by the architect Neri Oxman, has developed the additive manufacturing method *G3DP* (glass 3D printing), which can print glass in a variety of shapes, sizes, and colors with different optical properties and qualities of translucency.[19] (See Figures 2.28 and 2.29.)

Figure 2.28. Mediated Matter Group, MIT Media Lab, G3DP: additive manufacturing of optically transparent glass. Glass 3D printing process. Photograph by Steven Keating. *Courtesy of the Mediated Matter Group.*

Figure 2.29. Mediated Matter Group, MIT Media Lab, G3DP: additive manufacturing of optically transparent glass. Caustic patterns of a 3D printed glass structure. Photograph by Andy Ryan. *Courtesy of the Mediated Matter Group.*

Plastic materials can also be extruded through hand-held devices such as the 3Doodler, a 3D printing pen that extrudes plastic filament through an analog pen-shaped device. This allows the designer to hand-draw freely in 3D space, or on objects, to create three-dimensional drawings out of plastic materials that are available in various colors. (See Figure 2.30.) Projects such as *Guided Hand,* by the hybrid designer and developer Yeliz Karadayi, extend the capabilities of handheld 3D printing devices, with a haptic feedback device, the Geomagic Touch, which uses a robotic arm to push and pull the tip of the handheld pen. This produces the sensation of touching digital models, in the same manner as touching real objects with a pen, to combine the physical craft of modeling making with the precision and accuracy of digital models. (See Figure 2.31.)

Figure 2.30. *Parametric Patterns, Plastic 3D Drawings*, 2017. Plastic 3D drawings created by first-year undergraduate architecture students using 3Doodler pens to create structural patterns. Instructor, Frank Melendez. The Bernard and Anne Spitzer School of Architecture, City College of New York. *Courtesy of the author.*

Figure 2.31. Yeliz Karadayi, *Guided Hand*, 2016. A 3D printing pen used with the Geomagic Touch to create haptic feedback to constrain the user's movements and provide haptic textural effects. *Courtesy of Yeliz Karadayi.*

Robotic Fabrication

Advances in robotic technologies are providing architects and designers with new opportunities to fabricate architectural projects through the use of robots, programmable machines that can be automated to perform tasks. The field of robotics and the research for using robotics in architectural design is vast and will be discussed in greater detail in Chapter 15, "Robotics and Physical Computing." Industrial robots are one category of robots that are typically used for manufacturing. Industrial robots have two or more axes allowing the machine to move in a similar manner to a human arm. The tooling at the end of the robotic arm is known as the *end effector*. One of the advantages of robotic fabrication is the ability to change the end effector to various tools, which provides opportunities to use the machine for both additive and subtractive fabrication processes, as well as other methods of assembly. For example, using a drill bit as the end effector allows the industrial robot to cut and remove material in a similar manner to a CNC router; however, the robotic arm's multi-axis capabilities can be used to cut material from multiple angles, such as from the side or below, allowing for *undercuts*. (Figure 2.32.) Other end effectors, such as grippers and vacuums, can be used to pick up and move objects. In 2006, Gramazio Kohler Architects designed the Gantenbeim Vineyard Facade in Fläsch, Switzerland. Using a robotic production method that they developed at the ETH Zürich, they designed a masonry facade for the vineyard's fermentation room, which served as a temperature buffer and daylighting filter for the room. The facade was fabricated through the use of an industrial robot with a gripper end effector, which was programmed to lay over 20,000 bricks precisely according to parameters, the desired angle at the exact prescribed interval. (Figure 2.33.) The bricks are rotated and offset to allow daylight to enter while excluding direct sunlight, and to form a pictorial three-dimensional effect of round grapes. (See Figure 2.34.)

Today, physical models, 3D models, and digital fabrication processes are used in a variety of ways throughout the architectural design process. Physical models and artifacts can be scanned to create 3D models, and 3D models can be output and produced as physical objects through the use of digital fabrication tools. This ability to work back and forth between physical and virtual models has altered traditional design and construction workflows and, with advances in technology, continues to open up new opportunities for architecture.

Figure 2.32. Armand Graham, Timbr, 2016. Robotic arm using a drill bit end effector to fabricate the sustainable wood furniture. Fabricated by Timbur, LLC, Ezra Ardolino. *Courtesy of Armand Graham.*

Figure 2.33. Gramazio Kohler Research, ETH Zürich, Gantenbeim Vineyard Facade, 2006, Fläsch Switzerland. Industrial robot programmed to grab and stack bricks using a gripper end effector. *© Gramazio Kohler Research, ETH Zürich.*

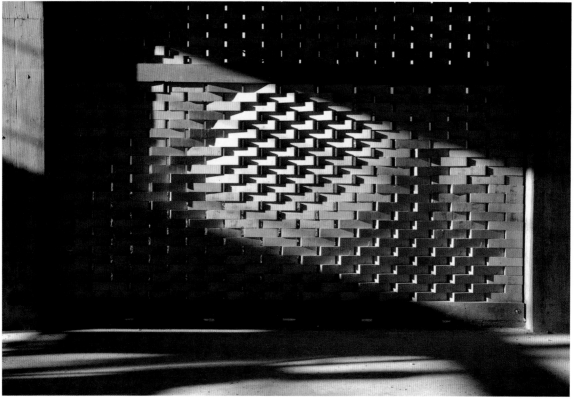

Figure 2.34. Gramazio Kohler Architects, Gantenbeim Vineyard Facade, 2006, Fläsch Switzerland. Nonstandardized brick facade fabricated by industrial robot. *© Gramazio Kohler Architects*

Endnotes

1. Milena Stavric, Predrag Sidanin, and Bojan Tepavcevic, *Architectural Scale Models in the Digital Age: Design, Representation, and Manufacturing* (New York: Springer Wien, 2013).

2. Vitruvius Pollio, Marcus, "Measures of Defense" in *De architectura* (*The Ten Books on Architecture*, trans. Morris Hickey Morgan), (Cambridge, MA: Harvard University Press, 1914).

3. Richard Garber, guest ed., *Architecture Design: Closing the Gap-Information Models in Contemporary Design Practice* (London: John Wiley & Sons, March–April 2009).

4. Yehuda E. Kalay, *Architecture's New Media: Principles, Theories, and Methods of Computer-Aided Design* (Cambridge, MA: MIT Press, 2004).

5. Ibid.

6. Greg Lynn, *Animate Form* (New York: Princeton Architectural Press, 1999).

7. Howard Schubert, "Embyrological House, *Origins of the Digital*, Article 4, Canadian Center for Architecture, https://www.cca.qc.ca/en/issues/4/origins-of-the-digital/5/embryological-house.

8. Branko Kolarevic, *Architecture in the Digital Age: Design and Manufacturing* (New York and London: Routledge, Taylor & Francis, 2005).

9. Michael Weinstock, *The Architecture of Emergence: The Evolution of Form in Nature and Civilization* (Chichester, UK: Wiley, 2010).

10. Craig Reynolds, "Flocks, Herds, and Schools: A Distributed Behavioral Model," *SIGGRAPH '87 Proceedings of the 14th Annual Conference on Computer Graphics and Interactive Techniques,* Maureen C. Stone, ed. (New York: ACM, 1987).

11. Neil Leach, guest ed., "Swarm Urbanism," *AD: Digital Cities* 79 (4, July–August 2009), general ed., Helen Castle.

12. Ibid.

13. Yidong Ma and Wieguo Xu, "Physarealm: A Bio-inspired Stigmergic Algorithm Tool for Form-Finding," in *Protocols, Flows and Glitches,* Proceedings of the 22nd International Conference of the Association for Computer-Aided Design Research in Asia (CAADRIA), Hong Kong, P. Janssen, P. Loh, A. Raonic, and M. A. Schnabel, eds. 2017, pp. 499–509.

14. Steve Aukstakalnis, *Practical Augmented Reality: A Guide to the Technologies, Applications, and Human Factors for AR and VR* (Boston: Pearson Education, Addison-Wesley, 2017).

15. Ibid.

16. Howard Rheingold, *Virtual Reality* (New York: Touchstone, Simon & Schuster, 1991).

17. Alicia Imperiale, *New Flatness: Surface Tension in Digital Architecture* (Basel, Boston, Berlin: Birkhäuser, 2000).

18. Lisa Iwamoto, *Digital Fabrications: Architectural and Material Techniques* (New York: Princeton Architectural Press, 2009).

19. Brian Krassenstein, "G3DP Project: Mediated Matter and MIT Glass Lab Develop Advanced Glass 3D Printer," 3DPrint.com, August 20, 2015, https://3dprint.com/90748/g3dp-glass-3d-print/.

Chapter 3
Architecture and Computing

Chapter 3 introduces digital concepts and terminologies related to computing and 3D modeling. The methods in which geometry is defined within 3D models builds upon historical methods of descriptive geometry and projection. This includes using the Cartesian coordinate system to define the locations of points in space, which can be utilized to define other geometric elements such as lines, curves, and surfaces. As computing technologies evolve, providing faster processing speeds and enhanced graphics, so do 3D modeling platforms and their capabilities.

This chapter provides an overview of early computer-aided design (CAD) models and graphics, the development of digital surface and solid modelers, advances in parametric and associative models, and the use of building information models (BIM) that contain blocks of parametric objects that store data and information. These advances in 3D modeling provide architects and designers with agency to create complex geometries, produce and test design iterations quickly, associatively link drawings and models, and streamline methods of collaboration.

3.1 Digital Concepts

Cartesian Coordinates

The French mathematicians René Descartes (1596–1650) and Pierre de Fermat (1607–1665) introduced the concept of coordinates on a plane through the use of two directions on a plane that intersect at a perpendicular angle. Descartes presented an algebraic approach to geometry by measuring distances in the directions of axes and defining an origin. He used geometric techniques to visualize algebraic equations, opening up new methods for studying classes of curves through the new analytic geometry. This led mathematicians about a century later to use a systematic algebraic approach to geometry based on coordinates called Cartesian coordinates, named after Descartes.[1]

Cartesian coordinates can be understood as a planar grid with positive and negative values running along two axes. The X axis runs horizontally and the Y axis runs vertically. The intersection of the X and Y axes is called the *origin*, which has an X value of zero and a Y value of zero that is defined as (0,0). X and Y values are variables that can be entered as coordinates to specify a point within the grid, measured from the *origin*. For example, a point with an X value of +4 and a Y value of +3 defines a point 4 units to the right of the origin and 3 units up from the origin, and is represented by the coordinates (4,3). (See Figure 3.1.)

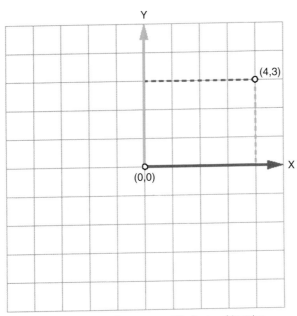

Figure 3.1. Cartesian coordinate system, 2D. *Courtesy of the author.*

X, Y, Z Axes

The introduction of a third axis that is perpendicular to the XY plane and passes through the *origin* produces the Z axis. This provides a third direction, which can be used to locate a point in three-dimensional space, with the origin coordinates defined as (0,0,0). A point with the same X and Y values specified in the previous example, plus a Z value of +5 is represented by the coordinates (4,3,5). (See Figure 3.2.)

Cartesian coordinates include both positive and negative values in the X, Y, and Z axes. Through the location of points within the Cartesian coordinate system, lines, surfaces, and volumes can be described. The Cartesian coordinate system is the basis of measuring points in space within two-dimensional and three-dimensional space, and are used to define *pixel* grids within *raster* graphics, and *path* control points within *vector* graphics.

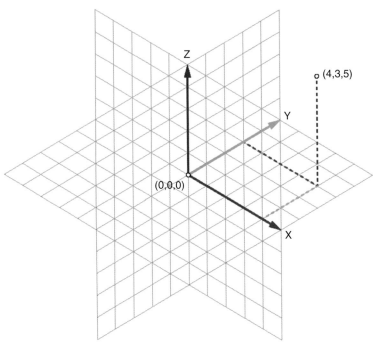

Figure 3.2. Cartesian coordinate system, 3D. *Courtesy of the author.*

Raster and Vector Graphics

Raster and *vector* graphics both utilize the Cartesian coordinate system to create images. *Raster* graphics use the two-dimensional Cartesian coordinate system to define a grid of cells, known as *pixels,* a portmanteau for *picture element.* In light-emitting surfaces, such as computer screens and television screens, color is achieved by various *additive* combinations of red, green, and blue color values, known as the RGB color model. In raster graphics, each *pixel* is filled with an RGB color value, resulting in the representation of an image. The clarity of the image depends on the number of pixels within a designated area, which is known as the image *resolution.* The resolution is measured according to the number of pixels per square inch (*ppi*). The more pixels per square inch, the higher the resolution; the fewer pixels per square inch, the lower the resolution. Raster graphics are best suited for photographic imagery, and are utilized in image-editing software. When raster graphics are scaled up, the pixels may be visible, resulting in a loss of quality in the image and making it appear *pixelated.* Because architectural drawings are typically printed at various scales, this makes raster graphics less suitable for creating linework within architectural drawings. (See Figure 3.3.)

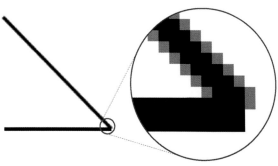

Figure 3.3. Linework from a raster graphic image with a portion of the polyline scaled up to illustrate that the linework edges appear pixelated. *Courtesy of the author.*

Vector graphics utilize the Cartesian coordinate system to define points, which are connected to form *paths*. A path can be defined as a line segment, curve, or closed polygon shape. Vector graphics utilize stored sets of mathematical equations to define paths. The path can be assigned attributes, such as a width and an RGB color value, to define a line segment. A *path* with attributes is called a *stroke*. The points and paths can be scaled up or down and will retain the same mathematical relationship; therefore, there is no loss in image quality when changing scale. This makes vector graphics much more suitable for architectural drawings, linework, and graphics. (See Figure 3.4.) Computer-aided drafting software and 3D modeling software utilize vector graphics.

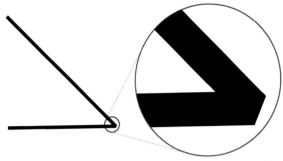

Figure 3.4. Linework from a vector graphic image with a portion of the polyline scaled up to illustrate that the linework maintains sharp edges. *Courtesy of the author.*

Bits and Bytes

A *bit* is the basic unit of information in computing and digital communications. The term *bit* is a portmanteau for *binary digit*, and has one of two values, which are commonly represented as either a 1 or a 0, and as logical values such as yes (1) or no (0), true (1) or false (0), and on (1) or off (0) [2] A *byte* is a unit of digital information in computing that commonly consists of eight bits, forming a series of eight 0s and 1s. The exponentiation with 2 as the base and 8 as the exponent allows for 256 combinations. This creates a range of values from 0 to 255, with 0 being the first value. Originally, the byte was developed to store a character with a range of 256 values, which was sufficient to store uppercase and lowercase letters, numbers, and symbols. The range of 0 to 255 is also used in the RGB color coding system, which allows for a range of 256 shades of red, 256 shades of green, and 256 shades of blue, which can be combined to create over 16 million possible colors.[3] The 8-bit system was expanded to adopt languages that exceeded 256 values, and other uses for storing information, resulting in the development of 16-bit, 32-bit, and 64-bit systems. The byte is the standard unit of measurement for all data storage.[4]

3.2 Computing in Architecture

Sketchpad

The first vector graphic systems were utilized by the U.S. Air Force to convert collected data from radars into single images. This led to the first modern concept of a computer-aided design (CAD) system, which was developed in 1963 at the Massachusetts Institute of Technology by the computer scientist and electrical engineer Ivan Sutherland. Sutherland's invention, a program called Sketchpad, allowed users to draw with a light pen on a graphical user interface (GUI).[5] Point coordinates could be defined on the screen with the light pen to draw lines and shapes, and constrained to precise directions, angles, and dimensions. (See Figure 3.5.) In addition to conceptualizing and developing an interactive computational device, this invention was the beginning of computer-aided drafting and paved the way for CAD systems to eventually become the primary method for creating architectural drawings and models.

Figure 3.5. Ivan Sutherland, Sketchpad, 1963. Massachusetts Institute of Technology.

Computer-Aided Design (CAD)

Early developments in the ability to digitally model and represent polyhedral forms were developed through research within various academic and industry settings, including mechanical engineering, architecture, movies, and games. Initial building-specific CAD systems were led by university-based research groups in the United States and Britain. This included a focus on developing systems to support building-related operations, led by Chuck Eastman; an artificial intelligence approach to developing architectural computing applications, led by Nicholas Negroponte; and computer applications that capitalized on the coordination of modular building components, led by Aart Bijl.[6] These developments encompassed architectural design processes, but were often too cumbersome and specific to use in practice.[7] In other industries outside of architecture, such as mechanical engineering, the development of CAD systems was led by industry-based research groups and focused on geometric modeling. Industries such as the aerospace, automotive, and manufacturing fields recognized the potential of 3D solid modeling to analyze geometry, reduce errors, and automate fabrication.[8] This led to the development of 3D modeling and CAD software, such as CATIA, which became the aeronautical applications leader in the mid-1980s.[9] Other developments in the representation of polyhedral forms were utilized in videogames, such as Atari's Battlezone (1980), and movies, such as *Tron* (1982), the first computer-graphics film. (See Figure 3.6.) These forms were primarily representational, and were used to create graphic images from vector wireframe models. However, they were limited in their ability to be quickly edited and modified, which was a necessary feature in the architectural design process.[10]

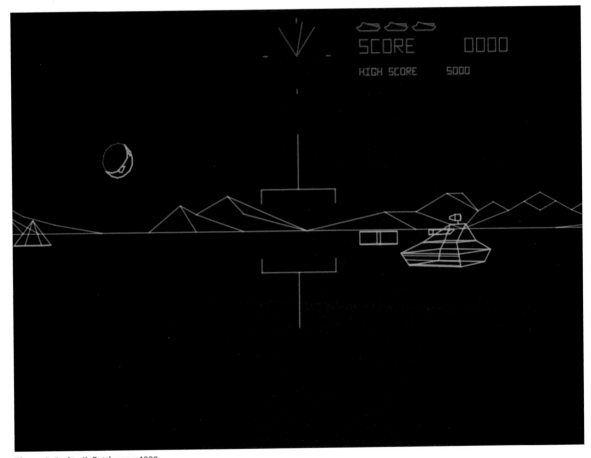

Figure 3.6. Atari's Battlezone, 1980.

As advances in computing were made, with the development of faster processing, personal computers, and graphic interfaces, the geometric modeling approach was implemented in the architectural industry and developed for computer-aided drafting. While there were many benefits associated with computer-aided drafting, such as increased precision and drawing production speed, these tools were utilized primarily to augment traditional two-dimensional hand-drafting methods. As computational tools continued to develop, three-dimensional geometric models were used to design and visualize forms through surface and solid modeling methods.

3.3 Developments in 3D Modeling

Surfaces and Solid Modeling

Just as a line segment can be defined by two points, a two-dimensional polygon can be defined by bounding line segments to produce a *surface*. Specifying *points* (vertices) in the modeling space defines *line segments* (edges), which are used as the input to define a *surface* (face). Surfaces can also be created by *sweep operations*. Just as a single point can be moved in a straight direction to define a straight line, a profile line or curve can be swept along straight or curved paths to define a surface. These operations include extruding, rotating, and sweeping.[11] Combining surfaces to create 3D, solid, volume-enclosing forms is known as *solid modeling*. Initial *solid models* were developed using two different approaches, a *boundary representation (B-rep)* approach and a *constructive solid geometry (CSG)* representation approach. *B-rep models* represent solid forms by connecting a series of surfaces that enclose a volume. These surfaces are created by defining vertices, edges, and faces, and by sweep operations. Additionally, complex surfaces and forms can be created through *Boolean operations*, which unite, intersect, and subtract overlapping geometry, for example, by subtracting a cylinder from a block form to create a hole.[12] *CSG models* also create forms through Boolean operations; however, the Boolean operations are stored as sequential sets of mathematical equations. Boolean operations are applied to Boolean operations, and so on, to produce CSG trees.[13] The starting elements in the tree define geometrically simple solid models, which go through a set of sequential Boolean operations, until converging to yield the final, geometrically complex solid model. CSG models display the shapes as wireframe geometry but without boundary surfaces, allowing the model to be edited and regenerated quickly. Today, parametric modeling tools and building models incorporate both B-rep and CSG-like methods, for visualizing and editing models.[14]

Parametric Models

Many current 3D modeling programs incorporate *parametric* capabilities. The geometry in *parametric models* can be defined with numerical inputs and relationships. These values can be shared with other geometric entities in the model. For example, multiple surfaces can be extruded to a specified height that is defined by a numerical value. When this numerical value that defines the height is changed, all of the surfaces are updated to reflect the updated value. Geometric constraints can also be applied to geometry. For example, the center point of a circle can be constrained to the endpoint of a line segment. Therefore, when the line is moved the circle moves with it, remaining constrained to the line's end point. This establishes a hierarchy of dependencies within the geometric entities of the 3D model, as the definition of one geometry (the circle) is dependent on another (the line). This allows elements lower down in the chain of commands, *downstream*, to respond to changes made to elements higher up in the chain of commands, *upstream*, providing the model with a rudimentary intelligence.

Early parametric modeling programs, such as Dessault Systèmes CATIA V5, display the parametric values and geometric constraints within a "tree", along with the 3D model. (See Figure 3.7.) This serves as a visualization of the geometric hierarchies and dependencies, and also provides the ability to edit and make changes to the model *parameters* directly within the tree. In addition to the 3D modeling space, a 2D paper space is provided to view and create various orthographic projections and section cuts to the parametric model. As changes to the 3D model are made, the 2D projections are automatically updated. This links the 3D modeling space with the 2D drawing space, making them *associative*. Other parametric modeling programs, such as Bentley's GenerativeComponents (GC), display the parametric properties of a feature within a table. (See Figure 3.8.) A feature such as a point on a plane displays the parameters that are required to define the point; a specified plane, an X value, and a Y value. Additionally, computational *functions*, such as defining the point as a *series*, can be specified, to create multiple point values for a single point. As opposed to a tree, GenerativeComponents displays the geometric elements and their relationships in a visual "symbolic diagram." (See Figure 3.9.)

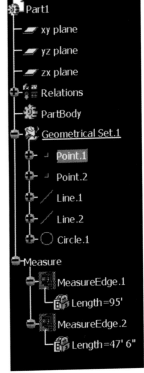

Figure 3.7. The tree in Dessault Systèmes CATIA V5. *Courtesy of the author.*

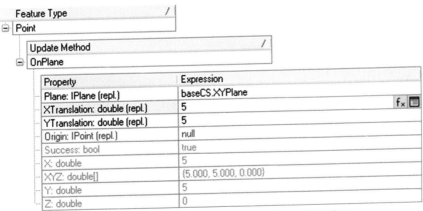

Figure 3.8. The feature table in Bentley's GenerativeComponents. *Courtesy of the author.*

These early parametric modeling platforms led to current developments of visual programming languages, such as Grasshopper, a node-based algorithmic editor for Rhino. Within the Grasshopper interface, individual components can be placed onto a canvas and connected in various ways to create programs. (See Figure 3.10.)

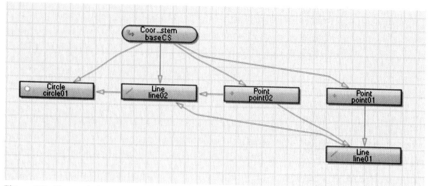

Figure 3.9. The symbolic diagram in Bentley's GenerativeComponents. *Courtesy of the author.*

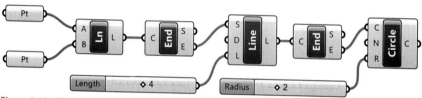

Figure 3.10. Visual programming components in Grasshopper for Rhino. *Courtesy of the author.*

Building Information Models (BIM)

Programs such as CATIA can also describe geometry with additional information, such as material properties. The ability for geometric entities to contain additional information and data is one of the fundamental principles of building information modeling (BIM). Programs such as Bentley's GenerativeComponents, Gehry Technologies' Digital Project (developed from CATIA), and Autodesk's Revit are current BIM architectural design tools. In BIM models, instead of modeling a particular element, an object family is defined with parametric geometry and a set of relations and rules to control the parameters.[15] For example, a wall family object can contain various information that makes up the wall, such as the inside finish, outside finish, internal construction, and internal layers. This object can then be assigned parameters, or placed within a context that will define the shape, such as the wall's length and height. Various "information" (the "I" in BIM) can be associated with parametric objects, such as material attributes, costs, and other data relevant to architecture, engineering, and construction (AEC). The BIM model is typically controlled by the architect, but can be shared with other project team members, such as engineers, contractors, clients, and so on, and serves as a "master model" that provides current and updated information and data related to the building and project. (See Figure 3.11.)

Figure 3.11. Gehry Partners, LLP, Walt Disney Concert Hall, Los Angeles, CA (completed) 2003. BIM 3D model. *Courtesy of © Frank O. Gehry. Getty Research Institute, Los Angeles (2017.M.66), Frank Gehry Papers.*

Although BIM platforms have many benefits that are impacting the architecture profession and changing the role of the architect in many ways, there are differences from surface modeling. BIM models are designed to streamline processes in architectural practice, which see projects through construction, over longer spans of time, and within larger interdisciplinary teams, including engineers, contractors, and other consultants. However, for schematic design phases, and in academic environments such as architectural design studios, surface modelers such as Robert McNeel & Associates Rhinoceros allow for more flexibility and ease in generating geometry, shapes, and forms. Additionally, visual programming interfaces, such as Grasshopper, which is included in Rhino 6 for Windows, provide parametric and algorithmic design capabilities for quickly generating iterative models and using scripting procedures for generating complex geometries.

Endnotes

1. Francis Borceaux, *An Algebraic Approach to Geometry: Geometric Trilogy II* (New York: Springer, 2014).
2. Per Christensson, "Bit Definition," *TechTerms,* April 20, 2013, accessed November 15, 2017, https://techterms.com/definition/bit.

3. Casey Reas and Chandler McWilliams, *Form + Code: In Design, Art, and Architecture* (New York: Princeton Architectural Press, 2010).

4. Per Christensson, "Byte Definition," *TechTerms,* November 30, 2011, accessed November 15, 2017, https://techterms.com/definition/byte.

5. Ivan E. Sutherland, "Sketchpad: A Man-Machine Graphical Communication System," *SIMULATION* 2, no. 5 (May 1964), R-3–R-20.

6. Yehuda E. Kalay, *Architecture's New Media: Principles, Theories, and Methods of Computer-Aided Design* (Cambridge, MA: MIT Press, 2004).

7. Ibid.

8. Chuck Eastman, Paul Teicholz, Rafael Sacks, and Kathleen Liston, *BIM Handbook: A Guide to Building Information Modeling for Owners, Managers, Designers, Engineers, and Contractors,* 2d ed. (Hoboken, NJ: John Wiley & Sons, 2011).

9. Marian Bozdoc, "CAD Chronology: 1970–1989," iMB: Resources and Information for Professional Designers, http://mbinfo.mbdesign.net/CAD1970.htm.

10. Eastman et al., *BIM Handbook.*

11. William J. Mitchell and Malcolm McCullough, *Digital Design Media* (New York: Van Nostrand Reinhold, 1995).

12. Ibid.

13. Ibid.

14. Eastman et al., *BIM Handbook.*

15. Ibid.

Part 2
3D Modeling and Geometry

Part 2 provides an overview of the 3D modeling environment, as well as concepts and techniques that demonstrate methods for generating two-dimensional projections from 3D models. The ability to create 3D models with precision and efficiency requires an understanding of coordinate systems, metrics, and conventions of architectural drawing. This section introduces fundamental geometries for creating digital drawings and models, such as points, lines, and surfaces. Descriptions of vectors, splines, and NURBS geometry provide an understanding of the mechanics of 3D models and geometry, which can be created and manipulated to represent various shapes and forms ranging from simple to complex.

This section introduces tools, techniques, and workflows for generating geometry with extrusions, translations, rotations, and lofts. These processes yield various types of surfaces, such as planes, ruled surfaces, and doubly curved surfaces, which are defined and depicted through examples of paradigmatic works of architecture. The role of the 3D model has become the new convention in generating architectural projections and drawings in both academia and practice. Two-dimensional linework of three-dimensional forms can be generated by projecting point, line, and surface geometries onto planes, resulting in curve objects that can be used for creating architectural drawings and representations. Additionally, surfaces can be used to generate linework by extracting isocurves, contouring, and subdividing. This linework enhances architectural drawings through the representation of patterns and textures. The process of working from the 3D model to the drawing has created a paradigm shift in architectural pedagogy and methods of teaching architectural representation.

Chapter 4
The 3D Modeling Environment

Chapter 4 describes 3D modeling surface types and provides an overview of the Rhino 6 for Windows modeling environment. This chapter also describes the organization of the interface, which includes the 3D modeling viewports, toolbars, and menus for accessing commands that create and transform geometric objects. Units, modeling aids, layers, and object properties, can be utilized for creating accurate, precise, and organized, two-dimensional drawings and three-dimensional models. These drawings and models can be visualized in various formats, such as wireframe, shaded, and rendered views.

4.1 Surface Types

3D modeling environments use Cartesian coordinate systems to define the locations of points in space based on their distances from the origin of the X, Y, and Z axes. Points are used as the underlying elements that define other geometry, such as lines, curves, planes, and surfaces. Two points can be used to describe a line, two intersecting lines can be used to describe a plane, and so on. In Rhino, these geometrical elements are various types of *objects*. Objects can be created and juxtaposed in the virtual three-dimensional environment to simulate a building, structure, landscape, or any other three-dimensional form. Similar to a physical model, users can move, rotate, and zoom in and out of the 3D model to obtain a different view of the forms and spaces in the virtual environment.

There are various 3D modeling types and methods for 3D modeling. Two primary surface modeling types are *polygonal* modeling and *NURBS* modeling. Polygonal models consist of polygon meshes, closed figures that are bound by straight line segments to define surfaces, typically through triangular and rectangular polygons. Within polygon models, these points, lines, and surfaces form the vertices, edges, and faces, respectively. In polygon models, curves are approximated through the use of individual line segments. The more line segments, the smoother the curve appears. This is also similar for curved surfaces, which are approximated by the number of polygons faces within the surface. By increasing the number of polygon faces in the model, the appearance of a smoother surface is achieved. (See Figure 4.1.)

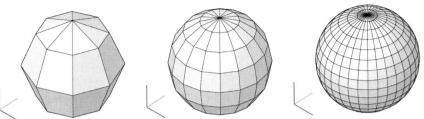

Figure 4.1. Mesh models of spheres consisting of a various number of polygons, from a low polygon count (left) to a high polygon count (right). *Courtesy of the author.*

In *NURBS (nonuniform rational B-spline)* modeling, curves are the basis of form generation, and utilize algorithmic formulas to continuously adjust and recalculate curves and surfaces.[1] This calculus-based system allows for the creation of smooth and fluid curves. NURBS models use *control points* to define curve and surface geometry, which are based on X, Y, and Z coordinates. Additionally, NURBS surfaces utilize a U, V space along the surface. These surfaces can be edited globally, by editing the surface control points through translations. (See Figure 4.2.)

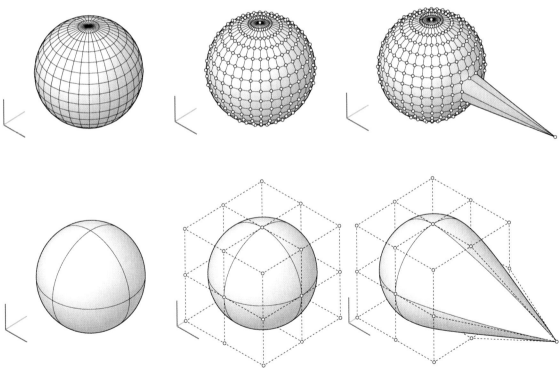

Figure 4.2. A comparison between a polygon sphere and a NURBS sphere: polygon sphere with the vertices displayed, and one vertex translated (top row); a NURBS sphere, with the control points displayed, and one control point translated (bottom row). *Courtesy of the author.*

4.2 The Rhinoceros Interface

To begin to construct virtual 3D models, one should understand the interface of the software in which they are working. Interfaces vary depending on the software; however, most 3D modeling software interfaces consist of command lines (to type commands), viewports (to view the 3D model), and toolbars consisting of tool icons (icons that are clicked to activate commands). The primary organization of the Rhino 6 for Windows interface includes drop-down menus, the Command line, tabs and toolbars, main toolbars, panels, viewports, and modeling aids. In Rhino, commands can be executed in three ways: by selecting the command from drop-down menus, by typing the command in the Command line, or by clicking on the tool icons that graphically depict the various commands. (See Figure 4.3.)

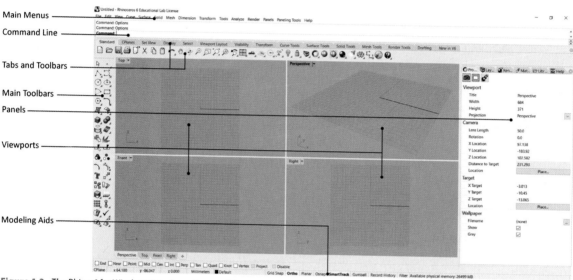

Figure 4.3. The Rhino 6 for Windows interface. *Courtesy of the author.*

Main Menus

The Main Menus provide drop-down menus with commands that are organized according to the menu titles. For example, the File drop-down menu provides commands for creating, opening, and saving files. Clicking on the Curve drop-down menu, will provide a list of the various commands associated with creating, editing, and generating curves. Selecting other titles in the Main Menu will provide a list of all of the commands associated with that category. Some titles provide subtitles, which are indicated by a small black arrow pointing toward the right. For example, after clicking the Curve drop-down menu, hovering the mouse over the Line subtitle expands a sublist of various commands for making and editing lines. (See Figure 4.4.) Clicking on one of the line options—such as, Single Line—prompts the command and displays the next steps needed to complete the command in the Command line.

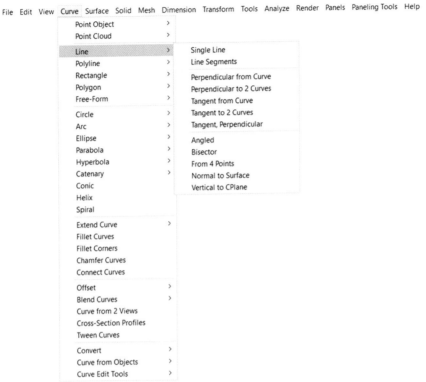

File Edit View Curve Surface Solid Mesh Dimension Transform Tools Analyze Render Panels Paneling Tools Help

Figure 4.4. Rhino Main Menus, Curve drop-down menu, and Line submenu. *Courtesy of the author.*

The Command Line

Many commands can be executed by typing directly into the Command line. This provides an intuitive method for communicating to the software the desired command you wish to execute. After executing a command, additional information is needed as input to complete the command. For example, if the user types the command "Circle" in the Command line and presses the Enter key on the keyboard, text for the following steps appear, which includes specifying "Center of circle" by clicking in the modeling space, which defines the center of the circle. The next step includes defining the size of the circle by entering the value for Radius. Commands executed in the Command line typically have a series of alternative options for defining the object within a set of parentheses ( ). These options can be changed by hovering the mouse over the text and clicking the left mouse button to change the input option, such as switching from defining the "Radius" to defining the "Diameter" of the circle. The value of the diameter can be typed in units (for example, 1'6"). Press the Enter key on the keyboard to complete the command. (Figure 4.5).

Command: Circle

Center of circle (Deformable Vertical 2Point 3Point Tangent AroundCurve FitPoints):

Radius <12.000> (Diameter Orientation Circumference Area):

Diameter <24.000> (Radius Orientation Circumference Area): 1'6"

Figure 4.5. Rhino Command line. A list of the command prompts and options used to create a circle. *Courtesy of the author.*

75

Tabs and Toolbars

A series of tabs can be selected that each contain different sets of toolbars and tool icons. The tool icons graphically depict the function of the command. When the tab heading is clicked, the icons associated with these headings appear. For example, under the Set View tab, we can find many of the tool icons related to views. This includes navigation tools for changing the views, and different viewports. (Figure 4.6.)

Figure 4.6. Rhino tabs and toolbars. *Courtesy of the author.*

Main Toolbars

The main toolbars contain the tool icons of commands that are frequently used for modeling and editing geometry. These include commands for creating, editing, and transforming geometry. Some tool icons contain a small black arrow in the bottom right corner of the icon. These arrows can be clicked to expand and reveal other commands that are closely associated with the expanded icon. (Figure 4.7.)

Panels

The far-right side of the screen contains panels organized as six tabs: Properties, Layers, Rendering, Materials, Library, and Help. The Properties tab provides information about a selected object in the 3D model. This can include virtually any object, such as a curve, surface, or viewport. The Properties tab lists information and settings for the selected object under four different subcategories: Object, Render Mesh Settings, Rendering, and Isocurve Density. The Properties tab is useful for providing information about the object, such as the object type, the layer in which it is located, the display color, and isocurve density and visibility. (Figure 4.8.)

The use of layers is a conventional method for organizing elements in digital image editing, computer-aided drawings, and 3D modeling. The Layer tab lists default layers in the model and allows users to create new layers, name and rename layers, and reorganize the order in which layers are listed. (Figure 4.9.) In architectural 3D models, layers are very useful for organizing the various geometry, elements, and features that are associated with a building. For example, the elements that make up the exterior walls, interior walls, doors, windows, and so on can all be assigned to their specified layers. Layers can be turned on or off, to show and hide all of the elements on each layer. They can also be locked or unlocked, which toggles the ability to select elements in the layer. Layers can be assigned specific colors, which is a useful method for graphically differentiating between the various elements of the model.

Figure 4.7.
Rhino main toolbar and tool icons.
Courtesy of the author.

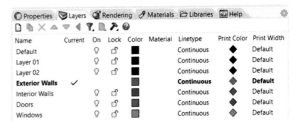

Figure 4.8. Rhino Panels, Properties tab. *Courtesy of the author.*

Figure 4.9. Rhino Panels, Layers tab. *Courtesy of the author.*

The Rendering, Materials, and Library tabs provide settings and options for rendering scenes and assigning materials. This includes various setting for the the render view, image resolution, and background, as well as various types of materials and material attributes, which can be selected and modified. The Help tab provides an interface for accessing Rhino's help topics and command descriptions.

Viewports

3D modeling software interfaces contain viewports, which are the camera views into the virtual modeling space, and are used to see and represent the model as orthographic, perspective, and axonometric projections. The four default viewports in most 3D modeling software are labeled as Top, Front, Right, and Perspective views. (Figure 4.10.) The Top, Front, and Right views are orthographic projections and represent the plan, south elevation, and east elevation, respectively. The Perspective viewport represents a one-point perspective view and is the view that is used to rotate around (orbit), and zoom in and out of the 3D model. Rhino viewports contain a default grid. This grid, which is called the construction plane (CPlane), has grid axes, the X axis represented as a red line, and the Y axis represented as a green line. The point at which the axes of a coordinate system intersect is called the *origin*. Each viewport also contains a graphic icon indicating the direction of the world XYZ axes in the bottom left corner of each viewport.

The default viewports can be modified to customize their organization and appearance on the screen. The sizes and layout of the viewports, the views of the 3D model, and the graphic appearance of the 3D model can all be changed. Additional views are available, such as isometric and two-point persepective views.

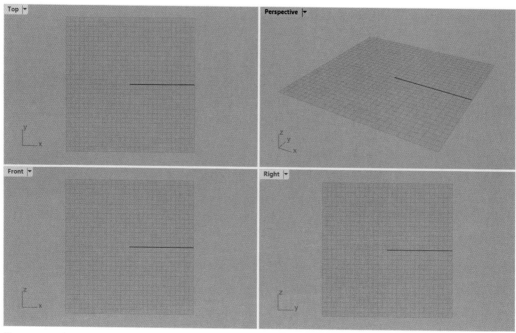

Figure 4.10. Rhino viewports, consisting by default of Top, Front, Right, and Perspective views. *Courtesy of the author.*

Modeling Aids

Architectural drawings require a high degree of precision in order to ensure that a constructed building is built accurately. Traditional hand-drafting tools, such as straight edges and triangles, were originally developed to aid in creating precise drawings with accurate measurements. Many of these tools were designed to draw straight lines, orthogonal geometry, precise angles, and so on. Modeling aids provide methods for controlling the geometry in a drawing or model. Modeling aids can be activated by clicking on their icons to toggle them on or off. (Figure 4.11.) Grid Snap constrains the starting position for geometry to the grid system. The Grid Snap settings can be changed by typing "Grid" in the Command line and changing the Grid Snap spacing. The Ortho setting (which is an abbreviation for Orthogonal, meaning two lines that are perpendicular at their point of intersection) constrains the location of the points that are defining geometry, lines, curves, surfaces, and the like, to run parallel to the X, Y, and Z axes. The Planar setting allows you to begin creating geometry in one viewport, and constrains the other points that are defining the geometry to the same plane, if you continue in another viewport.

The Osnap (object snap) setting constrains geometry to "snap" to other object geometry. When the Osnap setting is activated (checked), the submenu is enabled. The snap controls can be selected and constrained to an object's End (endpoints),

Mid (midpoints), Cen (centerpoints), and so on. The SmartTrack setting can be used to constrain geometry to existing geometrical relationships in the model. This is useful for aligning objects along the same axis and finding other relationships that are not modeled, such as the apparent intersection of two lines that do not actually intersect. When SmartTrack is enabled, the features of other objects (such as axes, endpoints, and midpoints) can be referenced to define points in space when creating new objects. The Gumball feature enables the navigational tool for translating objects. The Gumball tool will be further explained in section 5.4.

Figure 4.11. Rhino modeling aids. *Courtesy of the author.*

4.3 Units and Scale

The two primary systems for measuring are *imperial* and *metric*. The imperial system uses feet as the unit of measurement, while the metric system uses meters. The Document Properties and Options commands in Rhino open the same dialog box, which has many of the Rhino modeling and interface settings. Units can be specified by expanding the Units options and setting the Model units to the preferable system of measurement. (Figure 4.12.)

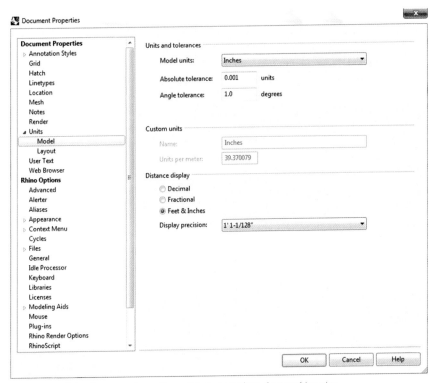

Figure 4.12. Rhino Document Properties and Options window. *Courtesy of the author.*

4.4 Navigation

Navigating within the 3D modeling environment is based on the view from and the movement of a virtual camera. A camera represents the position of a lens (eye) and a "target" location on which the view is focused. *Panning, zooming*, and *orbiting* change the view, or camera and target location, of the 3D model. Panning slides the view up, down, left, and right. Zooming moves the virtual camera forward and backward, or closer and further away from the model. Orbiting rotates around the model. Panning and zooming can be utilized in any view, while orbiting can only be used while in a three-dimensional view.

4.5 Visualization Methods

The graphic representation of geometry in the viewports of the 3D model can be visualized in different ways. (Figure 4.13.) The default method for visualizing surfaces is the wireframe method. This method illustrates the edges and isocurves of surfaces and renders the surface as transparent. The shaded method visualizes the edges and surface as opaque, and with an assigned color that is based on the color of the layer in which the geometry is located. The rendered method visualizes the surfaces as materials, which are assigned based on the material assigned in the layer in which the geometry is located. Materials can be assigned various amounts of transparency, which allows surfaces in the rendered viewport setting to be visualized as transparent, translucent, or opaque. Additional viewport visualization options include ghosted, artistic, pen, and more.

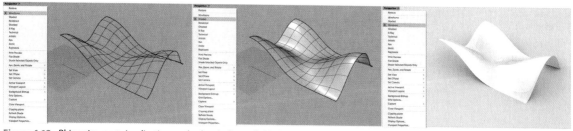

Figure 4.13. Rhino viewport visualization methods: wireframe (left), shaded (middle), and rendered (right). *Courtesy of the author.*

Endnote

1. Alicia Imperiale, *New Flatness: Surface Tension in Digital Architecture* (Basel, Boston, Berlin: Birkhäuser, 2000).

Chapter 5
2D Drawing

Chapter 5 describes some of the primary geometric elements that are used to create two-dimensional drawings within the 3D modeling environment, including points, line segments, and curves. This overview of point and curve objects, B-splines, Bézier curves, and NURBS (nonuniform rational B-splines) is intended to provide the reader with a better understanding of the computations utilized for generating curves within the Rhino 3D modeling environment, and a foundation for learning more advanced concepts related to programming. Methods for editing curve control points, and tools and techniques for creating, replicating, editing, and transforming two-dimensional geometry are provided as a means for creating design drawings and 3D models.

5.1 Drafting

Architectural drawings are two-dimensional projections that describe three-dimensional forms and spaces. Historically, two-dimensional architectural drawings, such as floor plans, elevations, sections, and axonometrics, were produced using drafting tools, such as straightedges, T-squares, triangles, and compasses. These drafting instruments gave architects and designers the ability to create drawings with precision and accuracy. In addition to many other factors pertaining to architectural design and production, the invention of the computer had a profound impact on architectural representation. The invention of computer aided-design (CAD) systems eventually revolutionized the methods by which two-dimensional drawings are produced.

The ability to use CAD software to draw two-dimensional geometry is useful not only for creating architectural drawings but also for 3D modeling. As stated earlier in the book, surface models are often created with sweep operations, such as extruding and revolving. These operations utilize two-dimensional profiles as input elements that define surfaces; therefore, a proficiency in drafting two-dimensional geometry, accurately and with precision, is a useful skill for creating both two-dimensional drawings and 3D models.

5.2 Points and Lines

Within 3D modeling environments, Cartesian coordinates are used to define points in a virtual space. A *point* is an element that does not have dimensional attributes and, within a Cartesian coordinate system, is defined with an XYZ value. The point at which the axes of the Cartesian coordinate system intersect is called the *origin*. A point located at the origin of the model has XYZ values of (0,0,0) where X = 0, Y = 0, and Z = 0. Figure 5.1 shows a series of points located on the XY plane and their XYZ values.

P1: X = 9, Y = 6, Z = 0

P2: X = −6, Y = 5, Z = 0

P3: X = −7, Y = −4, Z = 0

P4: X = 5 , Y = −2, Z = 0

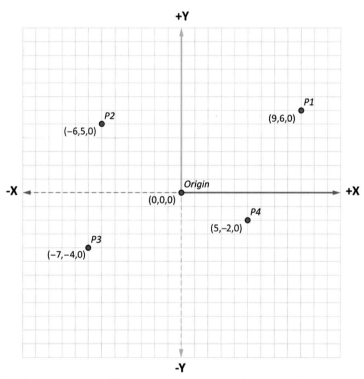

Figure 5.1. Various points on the XY plane and their Cartesian coordinate values. *Courtesy of the author.*

Point objects can be modeled within the 3D modeling space, using the Point command. Point coordinates are also used to define other geometrical objects, such as lines, surfaces, and volumes. For example, two points can be connected to define a line segment in the 3D modeling space. (See Figure 5.2.)

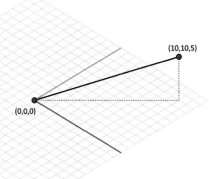

Figure 5.2. Two points in 3D space to define a line segment. *Courtesy of the author.*

Points can be generated from other geometry in the model. For example, curve objects can be *divided* into a specified number of segments. *Dividing* curve objects creates points that are evenly distributed by a specified number of segments, or based on a specified distance, and can be used to *split* the curve into smaller curve segments. (See Figure 5.3.)

Figure 5.3. The division of a line segment into two line segments (left) and ten line segments (right). *Courtesy of the author.*

Points can also be generated from Mesh and NURBS surfaces. For example, point grids can be created on a surface by specifying the number of points in the U and V direction. (See Figure 5.4.)

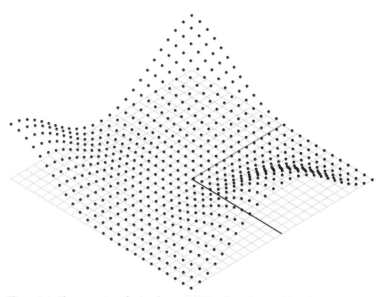

Figure 5.4. The generation of points from a NURBS surface. *Courtesy of the author.*

Points can also form entire 3D digital models. *Point cloud* models are data sets of points that can be produced by 3D laser scanners to create three-dimensional 3D models of physical objects and forms, such as buildings, landscapes, and urban environments. 3D laser scanners create models that use points within an XYZ coordinate system to create the *point cloud*. These points can serve as data to create Mesh and NURBS surface models, which can be used for other purposes, such as producing drawings, renderings, and BIM models. The images of a *point cloud* model produced by the 3D laser scanning and architectural surveying firm MYND Workshop are part of a series titled *Central Park & Sheep Meadow: Capturing New Yorkers and Their Park.* (See Figure 5.5.) The *point cloud* model was created with a LIDAR scanner to digitally model a portion of Central Park, accurately depicting the rocky landscape formations with a high resolution of detail. The individual points that define the geometry become more apparent when zooming into the digital point cloud model.

A *line* is a straight, infinite, one-dimensional geometric figure in space. A *line segment* is the portion of a line that is defined between two points. In Rhino, the Line or Line Segments commands can be executed to draw a line segment by left-clicking to specify the start point and end point that define the line segment.

Figure 5.5. MYND Workshop, *Central Park & Sheep Meadow: Capturing New Yorkers and Their Park*, New York. 3D laser scan point cloud model (top) and point cloud model detail (bottom). *Courtesy of MYND Workshop.*

A *polyline* is a collection of line segments that are joined together. Polylines can be open or closed. An open polyline does not return to its starting point, and a closed polyline does return to its starting point. Polylines can be "exploded" to separate the joined lines into discrete line segments. In Rhino, the Polyline command can be executed to draw a polyline by left-clicking to specify the start point and the following points that define the polyline. (See Figure 5.6.)

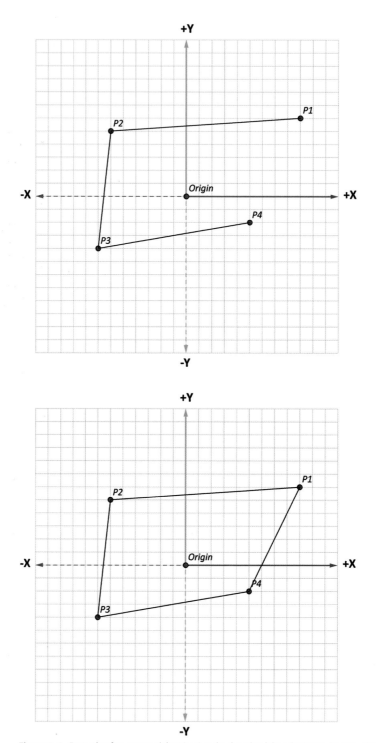

Figure 5.6. Example of an open polyline (top) and a closed polyline (bottom). *Courtesy of the author.*

Polygons are two-dimensional shapes that are defined by straight line segments or polylines that are closed. Triangles, quadrilaterals, and other closed *n*-sided shapes are examples of polygons. (See Figure 5.7.)

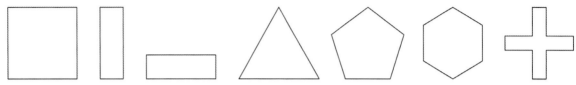

Figure 5.7. Examples of closed, two-dimensional polylines that form polygonal shapes. *Courtesy of the author.*

Two-dimensional shapes that are defined by straight line segments or polylines that are open are not polygons. (See Figure 5.8.)

Figure 5.8. Examples of open, two-dimensional polylines. *Courtesy of the author.*

Various types of architectural drawings can be drafted through the use of points, line segments, polylines, and curve objects that are created and edited within a two-dimensional construction plane (CPlane). Architectural drawings, especially floor plans, are typically drafted within the World XY CPlane, which is the active CPlane in the Top viewport. (See Figure 5.9.)

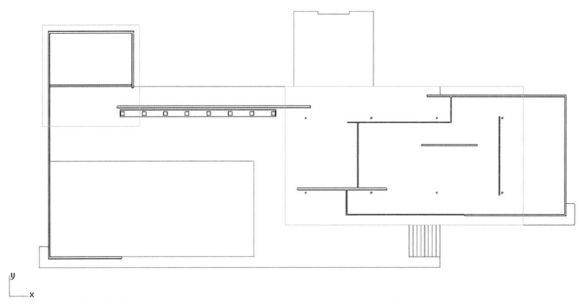

Figure 5.9. Digitally drafted linework of Ludwig Mies van der Rohe's Barcelona Pavilion. *Courtesy of the author.*

Images can also be imported into the 3D modeling space and used as underlays or guides for creating drawings. The Picture command in Rhino can be used to place bitmap images, such as JPEG and TIFF images, on a CPlane. The Picture image can be scaled and placed on a locked layer, and used as an underlay, reference, or template, to "trace" over with drafted linework.

The following sections will describe the terminology that is associated with NURBS curve objects and the methods for transforming, editing, and replicating curve objects.

5.3 Curve Control Points

Curve objects in the 3D modeling environment are defined by points and lines, which are used to calculate the curvature of the *spline*. These points, called *control points*, and the lines connecting them, form the *control polygon*, which defines a the curve by points *near* the curve, instead of points *on* the curve. By moving the control points of the control polygon, the curve follows in a very intuitive way.[1] There are various degrees of curvature based on the number of control points. A curve object that has two control points results in a one-degree curve, which is essentially a line segment. A curve object that has three control points results in a two-degree curve, such as a parabola. Curve objects with four or more control points result in three-degree curves, which can exhibit concave and convex curvature. (See Figure 5.10.)

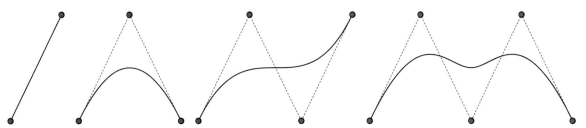

Figure 5.10. Examples of Bézier curves with increasing numbers of control points (from left to right). *Courtesy of the author.*

Today, many CAD softwares and computer graphics programs use NURBS technology to calculate smooth curves and surfaces. NURBS (nonuniform rational B-splines) curves and surfaces are based on Bézier curves and B-splines. Bézier curves were used and publicized by the French engineer Pierre Bézier, who headed the design department of the car manufacturing company Renault during the early 1960s.[2] Bézier curves are calculated based on the number of control points and control polygons. The curves are evaluated between two points restricted to a value between 0 and 1. A two-point Bézier curve is a one-degree curve and results in a line segment. (See Figure 5.11.)

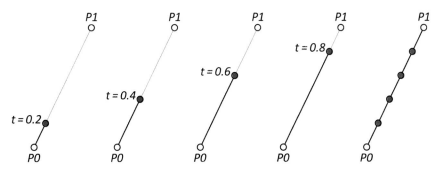

Figure 5.11. Example of a two-point Bézier curve. *Courtesy of the author.*

A three-point Bézier curve is a two-degree curve and bends in one direction. If two line segments defined by three points are measured by the same proportional distance, value *t*, to create two new points, a third line segment can be defined. If a point is placed at the same proportional distance, value *t*, of this third line segment, this point can be used to define the Bézier curve. Continuing to plot a series of points at their respective *t* value will result in the Bézier curve. (See Figure 5.12.)

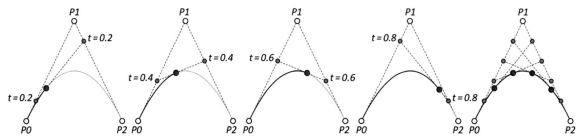

Figure 5.12. Example of a three-point Bézier curve. *Courtesy of the author.*

A four-point Bézier curve, is a three-degree curve, and can bend in two directions. The curve is calculated with the introduction of an additional subdivision line.[3] (See Figure 5.13.)

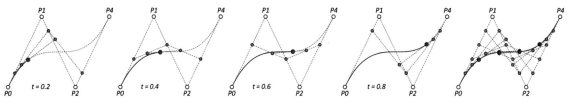

Figure 5.13. Example of a four-point Bézier curve. *Courtesy of the author.*

Bézier curves can be combined to form larger splines. B-splines use the minimum amount of support to create continuously smooth collections of Bézier curves. NURBS curves are B-splines that have an additional feature of a "weight" parameter on each control point. By increasing or decreasing the weight, the curve is pulled toward or pushed away from the control point, allowing for more control in drawing and refining the curve. (See Figure 5.14.)

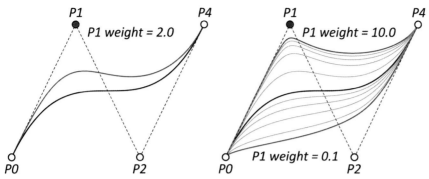

Figure 5.14. Example of a NURBS curve modified by increasing and decreasing the weight parameter of a control point (P1). *Courtesy of the author.*

In Rhino, two methods for drawing curves are the *Curve* and *InterpCrv* commands. The Curve command generates a curve by defining the location of the curves control points. (See Figure 5.15.) The InterpCrv command generates a curve by defining the points through which the curve will pass. (See Figure 5.16.)

The control points and control polygons of spline geometries can be turned on or off to display or hide these elements. In Rhino, the command for displaying the control points on a curve is *PointsOn*. (See Figure 5.17.)

When turned on, control points can be moved to change the definition and appearance of the curve. For example, a planar curve with four control points that lies on the XY plane can be transformed into a three-dimensional curve by moving one of its control points along the Z axis. (See Figure 5.18.) Control points can also be added to, or subtracted from, existing curves.

Figure 5.15. The Curve command icon in Rhino.

Figure 5.16. The InterpCrv command icon in Rhino.

Figure 5.17. The PointsOn command icon in Rhino.

Figure 5.18. Example of modifying a 2D curve in the XY plane into a 3D curve by moving control points vertically (parallel to the Z axis). *Courtesy of the author.*

5.4 Working with Lines and Planar Curves

Some of the benefits that computer-aided drafting provides over traditional hand-drafting methods are the abilities to transform, replicate, and edit geometry with efficiency and speed.

Two-dimensional and three-dimensional curves can be modified and utilized to create various forms. Working within a two-dimensional plane, lines and planar curves can be used to draw various shapes and profiles. Through the use of modeling operations, lines and planar curves can be transformed, replicated, and edited to draft architectural drawings. Additionally, computer-aided drafting softwares provide resources for creating geometry with extreme precision and accuracy. The following paragraphs provide information on some of the most common methods and tools for working with and editing two-dimensional geometry.

Construction Planes (World)

Most 3D modeling environments, by default, contain three two-dimensional planes that are coplanar to the axes and that pass through the origin: the World XY plane, XZ plane, and YZ plane. These planes, which are infinite within the modeling environment, can be thought of as virtual drafting boards and are known as *construction planes*, or *CPlanes*, in the Rhino 3D modeling software. (See Figure 5.19.)

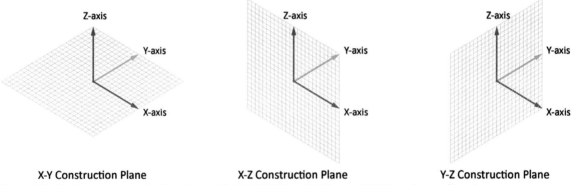

X-Y Construction Plane   X-Z Construction Plane   Y-Z Construction Plane

Figure 5.19. The three primary construction planes are the World XY CPlane, XZ CPlane, and YZ CPlane. *Courtesy of the author.*

The default Top, Front, and Right viewports in Rhino are orthographic projections that run parallel to the XY CPlane, XZ CPlane, and YZ CPlane, respectively. The default Perspective viewport displays the XY CPlane.

Architectural floor plans are typically drafted on, and/or parallel to, the horizontal XY CPlane within the Top viewport. This allows the Front and Right viewports, and their corresponding CPlanes, to be used for drafting architectural elevations and sections.

Modeling Aids

Architectural drawings require precision and accuracy, as they provide and communicate information that is necessary to construct buildings. The Modeling Aids portion of the Rhino interface provides options for constraining geometry to ensure precision and accuracy while drawing and modeling. (See Figure 5.20.) Many of the tools in the Modeling Aids palette can be toggled on or off. This includes the *Grid Snap* tool, which constrains the defining points of objects, such as the start point and end point of a line, to coincide with the grid of the CPlane. The *Ortho* tool constrains geometry to run parallel to the primary axes of the CPlane. The *Osnap*, or object snap tool, activates additional snap settings that can be toggled on or off. (See Figure 5.21.) This allows objects to be created and defined by "snapping" to the Endpoints, Midpoints, and Centers of other objects, or in relation to other objects, such as Perpendicular or Tangent to another line or curve. The *SmartTrack* tool is useful for snapping to apparent intersections, alignments, and other tracked features of geometry and objects within the 3D model through the use of temporary reference lines. The *Gumball* widget provides an interactive method for transforming geometry and is described in more detail in the following section. *Record History* stores the relationship between input geometry and the resulting output geometry. This allows for parametric associations within the 3D model. *Filter* allows for specific object types to be designated as selectable.

| Grid Snap | Ortho | Planar | Osnap | SmartTrack | Gumball | Record History | Filter |

Figure 5.20. The Modeling Aids toolbar in Rhino. *Courtesy of the author*

☑ End ☐ Near ☐ Point ☑ Mid ☐ Cen ☐ Int ☑ Perp ☐ Tan ☐ Quad ☐ Knot ☐ Vertex ☐ Project ☐ Disable

Figure 5.21. The Object Snap (Osnap) toolbar in Rhino allows for geometrical constraints to be toggled on (checked) or off (unchecked). *Courtesy of the author.*

Transformations

Architectural drawings are typically started by using a combination of the *Line*, *Polyline*, and *Curve* commands to draft geometric shapes. The XY CPlane is often used to begin drafting two-dimensional geometry, especially floor plans, as it represents a horizontal plane in 3D space. Maximizing and working within the Top viewport, is one method for ensuring that the drafted geometry is constrained to the XY CPlane. When geometric objects are drafted, it is common to edit and reposition them within the modeling space. This is achieved through "transformations," which include moving, rotating, and scaling objects. (See Figure 5.22.) The *Move* command allows geometry to be repositioned in space. Working within the XY CPlane, these objects can be moved to a specific distance, and constrained within the X and Y axes when the *Ortho* option is on. They can also be dragged in a freeform manner. (See Figure 5.23.)

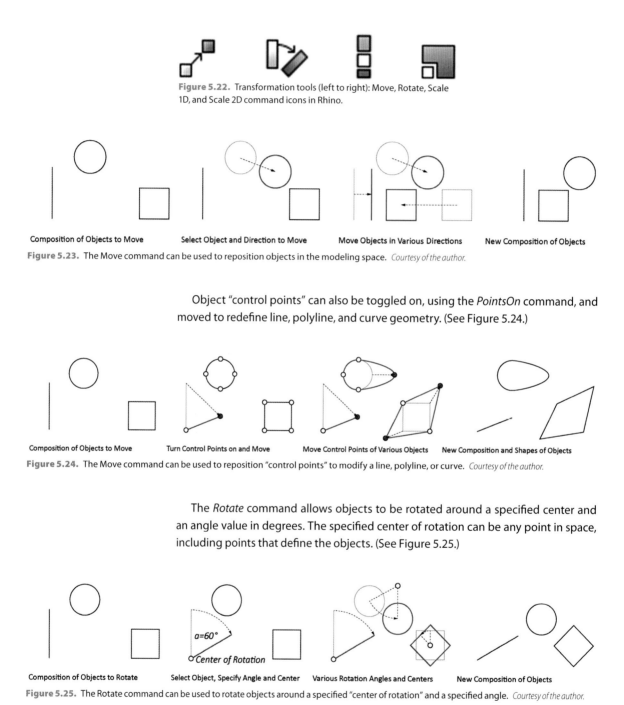

Figure 5.22. Transformation tools (left to right): Move, Rotate, Scale 1D, and Scale 2D command icons in Rhino.

| Composition of Objects to Move | Select Object and Direction to Move | Move Objects in Various Directions | New Composition of Objects |

Figure 5.23. The Move command can be used to reposition objects in the modeling space. *Courtesy of the author.*

Object "control points" can also be toggled on, using the *PointsOn* command, and moved to redefine line, polyline, and curve geometry. (See Figure 5.24.)

| Composition of Objects to Move | Turn Control Points on and Move | Move Control Points of Various Objects | New Composition and Shapes of Objects |

Figure 5.24. The Move command can be used to reposition "control points" to modify a line, polyline, or curve. *Courtesy of the author.*

The *Rotate* command allows objects to be rotated around a specified center and an angle value in degrees. The specified center of rotation can be any point in space, including points that define the objects. (See Figure 5.25.)

| Composition of Objects to Rotate | Select Object, Specify Angle and Center | Various Rotation Angles and Centers | New Composition of Objects |

Figure 5.25. The Rotate command can be used to rotate objects around a specified "center of rotation" and a specified angle. *Courtesy of the author.*

The *Scale* command can be used to change the dimensional values, or size, of an object in one, two, or three dimensions. (See Figure 5.26.)

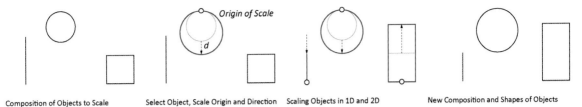

Composition of Objects to Scale   Select Object, Scale Origin and Direction   Scaling Objects in 1D and 2D   New Composition and Shapes of Objects

Figure 5.26. The Scale command can be used to scale objects in 1D, 2D, and 3D from a specified origin. *Courtesy of the author.*

In addition to executing transformation commands from the command line, or the command icons, Rhino features a *Gumball* widget, which can facilitate move, rotate, and scale transformations. (See Figure 5.27.) The Gumball widget can be toggled on or off, to appear or disappear, from the Modeling Aids interface. The Gumball widget consists of *Move* arrows, *Scale* handles, and *Rotate* arcs, which can be dragged or clicked to specify a value.

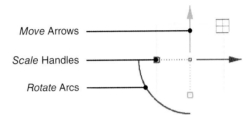

Figure 5.27. The Gumball widget provides an interactive method for applying transformations. *Courtesy of the author.*

Replicating Curves

When creating architectural drawings, it is often necessary to duplicate certain objects. Redrawing objects can be time consuming and can lead to mistakes in the process of creating duplicates of the same objects. CAD software provides various methods for replicating objects in various ways. These methods include copying, mirroring, offsetting, arraying, and tweening objects. (See Figure 5.28.)

Figure 5.28. Replication tools (left to right): Copy, Mirror, Offset, Array, ArrayPolar, and TweenCurves command icons in Rhino.

The *Copy* tool creates a duplicate of an object. This is useful for making duplicates of a single object or multiple objects simultaneously. Copies can be made randomly or with specific dimensions and directions. (See Figure 5.29.)

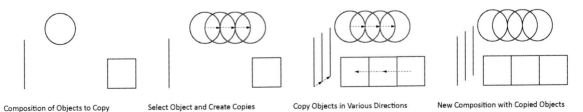

Composition of Objects to Copy   Select Object and Create Copies   Copy Objects in Various Directions   New Composition with Copied Objects

Figure 5.29. The Copy command can be used to replicate identical copies of objects in various directions. *Courtesy of the author.*

The *Mirror* tool creates a reflected image of an object along a reflection axis or plane. This tool facilitates the process of replicating objects to create geometrical configurations that are symmetrical. (See Figure 5.30.)

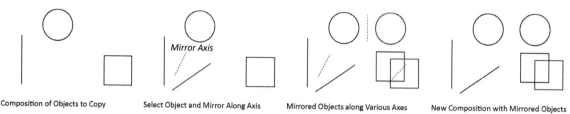

Composition of Objects to Copy   Select Object and Mirror Along Axis   Mirrored Objects along Various Axes   New Composition with Mirrored Objects

Figure 5.30. The Mirror command can be used to reflect an object along an axis. *Courtesy of the author.*

The *Offset* tool creates a copy of an object that is spaced within a specified distance from the original object. This is particularly useful for drawing walls with a specified width, or other materials that have a consistent thickness. Objects can be offset by specifying the side in which to place the offset and the distance from the object. (See Figure 5.31.)

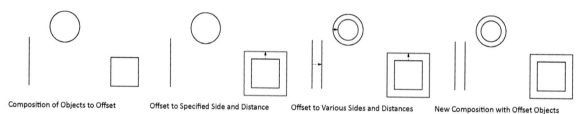

Composition of Objects to Offset   Offset to Specified Side and Distance   Offset to Various Sides and Distances   New Composition with Offset Objects

Figure 5.31. The Offset command can be used to copy a curve to either side of the original curve at a specified distance. *Courtesy of the author*

The *Array* tool facilitates the process of making multiple copies of an object by arranging them as columns and/or rows. The number of copies, the spacing between copies, and the direction in which the copies are created are input as values. In a similar manner, the *ArrayPolar* command creates multiple copies of an object; however, rather than arranging the copies orthogonally, the copied objects are arranged radially around a specified center point. The number of copies, the range of the angle in which the copies are placed, and location of the center point in which the copies are rotating around are input as values. (See Figure 5.32.)

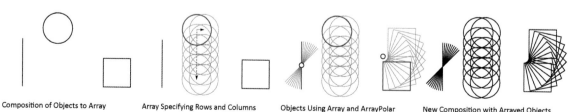

Composition of Objects to Array   Array Specifying Rows and Columns   Objects Using Array and ArrayPolar   New Composition with Arrayed Objects

Figure 5.32. The Array and ArrayPolar commands can be used to generate multiple identical copies of an object in a specified direction or radially around a specified center point. *Courtesy of the author.*

The *TweenCurves* command can be used to generate new curves that are the result of a transition between two curves. This technique derives from a process in the animation industry known as "inbetweening," in which intermediate frames are generated in between two images. This results in a series of frames that create a smooth transition from one image to another, yielding an animated effect. The TweenCurves tool generates a specified number of new curves that transform, or morph, from one curve to another. (See Figure 5.33.)

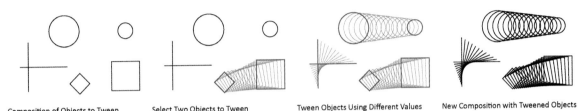

| Composition of Objects to Tween | Select Two Objects to Tween | Tween Objects Using Different Values | New Composition with Tweened Objects |

Figure 5.33. The TweenCurves command can be used to generate a specified number of iterative curves that morph between two specified input curves. *Courtesy of the author.*

Editing Lines and Curves

A number of tools are available to edit lines and curves. Some of the most common methods for editing lines and curves while drafting architectural drawings include trim, split, extend, fillet, and chamfer. (See Figure 5.34.)

Figure 5.34. Editing tools (left to right): Trim, Split, Extend, Fillet, and Chamfer command icons in Rhino.

The *Trim* command cuts and deletes the selected portion of a line or curve to a specified "cutting" object. The *Split* command is similar to the Trim command, and breaks a selected line or curve at its intersection with a specified cutting object. (See Figure 5.35.)

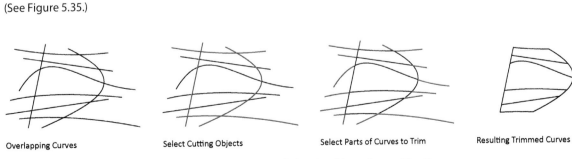

| Overlapping Curves | Select Cutting Objects | Select Parts of Curves to Trim | Resulting Trimmed Curves |

Figure 5.35. Sequence of steps for trimming lines and curves to specified cutting objects. *Courtesy of the author.*

The opposite of trimming lines is extending them. The *Extend* command can be used to lengthen, or extend, a line or curve to a specified boundary. (See Figure 5.36.)

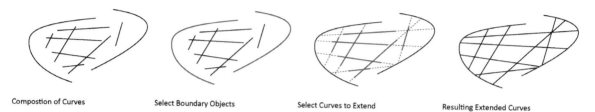

Compostion of Curves   Select Boundary Objects   Select Curves to Extend   Resulting Extended Curves

Figure 5.36. Sequence of steps for extending lines and curves to specified boundary objects. *Courtesy of the author.*

Two useful tools for creating rounded or angled corners are the *Fillet* and *Chamfer* commands. These commands extend and trim lines and curves to form rounded or angled corners with specified radii and distances. (See Figures 5.37 and 5.38.)

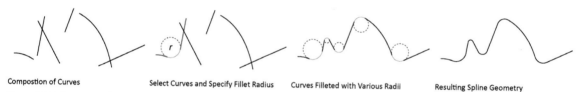

Compostion of Curves   Select Curves and Specify Fillet Radius   Curves Filleted with Various Radii   Resulting Spline Geometry

Figure 5.37. Sequence of steps for filleting lines and curves. *Courtesy of the author.*

Compostion of Curves   Select Curves and Chamfer Distances   Curves Chamfered with Various Distances   Resulting Line and Curve Geometry

Figure 5.38. Sequence of steps for chamfering lines and curves. *Courtesy of the author.*

Endnotes

1. Gerald Farin, Josef Hoschek, and Myung-Soo Kim, *Handbook of Computer-Aided Geometric Design* (Amsterdam, The Netherlands: Elsevier Science B.V., 2002).
2. Ibid.
3. Ching-Kuang Shene, "Finding a Point on a Bézier Curve: De Casteljau's Algorithm," *Introduction to Computing with Geometry Notes, Unit 5: Bézier Curves,* Michigan Technological University, 1997–2014, http://pages.mtu.edu/~shene/COURSES/cs3621/NOTES/spline/Bezier/de-casteljau.html.

Chapter 6
3D Modeling

Chapter 6 provides examples and descriptions of various types of surface geometries that are often used architectural design, including planar, ruled, developable, and doubly curved surfaces. The chapter introduces methods for creating and editing solid geometry, planar and space curves, and surfaces. These geometric objects can be edited, transformed, and replicated to create 3D models, ranging from simple shapes to complex volumes. The chapter introduces beginning and intermediate level concepts related to surface topology, and tools and techniques for working with surface control points.

6.1 Solid Models

Planar and Solid Geometry

Analytic geometry describes the location of a point in space based on the three axes of the Cartesian coordinate system. Some of the most common forms and volumes that have been used throughout the history of architectural design are based on Euclidean geometry. In his textbook on geometry *The Elements* (c. 300 BC) the Greek mathematician Euclid describes the logic of geometric systems through axioms and propositions. These geometries are rooted in measurements of the human body, a search for divine proportions, and beauty. Euclidean geometry includes planar and solid geometry. *Planar geometry* consists of two-dimensional planar shapes such as circles, squares, and polygons. *Solid geometry* is the branch of mathematics that deals with three-dimensional figures and consists of forms such as cubes, spheres, cones, and cylinders.

Euclidean geometry has influenced various cultures throughout history. The Florentine polymath Leon Battista Alberti (1402–72) used the text of Vitruvius, *De Architectura*, as a guide for interpreting classicism for his contemporaries. He pointed out that architects had to learn principles of primary, perfect geometric forms, as described by Vitruvius, which are related to the human form itself, in order to achieve "delight" and "beauty."[1] These concepts are based on the human mind's ability to visually complete and intellectually understand these forms through their simplicity and symmetry. As David Ross Sheer points out in *The Death of Drawing: Architecture in the Age of Simulation*, "The clarity of our mental image of these forms sets them apart in the realm of visual experience. Renaissance thought attributed the special quality of these forms to the common divine origin of the order of the world and human understanding. Modern architects have found their aesthetic value in their relationship of forms of thought."[2] As a result, Euclidean geometry can be found in various examples of art and architecture, and has influenced artists, architects, and designers throughout history including modern and contemporary designs. (See Figures 6.1 and 6.2.)

Figure 6.1. Carlo Scarpa, Brion-Vega Cemetery, San Vito d'Altivole, Italy, wall detail. *Courtesy of Jonathan Choe.*

Figure 6.2. Louis Isadore Kahn, Yale Center for British Art, New Haven, 1977 (completed). Court and drum, which encloses the stairs to the upper floors. Louis Isadore Kahn collection, 1951–1978 (inclusive), 1962–1977 (bulk). Manuscripts & Archives, Yale University Library.

3D modeling software provides tools for creating *solid geometries*. (See Figures 6.3 and 6.4.) This allows users to create forms without having to model points and lines to define the surfaces. Instead, the algorithms used to define the volume allow users to simply input the overall dimensions of the volume, for example, the length, width, and height of a cuboid form (box). The points, lines, and surfaces that are used to define a form are defined within the *solid model* as vertices, edges, and faces, respectively. This method of modeling is very useful for creating 3D models where high levels of detail are not necessary, such as *massing* models. (See Figure 6.5.)

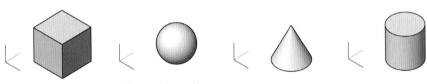

Figure 6.3. Solid geometrical forms. *Courtesy of the author.*

(a)   (b)

(c)   (d)

Figure 6.4. Solids tools: (a) Box, (b) Sphere, (c) Cone, and (d) Cylinder command icons in Rhino.

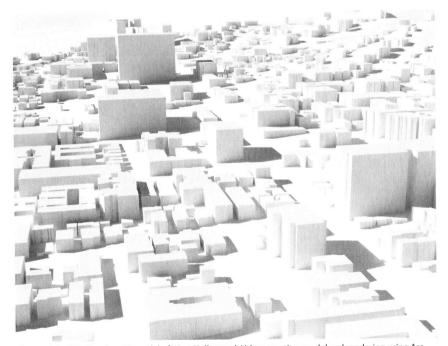

Figure 6.5. Billy Guarino, 3D model of West Hollywood. Urban massing model and rendering using Arc Map, Rhino 3D, and V-Ray. *Courtesy of Billy Guarino.*

As previously stated in section 5.2, a point can be described as an analytic entity, through numerical values in the X, Y, and Z axes: P1 = (X, Y, Z). Two points can be used to define a line segment: L1 = (P1, P2). Four points can be used to define four line segments: L1 = (P1, P2), L2 = (P2, P3), L3 = (P3, P4), L4 = (P4, P1). Four line segments can be used to define a surface: S1 = (L1, L2, L3, L4). (See Figure 6.6.) Through the sequence of defining points and line segments, various *n*-sided shapes can be modeled.

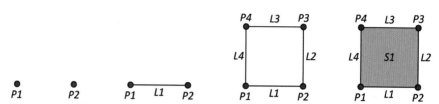

Figure 6.6. A surface defined by points and line segments. *Courtesy of the author.*

If the initial four points in the previous example are copied and moved in the Z direction, the eight points can be used to create a *solid model*, in this case a cube, by using the same analytic principles. (See Figure 6.7.) Through the use of points, lines, and surfaces, various types of *solid models* can be created, ranging from simple forms, such as *solid geometries*, to complex curved forms.

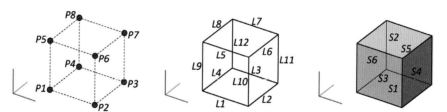

Figure 6.7. A solid defined by points, line segments, and surfaces. *Courtesy of the author.*

Boolean Operations

In architectural design, it is often necessary to combine objects or subtract objects from other objects in order to create apertures, pockets, fillets, chamfers, and other shapes that are more complex than common solid geometries. *Boolean operations* provide methods for combining, subtracting, and intersecting geometries to create forms that require more complexity. This can be useful for pragmatic reasons such as modeling an aperture in a form in order to represent a standard opening in a wall, or designing novel architectural forms. (See Figure 6.8.)

Figure 6.8. Moon Hoon Architect, Two Moon, South Korea. *Courtesy of Moon Hoon Architects and Namgoong Sun.*

Boolean operations include union, difference, and intersection. The *Boolean union* operation combines forms to create one single object. The *Boolean difference* operation can be used to subtract one object from another object. The *Boolean intersection* operation can be used to create a form that is the result of the portion of forms that are intersecting or overlapping. (See Figures 6.9 and 6.10.) Along with pragmatic modeling uses, Boolean operations can be used to quickly design and explore new geometrical configurations with outcomes that may be difficult to predict or time consuming to visualize with other methods of representation and physical modeling techniques.

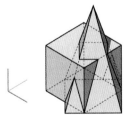 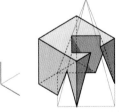 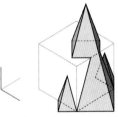 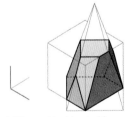

Figure 6.9. Boolean operations applied to a cube and a pyramid (left to right): Boolean union, Boolean difference A-B (pyramid subtracted from cube), Boolean difference B-A (cube subtracted from the pyramid), Boolean intersection. *Courtesy of the author.*

   (a)   (b)   (c)

Figure 6.10. Boolean tools: (a) Boolean union, (b) Boolean difference, and (c) Boolean intersection command icons in Rhino.

6.2 Planar and Space Curves

Although there are many options for working with solid geometry tools in 3D modeling software, it is common to use lines and curve objects to create surfaces, which can be juxtaposed to create three-dimensional forms. This requires an ability to modify *planar curves* and *space curves* that can be used to generate surfaces. Planar curves are two-dimensional and lie on a plane. Examples of planar curves include circles, parabolas, sinusoidal curves, spirals, as well as other types. (See Figure 6.11.)

Figure 6.11. Examples of planar curves. *Courtesy of the author.*

Space curves are three-dimensional and do not lie on a plane. Examples include helixes and conchospirals, as well as other types. (See Figure 6.12.)

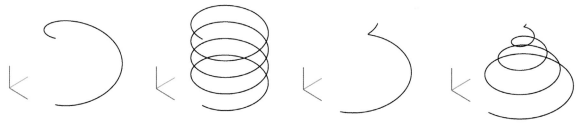

Figure 6.12. Examples of space curves. *Courtesy of the author.*

There are various methods for drawing curves in 3D space, including working with control points and applying object transformations to modify and edit curve objects, as described in Chapter 5. When curves are drawn on the XY CPlane, the curve control points can be turned on and moved in the Z direction. For example, a line segment with two control points that is drawn at a diagonal on the XY CPlane can be modified into a line segment that is not coplanar to any of the three primary XY, XZ, and YZ CPlanes, by moving one of the control points along the Z axis. (See Figure 6.13.)

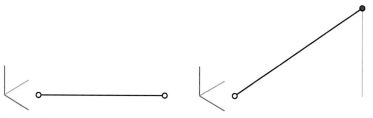

Figure 6.13. A line segment with two control points on the XY CPlane, modified to a line segment in 3D space by moving the end control point parallel to the direction of the **Z axis.** *Courtesy of the author.*

Line segments are curves with two control points and 1 degree of curvature. Line segments and curves can be *rebuilt* to change the number of control points and the degree of curvature. If the line segment that is drawn at a diagonal on the XY CPlane is rebuilt with four control points and three-degree curvature, the curve can be modified to turn upward by moving the end control point vertically along the Z axis. (See Figure 6.14.)

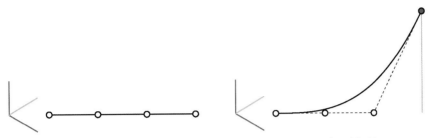

Figure 6.14. A line segment rebuilt with four control points on the XY CPlane, and modified into a curve by moving the end control point parallel to the direction of the Z axis. *Courtesy of the author.*

The previous two examples of a line segment and a curve have been modified so that they are not constrained to the default CPlanes; however, they remain *planar curves* because they lie within a plane. If a planar curve lies on the XY CPlane and multiple control points of the curve are moved to various distances along the Z axis, the resulting curve occupies three dimensions and no longer lies on a plane; therefore, it is a three-dimensional curve. (See Figure 6.15.) By working with a combination of planar and space curves, many types of surfaces can be modeled, ranging from simple to complex geometry.

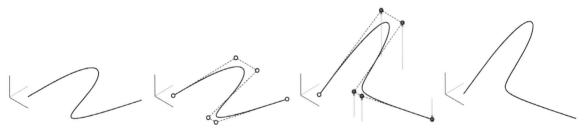

Figure 6.15. A planar curve with control points on the XY CPlane can be transformed into a 3D space curve by moving the control points to various distances parallel to the direction Z axis. *Courtesy of the author.*

6.3 Surfaces

In the physical world, a *surface* is the outermost layer of something, with material properties such as color and texture, such as the surface of the Earth, the surface of a body of water, the surface of a wall, or the surface of a piece of paper. In geometry, a *surface* is a continuous set of points that have length and width but no thickness. Both of these meanings can be considered in relation to 3D digital models. The former meaning typically applies to 3D digital modeling as the representation of materials properties through computational rendering methods that simulate real-world attributes, such as light, color, and texture. This section will focus on the latter definition, which deals with the geometric modeling of zero thickness surfaces within 3D modeling environments.

Surface Geometries

We experience many types of surfaces in the physical world that can be described through mathematics. Our ability to describe and visualize mathematical information has influenced our world in various ways. Architecturally, geometric configurations continue to be applied to design surfaces, forms, and spaces that strive to achieve beauty through the use of materials and fabrication methods. Although there are many different types of surface geometries, some common categories these surface types fall under include planar, ruled, developable, doubly curved, and freeform surfaces.

A *plane* is an infinitely extending, flat, two-dimensional surface. A *planar surface* can be defined with boundaries. For example, a cube is a volume that consists of six square planar surfaces. The simplicity of rectangular, planar surface geometries, and the ease in manufacturing and construction, have led to their application as one of the most commonly used surface geometries in architecture. One of the quintessential examples of modern architecture is the Barcelona Pavilion by Ludwig Mies van de Rohe. (See Figure 6.16.) The juxtaposition of planar surfaces, fabricated from various materials including glass, marble, and travertine, creates a "fluid space" that challenged the traditional understanding of architectural form and expressed the social and political context of the machine age.[3]

Figure 6.16. Ludwig Mies van de Rohe, The Barcelona Pavilion, 1929.

Ruled surfaces are surfaces that can be defined by a swept line in space. There are many types of ruled surfaces, including planes, helixes, and hyperbolic paraboloids. Ruled surfaces that can be unrolled or unfolded into a plane without stretching or tearing are known as *developable surfaces*. Developable surfaces bend in only one direction, for example, cylinders and cones. These types of surfaces are compelling for architectural design because they allow curved forms and shapes to be constructed out of flat sheet materials, such as plywood and sheet metal, when applied at an architectural scale.[4] A signature style of many buildings designed by Gehry Partners, LLP, includes the use of developable surface geometry to create sinuous architectural forms. Physical models used throughout the design process are made of various materials, such as wood blocks, acrylic, and paper. The curved, metallic colored paper surfaces on the physical models are often meant to represent the curved sheet metal panel surfaces on the building. (See Figure 6.17.) The paper surfaces are developable because they can be unrolled and flattened. Therefore, theoretically speaking, the curved surfaces in the digital models that match the developable properties of the paper can be fabricated as full-scale building envelopes, using flat sheet materials, such as sheet metal panels.

Figure 6.17. Gehry Partners, LLP, Walt Disney Concert Hall, Los Angeles, CA, (completed) 2003. Aerial photograph. *Courtesy of © Frank O. Gehry. Getty Research Institute, Los Angeles (2017.M.66), Frank Gehry Papers.*

Doubly curved surfaces are surfaces that bend in two directions, such as spheres and saddle-shaped surfaces. These types of surfaces are not developable; however, they can include surfaces that are made out of straight lines and are therefore ruled, such as the *hyperbolic paraboloid*. The architect and engineer Felix Candela explored the use of ruled, hyperbolic paraboloid surfaces to design thin-shell concrete structures. The straight rule lines of the geometry were used to design the curved surface formwork for casting concrete. (See Figure 6.18.)

Figure 6.18. Felix Candela, Los Manantiales Restaurant, Xochimilco, Mexico City, Mexico, 1958. Roof geometry. *© Avery Architectural & Fine Arts Library, Columbia University.*

The architect and engineer Frei Otto designed tensile membrane structures that exhibited doubly curved surface geometry, such as the Tranzbrunnen (Dance Pavilion) in Cologne, Germany. (See Figure 6.19.) Elastic materials that can be pulled

Figure 6.19. Frei Otto, Tranzbrunnen (Dance Pavilion), Cologne, Germany, 1957. Tensile structure. Photo: Christine Kanstinger. *Courtesy of Atelier Frei Otto + Partner, Kunstler + Ingenieure.*

and stretched are useful for exploring doubly curved surfaces. Frei Otto utilized physical devices, and the unorthodox model-making material of soap film, as a way to study and explore doubly curved, minimal surface geometry. These performative models, which investigated the natural geometric formations of minimal surfaces, were used as a design tool in many of his projects, including the Olympic Stadium in Munich, Germany.

The Dongdaemun Design Plaza, designed by Zaha Hadid Architects, is another example of a built architectural project that utilizes complex curvature. The project is a cultural hub in the center of Seoul, South Korea, consisting of a series of public spaces, museums, galleries, conference halls, media centers, and more. The Dongdaemun Design Plaza design and construction set many new standards for innovation, including the first public project in Korea to implement advanced 3D digital construction services. The building is clad with approximately 45,000 metal panels that wrap the complex curvatures of the structure. This was achieved with double-sided molding and cutting equipment for metal forming. (Figure 6.20.)

Figure 6.20. Zaha Hadid Architects, Dongdaemun Design Plaza, Seoul, South Korea, 2007-2013. Complex curvature of the metal-clad exterior envelope. *Courtesy of the author.*

6.4 Modeling NURBS Surfaces

Both 2D and 3D curves can be used to create surfaces through techniques based on extruding, translating, rotating, and lofting methods. *Extruded* surfaces are generated by moving curves along a straight line, or in a specified direction, for example, the Z axis. (See Figure 6.21.) This method of generating surface geometry is commonly used when transforming two-dimensional orthographic projections, such as linework from a floor plan, into 3D models. For example, two-dimensional profiles that lie on the XY CPlane can be extruded vertically along the Z axis. This results in surfaces that are perpendicular to the XY CPlane.

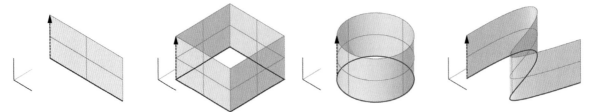

Figure 6.21. Extruded surface: curve profiles extruded parallel to the direction of the Z axis. *Courtesy of the author.*

Translational surfaces are generated by sweeping profile curves along defined path curves, or "rails." The profile curves for translational surfaces can typically be swept along one or two rails. (See Figure 6.22.)

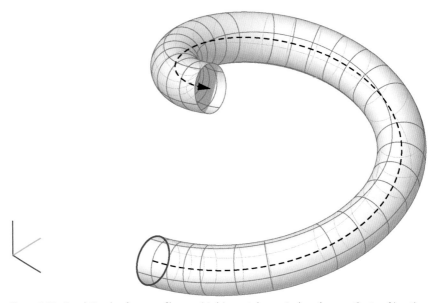

Figure 6.22. Translational surface: a profile curve (circle) swept along a single path curve. *Courtesy of the author.*

Rotational surfaces are generated by revolving profile curves around a specified axis. The axis can be defined by specifying the start and end points of a line segment. (See Figure 6.23.)

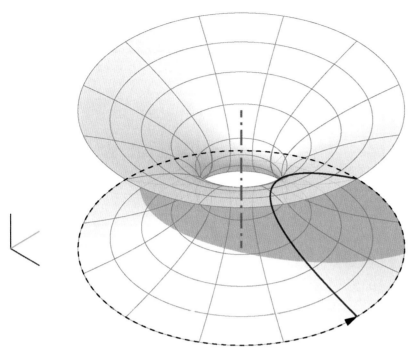

Figure 6.23. Translational surface: a profile curve (parabola) rotated around an axis. *Courtesy of the author.*

Lofted surfaces are generated by selecting a series of profile curves that are input to define the surface. Two or more curves can be used to define the lofted surface. (See Figure 6.24.)

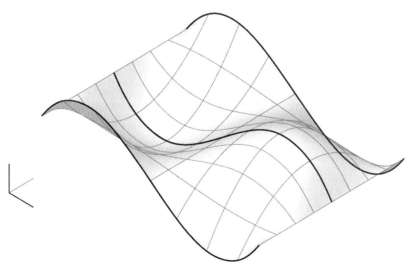

Figure 6.24. Lofted surface: three profile curves lofted to create a doubly curved surface. *Courtesy of the author.*

111

Heightfield surfaces are generated based on the color values of a bitmap image. When the bitmap image is selected as the *heightfield* image, the surface properties are defined by specifying the number of control points and height of the surface. (See Figure 6.25.)

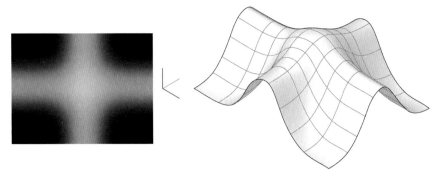

Figure 6.25. Heightfield surface: a grayscale bitmap image (left) used to assign Z values to generate a surface (right). *Courtesy of the author.*

6.5 Working with NURBS Surfaces

Construction Planes (Local)

The World XY, XZ, and YZ CPlanes can be repositioned within the Euclidean space as "local" CPlanes that are defined by other coordinates or geometry. This allows the CPlane to be repositioned to any direction or angle in space. This is very useful in modeling objects that are not orthogonal to the default World CPlanes. For example, to create a piped surface that is swept along a space curve, a local CPlane can be positioned normal to the tangent of the space curve at its endpoint. (See Figure 6.26.) A circle can be drafted on the local CPlane with its centerpoint at the origin (the space curve endpoint) and with a radius value. Using a translational method, the circle (profile curve) can be swept along the space curve (rail). The resulting surface will remain a circle in section when cut along a plane normal to the tangent of the space curve. (See Figure 6.22.)

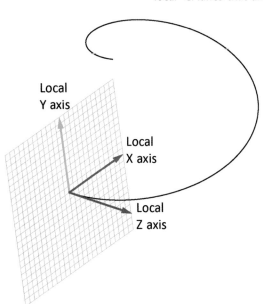

Figure 6.26. A local construction plane positioned normal to the endpoint of a curve. *Courtesy of the author.*

UV Values and Surface Control Points

The same PointsOn command that was described in Section 5.3 to display the control points of a curve can be used to display the control points of a surface. Editing surfaces by displaying and transforming their control points is a useful technique for sculpting and refining surface geometry. The number of control points on a surface depends on the number of U and V values that are defining the surface. One feature of NURBS surfaces is that they are defined by a coordinate system that is independent of the XYZ Cartesian coordinate system. NURBS surfaces utilize a UV coordinate system. All of the points that make up a NURBS surface can be located by their U and V values. To better visualize this, it is useful to understand curve directions.

In addition to control points, curves have a direction. The default direction of a curve is the same direction as the sequence of points that were used as input to define the curve. For example, if a curve is created by clicking to define four points sequentially, P0 to P3, the curve can be analyzed to view the curve direction, which runs in the same direction in which the sequence of points were created. In Rhino, the curve direction can be previewed by using the Dir command or Analyze direction tool in the Main Toolbars. (See Figure 6.27.)

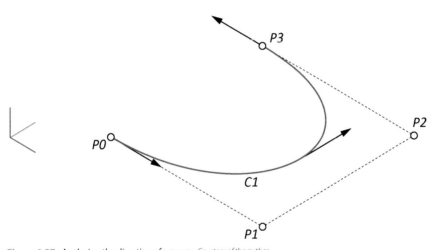

Figure 6.27. Analyzing the direction of a curve. *Courtesy of the author.*

If this curve (C1) is copied in the Z direction, and both of the curves are used to loft a surface, using the first curve (C1) as the first input and the copied curve (C2) as the second input, the surface has two directions, based on the input geometry, the direction of the two curves, and the direction of the loft. These are the U and V directions of the surface. The start point for each of these two directions is the origin, or U = 0, V = 0 values of the U-V coordinate system for the surface. The end point value will be the length and width dimensions of the surface, or the surface can be "normalized" so that the end point values are U = 1, V = 1 independent of the length and width dimensions of the surface. This establishes a surface "domain" between 0 and 1. (See Figure 6.28.)

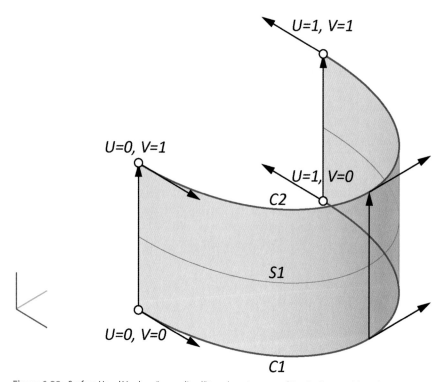

Figure 6.28. Surface U and V values "normalized" to a domain range of 0 to 1. *Courtesy of the author.*

An understanding of U and V coordinates is useful for editing surfaces and modifying the number of surface control points. Continuing with the example of a lofted surface, the PointsOn command can be used to turn on the surface control points. This surface has four control points in the U direction and four control points in the V direction, for a total of sixteen surface control points. These values also relate to the number of *isocurves*, or the vertical and horizontal curves that appear in the middle of the surface. Isocurves are not actual curve objects, but are a visual representation that describes the number of U and V divisions on the surface. (See Figure 6.29.)

The number of control points and isocurves that define a surface can be modified using the Rebuild command. (See Figure 6.30.) Rebuilding surfaces by specifying the U and V point count allows for the number of surface control points to be increased or decreased, which is useful for editing surface geometry. Changes to the U and V point count also increases or decreases the number of surface isocurves, which can be extracted from the surface and turned into curve objects. (See Figure 6.31.)

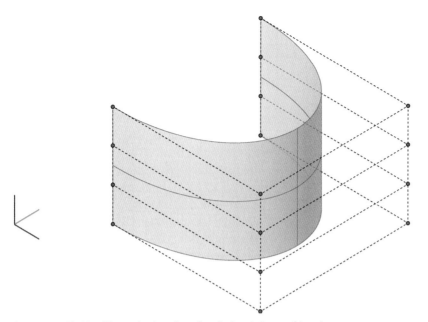

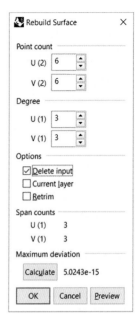

Figure 6.29. The U and V control points of a surface displayed. *Courtesy of the author.*

Figure 6.30. The Rebuild Surface dialog box in Rhino.

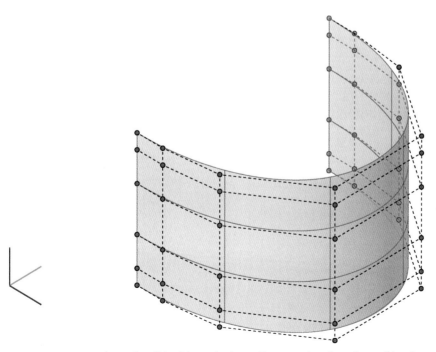

Figure 6.31. Increasing the number of U and V control points and isocurves of a surface. *Courtesy of the author.*

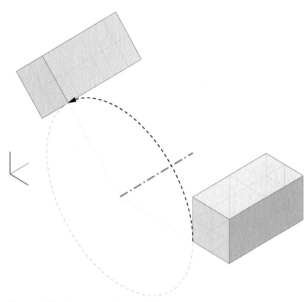

3D Transformations

Transformation methods of Move, Rotate, and Scale were described in Chapter 5 for editing two-dimensional geometry that is constrained to the XY CPlane. These same transformation methods can be applied to 3D geometry with the additional input of a value in the Z direction. Objects can be moved, rotated, and scaled in 3D by specifying these commands in the command line and using the tool icons, or by using the *Gumball* widget. Additional transformation methods are also available when working three dimensionally. For example, objects can be rotated in 3D by defining an axis of rotation and entering the angle of rotation as a value. (See Figures 6.32 and 6.33.)

Figure 6.32. 3D rotation of a cuboid form around a specified axis. *Courtesy of the author.*

(a)   (b)

Figure 6.33. 3D Transformation tools: (a) Rotate 3D and (b) Scale 3D command icons in Rhino.

Applying transformation methods to surface control points allows for a great amount of flexibility in modeling surface geometry. Surfaces can be rebuilt with lower or higher U and V values to decrease or increase the number of surface control points. By manipulating individual or multiple control points, surfaces can be pulled, stretched, and twisted into complex surface geometries. (See Figure 6.34.) Using transformation methods on surface control points also allows for an increased amount of control in modeling surfaces.

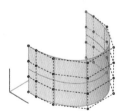 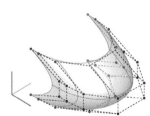 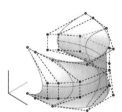 

Figure 6.34. Transformations applied to a selected set of surface control points (left to right): original surface, moved, rotated, scaled. *Courtesy of the author.*

3D Replications

The same methods for replicating curves apply to the replication of surfaces as well. Through the use of other geometrical objects in the model, surfaces can be trimmed and extended. Two sets of surfaces can be chamfered and filleted to create sharp, round, or angled corners. Surfaces can also be *arrayed, offset,* and *tweened* to create multiplicities of surfaces. (See Figures 6.35 and 6.36.)

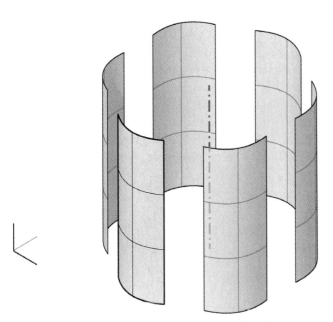

Figure 6.35. Surface replication with ArrayPolar. *Courtesy of the author.*

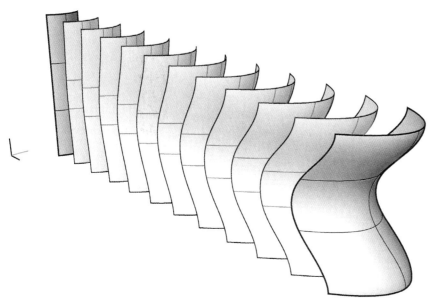

Figure 6.36. Surface replication between two specified surfaces using Tween surfaces. *Courtesy of the author.*

Cage Edit Transformations

Transformations can be applied to groups consisting of multiple surfaces. The Cage Edit command generates a bounding box around a selected set of surfaces. This bounding box, or "cage" can be aligned to the world coordinate system, and the number of control points in the X, Y, and Z directions can be specified. These control points can be turned on by selecting the cage and executing the PointsOn command. The control points can be selected and transformed by moving, rotating, and scaling operations, which will have an impact on all of the surfaces that are within the cage. (See Figure 6.37.)

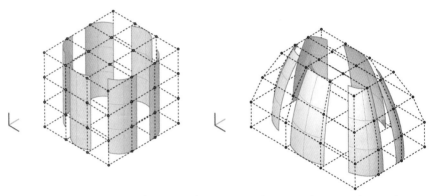

Figure 6.37. Creating a Cage Edit lattice around a selected set of surfaces (left) and transforming the Cage Edit lattice control points (right). *Courtesy of the author.*

Endnotes

1. Robert A. M. Stern, with Raymond W. Gastil, *Modern Classicism* (New York: Rizzoli International Publications, 1988).
2. David Ross Scheer, *The Death of Drawing: Architecture in the Age of Simulation* (New York: Routledge, 2014).
3. Toyo Ito, *N. 123 Toyo Ito 2001–2005* (Madrid, Spain: El Croquis, 2004).
4. Nettelbladt, Marten, *The Geometry of Bending,* http://thegeometryofbending.blogspot.com/.

Chapter 7
Generating Linework

Chapter 7 focuses on the use of three-dimensional forms and surfaces to generate curve objects. These curve objects can be generated and extracted from surfaces by rebuilding isocurves, working with point grids, and contouring. The tools and techniques for generating linework are very useful for enhancing architectural drawings, by visually suggesting and communicating notions of scale, materials and tectonics, curvature, spatial effects, and other design features.

7.1 Wireframe Linework

Wireframe models consist of points, lines, and curves to depict forms and surfaces. They are useful for visualizing and understanding the geometrical structure of an object. One of the earliest examples of a wireframe drawing is *Perspective Study of a Chalice*, created by the Italian Renaissance painter Paulo Uccello. (See Figure 7.1) This drawing was intended as a study of a perspectival method for creating the illusion of three-dimensional objects, and consists of a series of straight line segments and curves depicting the form of the chalice. The subdivisions of the surface geometry and the transparency through parts of the object allow for the reading of surface curvature and an understanding of the whole object.

Early 3D models depicted surface edges to represent three-dimensional objects. This was due to the ability to create wireframe models with relatively low computing power, in comparison to models with shaded surfaces. Wireframe linework is useful for understanding the shapes of three-dimensional objects. The subdivisions of surfaces with wireframe linework can be useful for representing curvature in a surface, in a similar manner that a rendering with tone or shade would allow for the illusion of curvature. Wireframes are also useful for articulating surfaces, which can allow architectural drawings to visually convey a sense of scale and tectonics. For example, wireframe geometry can be used to develop a tectonic strategy for panelizing architectural surfaces. The ability to generate wireframe geometry from a model is a useful technique for enhancing the representation of forms and surfaces in architectural drawings. (See Figure 7.2.)

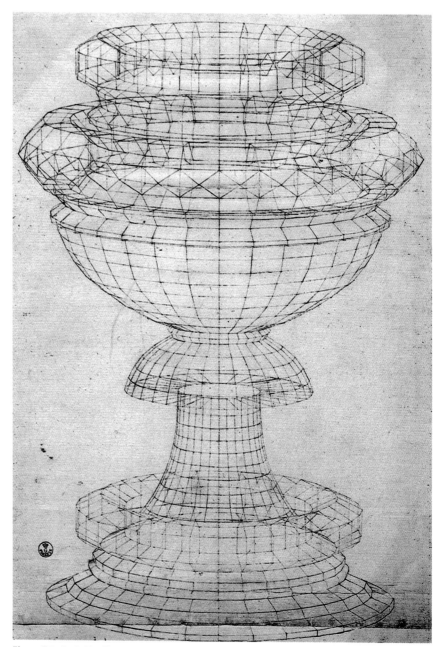

Figure 7.1. Paulo Uccello, *Perspective Study of a Chalice*, pen and ink on paper, 15th century. Gabinetto deí Disegni, Uffizi, Florence, Italy.

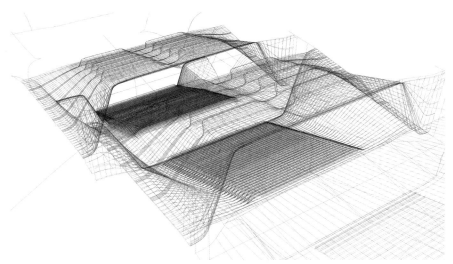

Figure 7.2. Architectures David Tajchman, *Stealth, New Maribor Museum*, 2010. Wireframe drawing of the doubly curved structural staircase. *Courtesy of Architectures David Tajchman.*

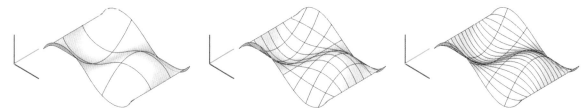

Figure 7.3. Rebuilding the same surface with various U and V values and displaying the surface isocurves. *Courtesy of the author.*

Current 3D modeling software provides the option to display the 3D model in wireframe mode within the viewport. This is useful for visualizing the edges of surfaces in the 3D model. However, wireframe curve objects can also be generated from NURBS and mesh surfaces. When working with NURBS surfaces, the U and V point counts can be increased or decreased to modify the number of isocurves. By adjusting the U and V values, many different variations of isocurve densities can be produced. The isocurves can be *extracted* from the surface to create curve objects, which can be added as wireframe linework to a drawing. (See Figures 7.3 and 7.4.)

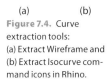

(a)   (b)

Figure 7.4. Curve extraction tools: (a) Extract Wireframe and (b) Extract Isocurve command icons in Rhino.

7.2 Contour Linework

Site plans are architectural drawings that indicate the location of a building on a site, as well as other information, such as vegetation, roads, and service lines. Typically, sites are not completely flat and may be located on landscapes that have drastic changes in topography, such as the Pizota Hotel in Puerto Vallarta, Mexico, designed by Estudio Carme Pinós. (See Figure 7.5.). Even if a site appears to be perfectly flat, the topography needs to be altered to produce a slope that allows for water drainage. Contour drawings are useful for understanding changes in elevation. *Contours* are lines and curves on a site plan, or map, that indicate elevation changes in the topography. (See Figure 7.5.)

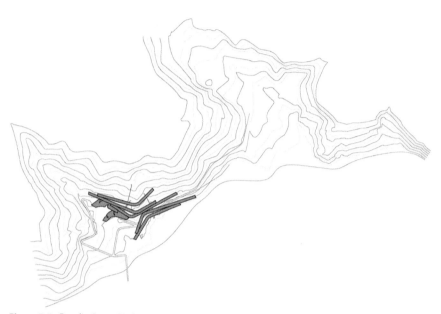

Figure 7.5. Estudio Carme Pinós, Pizota Hotel, Puerto Vallarta, Mexico, 2004. Site plan drawing. *Courtesy of Estudio Carme Pinós.*

In 3D models, contours are lines and curves that are generated by planar cuts that occur through the surface at consistent intervals in a specified direction. Contours can be extracted from surfaces in any direction, but typically lie on horizontal planes, parallel to the XY CPlane, and are spaced incrementally in the vertical direction, parallel to the Z axis. In this case, the XY CPlane represents a flat ground surface. In Figure 7.6, the undulating surface of the 3D model represents the topographical landscape of a cliff side. Contours can be generated at an incremental distance to any metric, such as every foot or every ten feet, depending on the scale of the drawing and the total area of the landscape that is being represented. To create contours, execute the Contour command, select the object to contour, specify the direction perpendicular to the contour planes, which in this example is the Z axis, and specify the distance between contours. (See Figures 7.6 and 7.7.)

The contour linework in the model can be projected onto the XY CPlane and exported as a site plan drawing to represent the topographical changes in a landscape. Areas of the drawing in which the curves are spaced closely together indicate steep inclines in the topography, whereas areas of the drawing in which the curves are spaced further apart indicate shallow inclines and gradual slope in the topography. In order to have a better understanding of scale, a drawing convention for site plans includes assigning different line weights to contour lines to show minor and major distances in elevation. For example, minor contour lines can be drawn at every foot, appearing as thinner lines, while major contour lines are drawn at every ten feet,

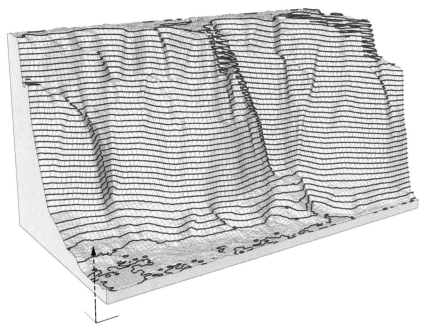

Figure 7.7. Curve Extraction tools: Contour command icon in Rhino

Figure 7.6. 3D model of a site landscape with topography "contours" generated at consistent intervals in the Z direction. *Courtesy of the author.*

appearing as thicker lines. This allows for clarity in the drawing, and provides a better visual understanding of the topographical changes in the landscape at every foot and at every ten feet. (See Figure 7.8.)

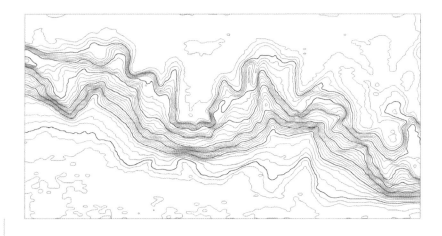

Figure 7.8. A site plan representing elevations in a landscape topography with contour lines. *Courtesy of the author.*

7.3 Paneling Linework

Architectural surfaces are often constructed with materials that are manufactured in the form of panels, such as plywood, sheet metal, glass, ceramic tiles, and the like. Determining how these panels are assembled, juxtaposed, and scaled to create architectural surfaces is part of the design process. The "panelization" of surfaces and materials can affect the experience of a space, lighting conditions, structural design, and other architectural qualities. 3D models can be used to explore and study various paneling patterns. The method in which digital surfaces are subdivided, or panelized, can have an impact on the final design and built work of architecture, as evident in COOP HIMME[L]BLAU's design for the BMW Welt in Munich, Germany. (See Figure 7.9.)

Figure 7.9. COOP HIMMELB[L]AU, BMW Welt, Munich, Germany, 2001–2007. Photo: Duccio Malagamba.
Courtesy of COOP HIMMELB[L]AU.

Through the use of additional tools available with the Rhino plug-in Paneling Tools, developed by Rajaa Issa, surface geometry can be used to generate 3D point grids based on the variable input numbers of U and V values. 3D point grids can then be used to generate curves that form various patterns.[1] For example, a *point grid* can be created by specifying the *surface domain number*. This point grid can be used to define a *point panel grid*, which provides various settings for generating panels. Commonly used patterns include quadrilateral, triangular, diagonal, and diamond shaped (See Figure 7.10), as these types of patterns are often used as shapes for fabricating and assembling materials. There are many methods and patterning possibilities when working with digital surfaces. Exploring these possibilities by altering the input values and combining patterns can yield new and unexpected ways of thinking about the design of architectural surfaces.

Figure 7.10. Surfaces panelized as (left to right) quad, triangular, diagonal, and diamond patterns using the same 3D point grid as input values. *Courtesy of author.*

Two-dimensional patterns that are drafted on planar surfaces can be transferred to other planar or nonplanar surfaces. This can be achieved with the Flow Along Surface command. (See Figure 7.11.) In this instance, the reference surface that has the two-dimensional pattern and the target surface (the surface where the pattern will be applied) are topologically the same, as they are both "normalized" surfaces with U and V domain values from 0 to 1. Regardless of the sinuous quality of a 3D surface, the pattern will be calculated using the same U and V values, and will appear stretched and distorted to "flow" along a surface. (See Figure 7.12.)

Figure 7.11. The Flow Along Surface command icon in Rhino.

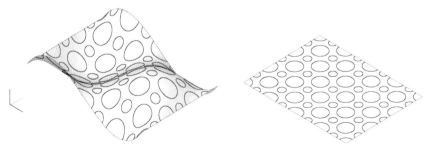

Figure 7.12. Two-dimensional patterns on planar surfaces (right) can be transferred to other planar or nonplanar, 3D curved surfaces (left). *Courtesy of the author.*

Endnote

1. Rajaa Issa, *Paneling Tools for Grasshopper* (Seattle, WA: Robert McNeel & Associates, 2013). Available at https://wiki.mcneel.com/_media/labs/panelingtoolsmanual.pdf, accessed February 4, 2019.

Part 3
Architectural Design Drawings and Graphics

Part 3 focuses on the use of linework to create and enhance architectural drawings. This section provides descriptions of orthographic and perspective projections and their application in producing conventional architectural drawings, such as plans, sections, elevations, axonometrics, and perspectives. Methods for creating these types of drawings within digital modeling environments include the use of viewports, cameras, and clipping planes, and processes for manipulating these tools.

This section describes workflows for exporting two-dimensional projections form 3D models into vector-based and computer-aided drafting software for enhancing linework with line weights, line types, color, text, and other graphic qualities. This includes an overview of tools and techniques within graphic design software for editing and generating additional linework, with symbols, gradients, and other effects using vector and raster-based graphics. This method of working requires an understanding of file formats and workflows that support interoperability between various software.

Chapter 8
Generating 2D Projections

Chapter 8 focuses on the generation of two-dimensional projections from 3D models. Geometric objects, such as points, lines, and curves, are created when 3D models are projected onto two-dimensional planes. This geometry can be exported to vector graphics and computer-aided drafting software to create architectural design drawings by assigning line weights, line types, color, text, and other graphic properties. This chapter describes the various types of conventional architectural drawings, which consist of *orthographic* and *perspective* projections. Generating projections from 3D models requires an understanding of viewports, cameras, and clipping planes. In addition to conventional architectural drawings, these digital workflows and tools can be implemented and modified to explore experimental methods of generating architectural drawings and representations.

8.1 Architectural Projections

Architectural drawings can be thought of as a step in the process of translating an idea into a work of architecture. Architecture has been thought of as an attempt to maximize the preservation of an idea by transporting it through drawing to building with minimum loss.[1] Alternatively, ideas can manifest through the drawing process, opening up new possibilities in which ideas are pushed into the representation of objects. Architectural drawings are two-dimensional representations of three-dimensional forms that are either abstract or optically accurate. Abstract drawings include *orthographic projections*, in which projection lines run perpendicular to the projection plane. Orthographic projections communicate metric information and are proportionally accurate. Optically accurate drawings include *perspectives projections*, in which lines converge at vanishing points and depict forms and spaces as we (humans) experience them through the sense of sight.

Orthographic projections include *elevations, plans, sections, auxiliary views*, and *axonometric* drawings. In *orthographic* projections, the projection lines run perpendicular to the projection plane. In *elevation, plan*, and *section* drawings, the primary axes of an object are orthogonal to the projection plane. An *elevation* drawing is a directional view from a vertical plane that typically runs parallel to the primary axes of the object. A multi-view drawing consists of the top and side elevations of an object.[2] (See Figure 8.1.) In architectural drawings, *elevations* can be used to represent the exterior facades of a building or interior surfaces. (See Figure 8.2.)

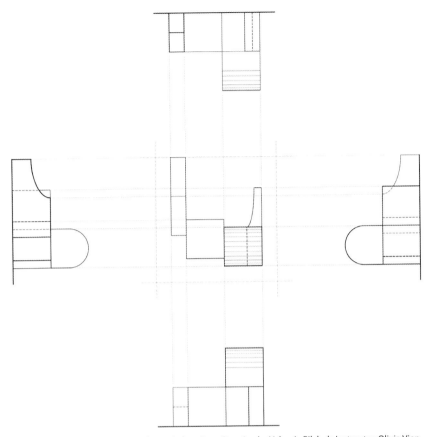

Figure 8.1. Multi-view drawing: plan and elevations. Drawing by Valeryia Pilchuk. Instructor, Olivia Vien. The Bernard and Anne Spitzer School of Architecture, City College of New York. *Courtesy of the author.*

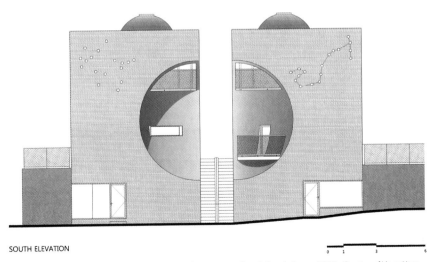

SOUTH ELEVATION

0   1   3   6

Figure 8.2. Moon Hoon, elevation drawing of Two Moon, Seoul, South Korea, 2015. *Courtesy of Moon Hoon.*

A *plan* drawing is a directional view from a horizontal plane, typically from above facing downward. A *section* drawing is also a directional view from a plane that cuts through an object, but in the vertical direction. (See Figure 8.3.) There are various types of *plan* drawings, including *site plans*, *roof plans*, and *floor plans*. In a *floor plan*, the horizontal plane cuts through the object. In architectural drawings, *floor plans* cut through the building, typically between 3-4 feet above the finished floor surface, illustrating the elements that are cut and the elements below the cut datum. Floor plans are useful drawings for communicating the building's dimensional attributes, architectural systems, spatial organization, relationship to the site, and more. For example, Estudio Carme Pinós floor plan drawing of a sports center and indoor and outdoor swimming pools in Sarriguren, Navarra, Spain. (See Figure 8.4.) In architectural drawings, *sections* cut through the building vertically, illustrating the interior elevations and the relationship between interior,

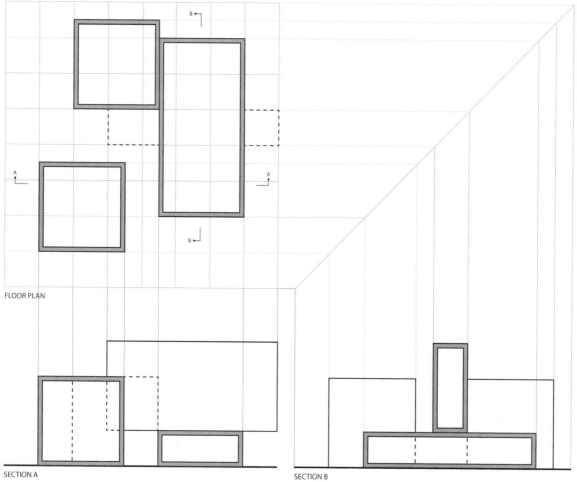

FLOOR PLAN

SECTION A

SECTION B

Figure 8.3. Plan and section drawings of cuboid objects. Drawing by Christopher Lin. Instructor, Frank Melendez. The Bernard and Anne Spitzer School of Architecture, City College of New York. *Courtesy of the author.*

exterior, and ground. For example, the section drawing of the International Terminal Waterloo in London designed by GRIMSHAW. (See Figure 8.5.) Although it is difficult (if not impossible) to understand what an object looks like in three dimensions with just a single plan, section, or elevation, a collection of drawings, elevations, plans, and sections can communicate the actual three-dimensional information about an object. In architectural design, these types of drawings provide metric information that is used to construct a building.

Figure 8.4. Estudio Carme Pinós, floor plan drawing of sports center and indoor and outdoor swimming pools, Sarriguren, Navarra, Spain, 2001–2008. *Courtesy of Estudio Carme Pinós.*

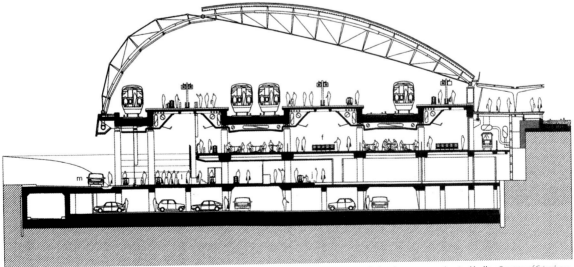

Figure 8.5. Grimshaw, International Terminal, Waterloo, London, UK, section drawing through the departure and arrival halls. *Courtesy of Grimshaw.*

Auxiliary views are additional views that can be created to further describe a three-dimensional object. They can be used to provide true length information of geometry that is nonorthogonal to the projection plane. When the surface of a form is oblique to the projection plane, auxiliary views can be used to project to a plane that is parallel to that surface. (See Figure 8.6.) Additional auxiliary views can be created to show multiple sides of a form. Typically, three primary projections are necessary to understand a three-dimensional form. However, complex forms require additional information. Auxiliary views can be useful to understand a form by providing multiple views from various angles. (See Figure 8.7.)

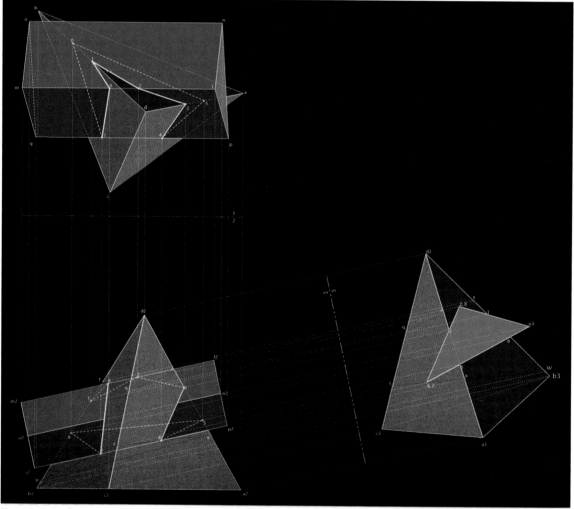

Figure 8.6. Auxiliary view used to describe the true length and shape of the triangular side of a triangular prism. Drawing by Nadeen Hassan. Instructor, Bradley Horn. The Bernard and Anne Spitzer School of Architecture, City College of New York. *Courtesy of the author.*

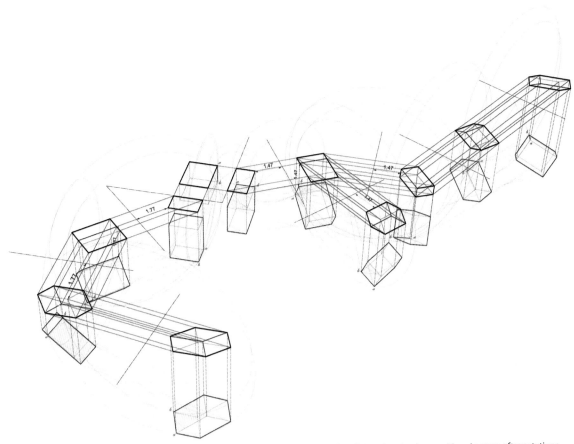

Figure 8.7. Matt Hutchinson, Descriptive geometry study of view relationships: inclined view showing box positions in space after rotations around axes, 2015. *Courtesy of PATH.*

In axonometric drawings, the projection plane is rotated, so that the objects primary axes are nonorthogonal to the projection plane. This allows multiple sides of the object to be depicted in the projection, which makes it easier to understand the three-dimensional qualities of an object. (See Figure 8.8.) In the architectural field, axonometric drawings are useful for viewing the roof and two facades in a single drawing, to understand the building as whole. (See Figure 8.9.)

Perspective projections include one-point perspectives and two-point perspectives. In perspective projections, the projection lines run oblique to the projection plane, and converge at vanishing point(s). In perspective drawings, the vanishing points (a single vanishing point in one-point perspectives and two vanishing points in two-point perspectives) are located on the horizon line, which represents the eye level of the observer. In one-point perspectives, the horizontal edges of the object in one direction run parallel to the projection plane, remaining as horizontal lines in the drawing, and the edges of the object in the opposite direction converge at

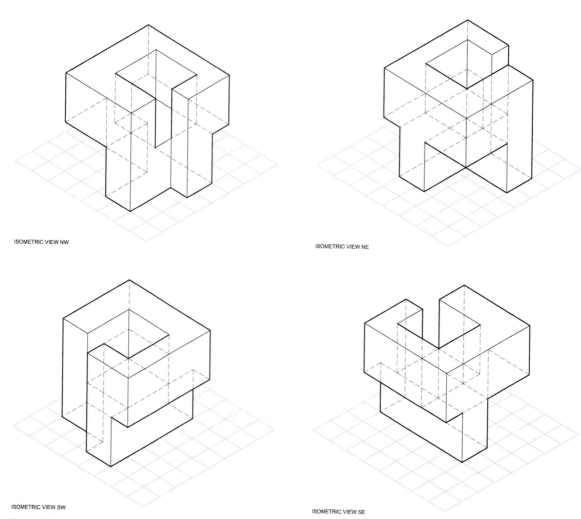

ISOMETRIC VIEW NW

ISOMETRIC VIEW NE

ISOMETRIC VIEW SW

ISOMETRIC VIEW SE

Figure 8.8. Axonometric drawings of an architectural massing model. *Courtesy of the author.*

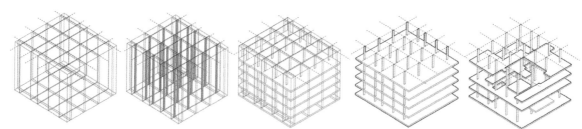

Figure 8.9. Axonometric drawings and analysis of the Villa Shodhan by Le Corbusier. Drawings by Renee Thomas. Instructor, Frank Melendez. The Bernard and Anne Spitzer School of Architecture, City College of New York. *Courtesy of the author.*

the vanishing point. The vertical edges of object are drawn as vertical lines. (See Figure 8.10.) One-point perspective drawings are useful for providing imagery that describes the visual experience of a space. It can also be used in tandem with section projections to reveal the interior spaces of a building. An example of a one-point perspective section is found in the hand-drafted representation of the School of Architecture at Yale University, designed by Paul Rudolph. (See Figure 8.11.)

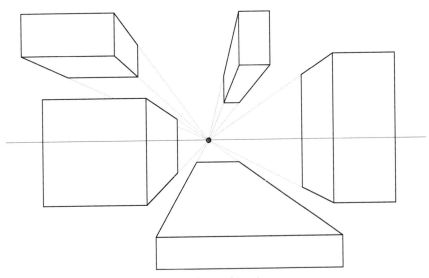

Figure 8.10. One-point perspective drawing. *Courtesy of the author.*

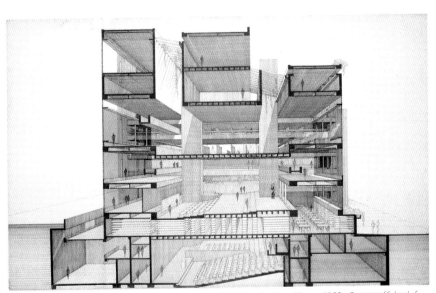

Figure 8.11. Paul Rudolph, School of Architecture, Yale University, New Haven, 1958. *Courtesy of School of Architecture, Yale University, Memorabilia, (RU 925). Manuscripts & Archives, Yale University Library.*

In two-point perspectives, the horizontal edges of the object in one direction converge at one vanishing point, and the edges of the object in the other direction converge at the second vanishing point. The vertical edges of the object are drawn as vertical lines. (See Figure 8.12.) Both one-point and two-point perspectives are pictorial effects that illustrate what an object looks like as viewed by the human eye. Perspective drawings depict three-dimensional objects as experienced in the real world through the human sense of sight. Architectural perspective drawings convey what the formal and spatial qualities of a building typically look like, as experienced from standing inside a building, or viewing the building from the outside. (See Figure 8.10.) An example of a two-point perspective drawing under construction is found in the hand-drafted representation of Frank Lloyd Wright's Fallingwater, in Mill Run, Pennsylvania. (See Figure 8.13.) In this perspective, the view of the building is experienced from a lower elevation on the site landscape looking up towards the building.

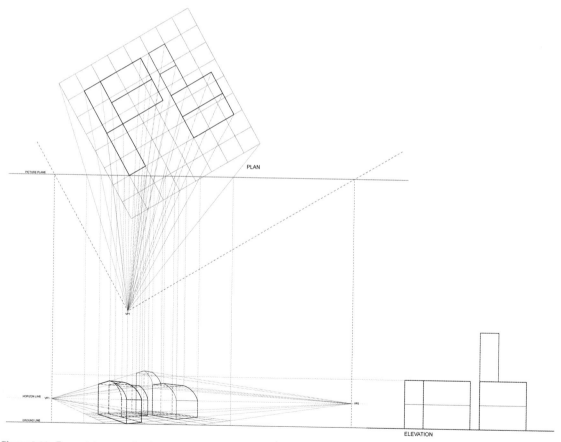

Figure 8.12. Two-point perspective drawing generated from a plan and elevation. Drawing by Brendan Murphy. Instructor, Olivia Vien. The Bernard and Anne Spitzer School of Architecture, City College of New York. *Courtesy of the author.*

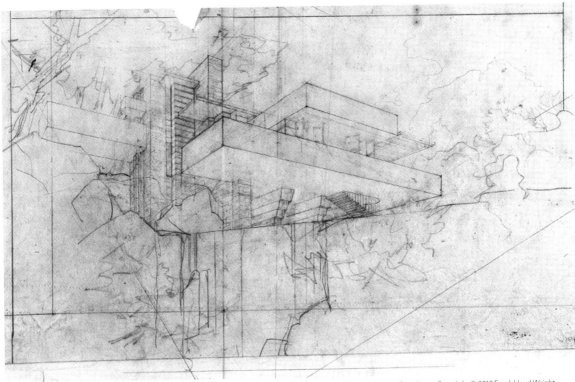

Figure 8.13. Frank Lloyd Wright, Fallingwater, Mill Run, Pennsylvania, 1914. Two-point perspective drawing. *Copyright © 2018 Frank Lloyd Wright Foundation, Scottsdale, Arizona. All rights reserved. Frank Lloyd Wright Foundation Archives (Museum of Modern Art | Avery Architectural & Fine Arts Library, Columbia University, New York).*

Through the manipulation of the structural elements that make up perspective projections, various effects can be achieved that distort the geometry, giving the appearance of a fish-eye lens, or wide-angle lens. This effect can be achieved through traditional hand-drafting techniques or by adjusting camera settings within 3D models. This is useful for creating perspectives that achieve or exaggerate a larger field of vision. Many of the drawings and paintings by the architect Zaha Hadid are well known for this style of representation, which express the sweeping forms, fragmentation, and energies of her architecture, such as the design and representation of the Vitra Fire Station in Germany. (See Figure 8.14.) The aerial perspective painting of the project illustrates the design of the fire station, which is conceptually sheared off from the adjacent factory blocks and shot through with a curving walkway, drawing forms out from the site.[3] Through a collection of orthographic and perspective drawings, architects and designers can communicate the design of three-dimensional objects, forms, and spaces. Collectively, these drawings can be used to understand the scale, metrics, composition, organization, and visual experience of an architectural design.

Figure 8.14. Zaha Hadid Architects, Vitra Fire Station, Weil am Rhein, Germany, 1990–1993. Aerial site plan painting. *Courtesy of © Zaha Hadid Foundation.*

8.2 Setting Up a View

Various types of *orthographic* and *perspective* projections can be created within the 3D model. Additionally, *orthographic* and *perspective* views, are typically preset views within the *viewports* of 3D modeling software. *Viewports,* which can be thought of as virtual windows that provide various views into the 3D model, are viewed on the flat screen of a computer or monitor, as *orthographic* and *perspective* projections. Typically, the interface of 3D modeling software displays four viewports that are simultaneously available on the screen while viewing a digital model. These include the Top, Front, Right, and Perspective views. The Top, Front, and Right views are orthographic projections, while the Perspective view is a one-point perspective projection. This allows users to simultaneously see the metric and visual results of a modeled object in each viewport, and is useful for providing more information about the geometry that is being modeled. A single viewport, however, can be *maximized* to occupy the majority of the interface, and set as the only current view of the model. This allows users to focus on one particular view of the model that is displayed at a larger scale. These views can be changed and specified for each viewport.

Each viewport has a virtual camera that is associated with generating the view. (See Figure 8.15.) The camera is defined by a camera viewpoint (the location of the eye of the observer), a camera target (the focal point of the camera), and a lens angle (the field of view). Navigating within the modeling environment by panning, zooming, and orbiting around the model is essentially moving and repositioning the camera; however, this is not visualized because the camera and its features are typically hidden by default. A camera's features and attributes can be revealed in other viewports, and, in Rhino, can be edited under the Viewport Properties. This includes the option to change the camera from Parallel (orthographic) to Perspective. In Perspective mode, the option to change the camera's Lens length (focal length), which is measured in mm, allows for exaggerating the perspective effect and widening the frame of a view. The viewport can also be set to two-point perspective. Camera views can be saved and provided with a unique name. This is useful when it is necessary to return to a specific view, or series of views, of the 3D model that are not available within the preset default options.

Figure 8.15. The camera attributes displayed in relation to the digital model (left) and the associated camera view of the digital model (right). *Courtesy of the author.*

8.3 Clipping Planes

Architectural floor plans and section drawings are orthographic projections that represent horizontal and vertical *cuts* through a building. *Clipping planes* are useful for visualizing the result of cutting through a digital model. They are virtual, infinite planes that cut all of the geometry in a model, visualizing the effect of the cut on the model by displaying the geometry that appears on one side of a plane, while hiding the geometry that exists on the opposite side of that same plane. (See Figure 8.16.) In

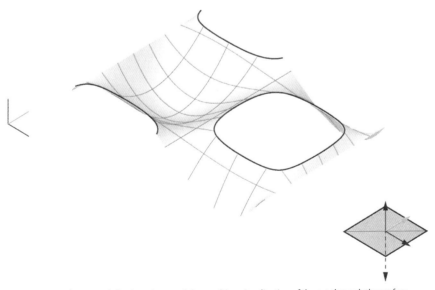

Figure 8.16. A horizontal clipping plane and the resulting visualization of the cut through the surface. Geometry below the clipping plane is visible, and the geometry above the clipping plane is hidden. *Courtesy of the author.*

Figure 8.17. The Clipping Plane command icon in Rhino.

Rhino, the Clipping Plane command can by typed in the command line, or by clicking on the Clipping Plane icon under the Display tab. (See Figure 8.17.) The clipping plane can be positioned in any direction and is defined by using an input of three points. Additionally, the side of the plane that displays or hides the model geometry can be flipped. By specifying three points that are orthogonal to the XY CPlane a horizontal clipping plane can be created and used to visualize a Floor Plan cut. The clipping plane can be moved vertically in the direction of the Z axis in order to provide a dynamic representation that visualizes the effect of the cut on the model. The Clipping Plane tool can be used to create various types of drawings, such as plans, sections, and axonometrics, that reflect cut objects. (See Figure 8.18.)

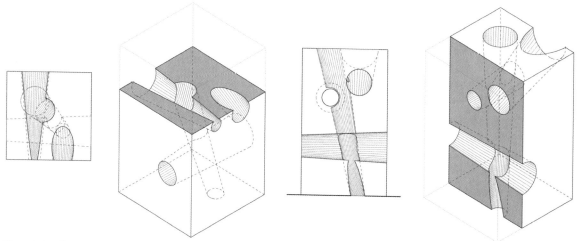

Figure 8.18. Plan, section, and axonometric drawings through a solid (stereotomic) model produced through the use of clipping planes. Drawing by Chaerin Kim. Instructor, Frank Melendez. The Bernard and Anne Spitzer School of Architecture, City College of New York. *Courtesy of the author.*

8.4 Orthographic Projections

Orthographic projections consist of points and lines that are projected parallel to each other and perpendicular to the projection plane. (See Figure 8.19.) Orthographic projections do not distort the representation of forms and spaces; therefore, they are useful for providing information related to proportion, scale, and composition. Orthographic projections such as elevations, plans, and sections are abstract drawings that can be measured to provide accurate dimensional information about forms and spaces. While these types of drawings are very useful for the reasons stated, they only reveal partial information about a three-dimensional objects. Typically, an additional collection of different types of orthographic projections is necessary in order to comprehend a three-dimensional object.

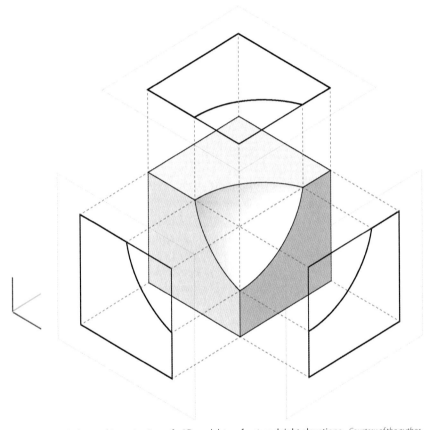

Figure 8.19. Orthographic projections of a 3D model: top, front, and right elevations. *Courtesy of the author.*

In the digital 3D modeling interface, default viewports include Top, Front, and Right views, which are orthographic projections that run parallel to the XY, XZ, and YZ construction planes, respectively. To generate linework (curve objects) of modeled geometry, orthographic projections can be created by selecting the modeled object to project, and specifying the orthographic view, or a construction plane, to project onto.

Elevations

Architectural *elevation* drawings are orthographic projections that represent the facades of a building. This includes the front, back, and side views of a building, which are typically titled based on the cardinal direction that the facade is facing, such as north, east, south, or west. An elevation drawing of the top facade, or roof, of a building, is plan drawing called a *roof plan*. In architectural plans, drawings are typically oriented with the north direction pointing upward, toward the top of the page. In digital models, this same convention applies within the Top View viewport of the model, with the positive Y axis running upward in the north direction. (This convention regarding cardinal directions matters when developing solar simulations, which will be described in Chapter 14). Therefore, the Front viewport represents a south elevation and the Right viewport represents an east elevation.

Creating Projections

Figure 8.20. The Make2D command icon in Rhino.

Orthographic projections can be created by selecting the objects in the model, activating the view in which to project the objects, and executing the Make2D command in Rhino. In the following example, the surface objects in a digital model of Ludwig Mies Van de Rohe's Barcelona Pavilion are selected and projected in Rhino using the Make2D command. (See Figure 8.20.) When this command is executed, and the objects to draw are selected, the 2-D Drawing Options dialog box appears. (See Figure 8.21.) The Make2D command can be used to project geometry from the model onto a CPlane, with options to select the View and to set the Projection to View, CPlane, Third angle projection, or First angle projection. Setting the Projection to View projects the current view. Setting the Projection to CPlane projects the selected elements to the current CPlane. Setting the Projection to Third angle projection or First angle projection provides two options for creating four projections of the active viewports simultaneously, to create a multiview projection. The projected geometry creates lines that are directly visible from an orthographic view, with options to include Hidden lines, the lines that are not directly visible from the orthographic view, and Scene silhouettes, to create outlines around objects. The Maintain source layers option is useful for organizing the projected linework by maintaining the new curve objects within separate layers that match the layers of the projected elements. The projected linework can be exported to other software to assign line weights and line types and develop the projected geometry into an architectural roof plan drawing. (See Figure 8.22.)

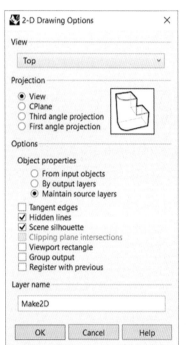

Figure 8.21. The 2D Drawing Options dialogue box.

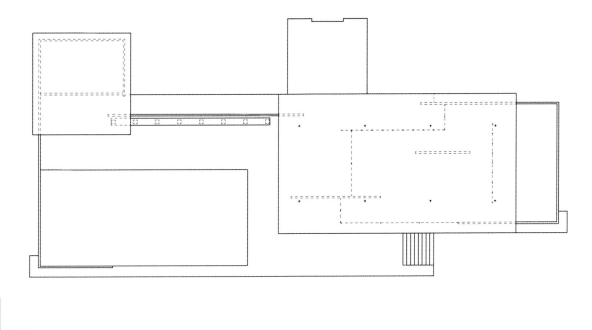

Figure 8.22. The orthographic projection (roof plan), of a 3D digital model of the Barcelona Pavilion, generated from the Top viewport. *Courtesy of author.*

Floor Plans and Sections

Architectural floor plans and sections are orthographic projections that represent directional views from horizontal and vertical planar cuts through a building. Architectural floor plans are horizontal cut views that are typically located 3'-0" above the finished floor, viewing downward. Floor plan drawings communicate many aspects of an architectural design, such as the building's organization, spatial relationships, wall thicknesses, or window and door locations. Architectural sections communicate the relationship between the building's exterior and interior, the relationship to the ground, and interior elevations. Through the use of clipping planes and the Make2D command in Rhino, the projected curve objects for architectural floor plans and sections can be generated. A clipping plane can be created and positioned horizontally, to create a *floor plan*, or vertically, to create a *section*, at the desired location of the orthographic projection. (See Figure 8.23.) The projection can be created from the viewport that is facing in the same direction as the cut. In Figure 8.23, a vertical clipping plane has been located through the 3D model to create a transverse section drawing of the Barcelona Pavilion. In this model, the projection was made from the Right viewport, which is facing in the same direction as the cut, the negative direction of the X axis. As with the previous example, these curves can be exported to other software to assign line weights and line types and develop the projected geometry into an architectural section drawing. (See Figure 8.24.)

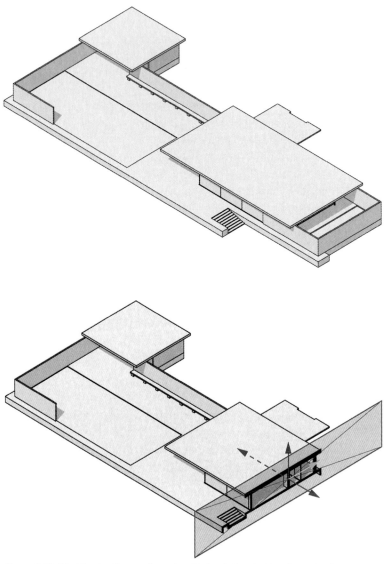

Figure 8.23. The Clipping Plane tool translated in the -Y direction in order to visualize a section cut in a 3D model of the Barcelona Pavilion. *Courtesy of the author.*

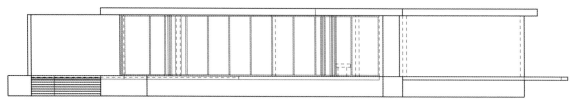

Figure 8.24. An orthographic projection (transverse section) generated from a clipping plane in the orthographic viewport of a 3D model of the Barcelona Pavilion. *Courtesy of the author.*

8.5 Axonometric Projections

Axonometric Projections

Axonometric projections are a type of orthographic projection, in which the projection plane is rotated, and therefore is not orthogonal to the object. (See Figure 8.25.) *Axonometric* projections are drawings that communicate the three-dimensional qualities of an object by depicting multiple sides of the object in a single drawing. There are three types of axonometric projections: *isometric, dimetric,* and *trimetric.* In *isometric* projections, three major axes make equal angles with the projection plane. (See Figure 8.26.) In *dimetric* projections, two of the three major axes make equal angles with the projection plane. In *trimetric* projections, the three major axes make different angles with the projection plane.[2] Axonometric drawings are useful because they allow for the viewing of three sides of an object simultaneously in one drawing. Additionally, they are not distorted, and they provide proportionally accurate information about the object.

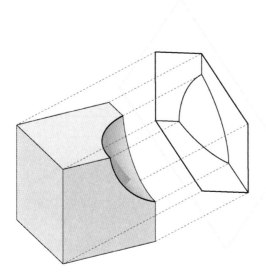

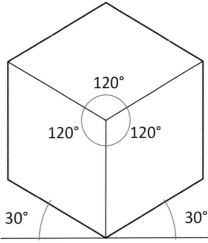

Figure 8.26. Diagram illustrating the angular relationships of a cube in an isometric projection. *Courtesy of the author.*

Figure 8.25. A 3D model projected onto a plane that is not orthogonal to the model in order to create an axonometric projection. *Courtesy of the author.*

Most digital 3D modeling software provides preset axonometric views. In the Rhino 3D modeling environment, the Top, Front, Right, and Perspective viewports can be changed to other views, including preset Isometric views. These views are labeled according to cardinal directions and include NE, NW, SE, SW isometric views, with the Y axis representing true north.

Exploded Axonometric Projections

An *exploded axonometric* drawing is a type of axonometric projection in which the multiple parts that form an object, building, or assembly are separated, or "exploded" into discrete elements or sets of elements. Typically, these elements are translated parallel to the primary axes, providing a clear visual illustration of the part-to-whole relationships between individual elements and the larger assemblies that are formed through their interconnectedness. (See Figure 8.27.) To create exploded axonometric projections, objects in the digital model can be translated, or moved, to new locations in the modeling space. In

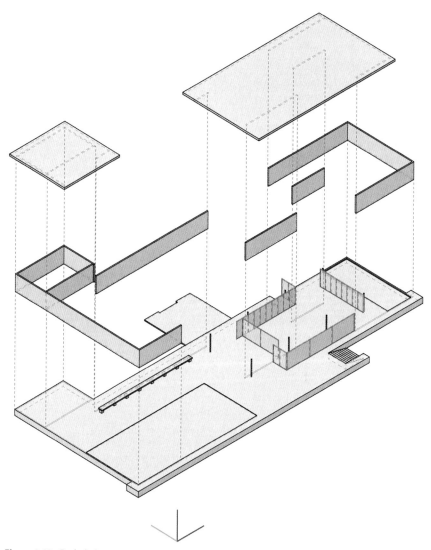

Figure 8.27. Exploded axonometric projection of a 3D model of the Barcelona Pavilion. *Courtesy of the author.*

the example, illustrated in Figure 8.27, the wall elements are moved in the Z direction to a specified distance, and the roof elements are moved in the Z direction twice this distance. Line segments are created that run parallel to the Z axis to connect the elements, and are included as part of the axonometric projection. The exploded axonometric projection can be generated by changing the viewport to one of the isometric views, selecting all of the objects in the model, and executing the Make2D command. This will generate the initial linework that can be exported to create the exploded axonometric drawing.

8.6 Perspective Projections

Perspective projections were developed as a method for accurately depicting the optical experience of human perception. Perspective drawings are intended to represent forms and spaces as we experience them through our sense of sight. One characteristic of human vision includes the receding of forms and spaces based on proximity and distance. Prior to the invention of perspective, the paintings and drawings of artists and architects attempted to depict three-dimensional forms and spaces; however, they often conveyed inconsistencies and inaccuracies in capturing true formal and spatial experiences. The Italian architect Francesco Brunelleschi is credited with inventing a pictorial system for creating optically accurate perspective projections. The Italian architect Leon Battista Alberti codified this system of measurement in his text *On Painting*, in which he described the pictorial system and process for creating perspective projections through the use of a vanishing point, picture plane, and station point.[4] (See Figure 8.28.) This discovery had a profound impact on the art world and became the basis for perspective drawing.

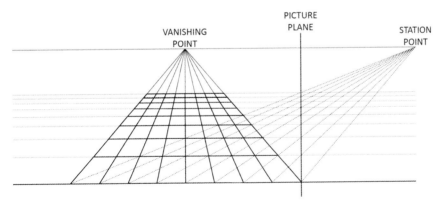

Figure 8.28. A diagram based on Leon Battista Alberti's system for creating perspective projections as described in his text *On Painting*. *Courtesy of the author.*

One-Point Perspective Projections

In *one-point perspective* projections, the vertical Z axis runs parallel to the picture plane and all of the vertical edges of the objects run parallel to the Z axis. One horizontal axis (i.e., the X axis) runs parallel to the picture plane and the other horizontal

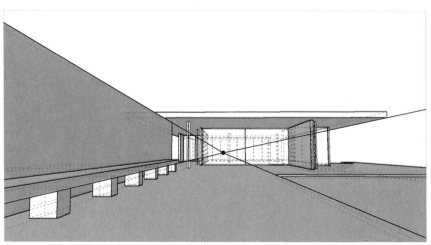

Figure 8.29. A one-point perspective projection of a 3D model of the Barcelona Pavilion illustrating lines converging at a single vanishing point. *Courtesy of the author.*

Figure 8.30. The Viewport (Camera) Properties dialog box in Rhino.

axis (i.e., the Y axis) runs perpendicular to the projection plane. The horizontal edges of objects in one axis remain horizontal, while the horizontal edges of objects that run along the other axis all converge at a single point, called the *vanishing point*. (See Figure 8.29.) The one-point perspective view is typically one of the default viewports available within the interface of 3D modeling software. In Rhino, this view can be selected, and represents the pictorial effects of a camera. Entering the Viewport Properties command in the command line will display the camera attributes. (See Figure 8.30). The projection types of Parallel, Perspective, and Two-Point Perspective can be selected from the Projection drop-down menu. The camera attributes can be modified, such as changing the camera's Lens Length, which modifies the amount in which the perspective is foreshortened.

Two-Point Perspective Projections

In *two-point perspective* projections, the vertical Z axis runs parallel to the picture plane and all of the vertical edges of the objects run parallel to the Z axis. The horizontal X and Y axes run oblique to the picture plane and all horizontal lines run parallel to these axes, which results in the convergence of lines at two vanishing points. (See Figure 8.31.) The two-point perspective view can be set as a current viewport as an option in the Viewport Properties window. Like the Perspective view, the camera's Lens Length, specified in the Viewport Properties, can be modified to change the amount of foreshortening in the two-point perspective.

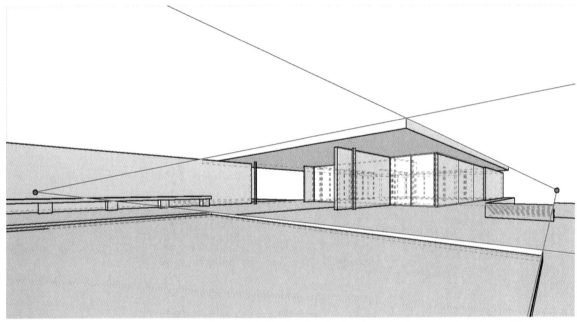

Figure 8.31. A two-point perspective projection of a 3D model of the Barcelona Pavilion illustrating lines converging at two vanishing points. *Courtesy of the author.*

Endnotes

1. Robin Evans, *Translations from Drawing to Building and Other Essays* (London: Janet Evans and Architectural Association, 1997).
2. Francis D. K. Ching and Steven P. Juroszek, *Design Drawing* (2nd ed.) (Hoboken, NJ: John Wiley and Sons, 2010).
3. Aaron Betsky, "Beyond 89 Degrees," in *Zaha Hadid: The Complete Buildings and Projects* by Zaha Hadid (London: Thames & Hudson, 1998).
4. Leon Battista Alberti, *On Painting,* trans. by John Spencer (New Haven, CT: Yale University Press, 1966).

Chapter 9
Architectural Design Drawings

Chapter 9 focuses on converting projected linework into architectural design drawings that communicate architectural forms and spaces. Architectural representations have been developed throughout the history of architecture and continue to evolve through the use of digital technologies. This chapter describes workflows for exporting linework from the 3D model, and importing linework into vector graphics and other computer-aided design (CAD) software. Additional topics include setting up drawing sheets and assigning line weights, line types, color, graphics, text, and other effects to convert projected geometry into architectural design drawings, through the use of Adobe Illustrator CC.

9.1 Linework Overview

The linework from projected geometry can be modified to reflect architectural graphic conventions. These convention or architectural drawings have developed throughout history and are intended to communicate architectural information through the use of linework, color, graphics, symbols, and text. Linework consists of line weights, line types, poché, and color.

Line Weights

Line weights refer to the thinness or thickness of a line. The Micromegas series of drawings by the architect Daniel Libeskind uses multiple lines to create fragments of architectural elements that depict a "new and ambiguous spatial world."[1] (See Figure 9.1.) By varying the thinness or thickness of a line, or "weight," lines can be read with a hierarchy of importance, and provide the drawing with a sense of depth. In analog drawings, a single pencil can provide a range of line weights based on the amount of pressure applied to the pencil tip and the angle at which it touches the paper or drawing surface. The less pressure and the more perpendicular the angle is to the surface, the thinner the line. The more pressure and the more oblique the angle is to the surface, the thicker the line. In computer-aided drafting, line weights can be applied to curve *paths*. These lines weights are available from preset values, or can be customized. Using a range of line weights in a drawing can produce a sense of depth. Thicker lines read as they are in the foreground, while thinner lines appear to recede into the background. Thicker lines can also be used to represent the profile boundaries of an object, allowing the complete shape to be easily read. In floor plans, a range of line weights can be used to indicate hierarchy. The thickest lines are typically used to represent the most important architectural features of the floor plan, and elements that are cut, such as the walls. The thinnest lines are typically used to represent less important architectural features in the floor plan, and elements that are below the datum of the cut, such as furniture.

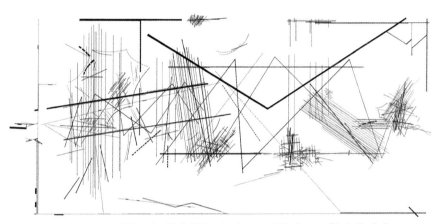

Figure 9.1. Daniel Libeskind, "Chamber Works I-H," series drawing, 1983. *Courtesy of Studio Libeskind.*

Line Types

Architectural line types are primarily used to represent visible and hidden architectural forms and objects, or to graphically communicate information that is not representational of an object. Visible elements are depicted with continuous lines, such as the elements that make up the facade in an elevation, or walls in floor plans and sections. Hidden objects and edges are depicted with dashed lines, also commonly referred to as hidden lines. Line types can be used to communicate information, as opposed to representing objects. For example, center lines can be used to represent a structural grid, indicating the center point alignments of columns. Dotted lines can be used to represent the relationship of one element to another.

Poché

Poché is a darkened portion of an architectural plan or section that represents cutting through a solid material. In architectural design drawings, poché is typically represented as a dark solid fill within the boundaries of walls and columns. This allows for a figural reading of the cut material, as illustrated in the floor plan drawing of Alcova, a speculative project designed by Britanny Utting and Daniel Jacobs. (See Figure 9.2.)

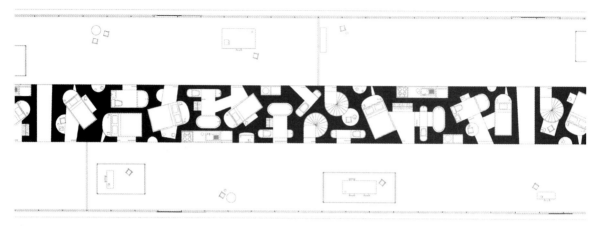

Figure 9.2. Brittany Utting and Daniel Jacobs, Alcova, 2014. Floor plan drawing. *Courtesy of Brittany Utting and Daniel Jacobs.*

Color and Graphics

Colors and graphics can be applied to provide drawings with additional effects and information. Color fills can be used to differentiate architectural elements or changes in materials. Color can also be used to create depth by indicating elements that are in shade or shadow. This is exemplified in the plan/section drawings for the project entry by Neil M. Denari Architects, for the Tokyo International Forum Competition. (See Figure 9.3.) Text can be added to label drawings and elements and specify numerical information. Graphic elements and symbols can be combined with text to call out specific elements in a drawing.

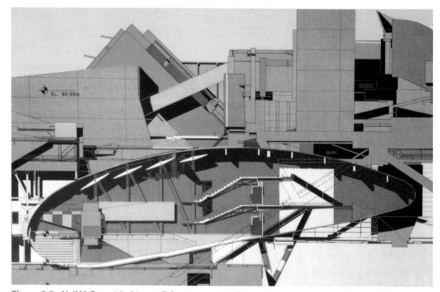

Figure 9.3. Neil M. Denari Architects, Tokyo International Forum Competition, 1989. Plan/section drawing. *Courtesy of Neil M. Denari Architects, Inc.*

9.2 Exporting Linework

Software is typically designed and optimized to perform specific operations and tasks. Therefore, different software packages are utilized throughout the architectural design process depending on the task at hand within various stages of design and production. It is often necessary to work with different digital tools that are best suited for completing a certain goal. While many 3D modeling software packages provide a broad range of tools and features to create architectural drawings, it is often necessary, and easier, to transfer data to other two-dimensional drafting and illustration software to develop and enhance two-dimensional projections into architectural drawings. The exception to this is building information modeling (BIM) software, in which 2D views are parametrically linked with the 3D model, to automatically generate architectural drawings. However, just as BIM software has many positive aspects in terms of architectural design and production, such as the ability to generate 2D drawings and link them with a 3D model, there are limitations as well, such as the ease and flexibility in creating more complex three-dimensional surfaces and forms.

While there is currently no single architectural design software that achieves all of the needs and demands of the contemporary architecture practice, software packages continue to evolve and include more features that improve workflows. Additionally, software *interoperability*—the ability to export and import useable data from one software to another—continues to improve. Although many 3D modeling platforms provide some basic tools for creating two-dimensional drawings, it is common practice to export two-dimensional point, line, and curve objects from the 3D model and import them into illustration and computer-aided drafting software. These environments provide more tools and features for assigning and controlling specific attributes that constitute architectural drawings, such as line weights, line types, poché, text, color, graphics, and plotting options. This chapter will present basic methods for exporting and importing geometry from the Rhino 3D model into Adobe Illustrator.

Raster and Vector Images

Digital graphics fall under two primary types of categories: *raster* graphics and *vector* graphics. A *raster* image consists of a grid of points within Cartesian coordinates, called pixels. Each pixel is assigned a numerical value that defines a color value, allowing a collection of pixels to form an image. The number of pixels that make up an image for a given physical size is known as *resolution*. Raster images are ideal for manipulating photographic imagery, but are restricted to size based on their resolution.[2] A program such as Adobe Photoshop© is an industry standard application for raster graphics. A more thorough explanation of raster images will be presented in Section 9.9.

A *vector* image is defined by points and paths, which are mathematically defined, and filled with a color. Instead of storing a value for each pixel in an image, vector graphics store equations that define geometrical shapes that form the image.[3] In addition to reducing the file size, this allows the image to be scaled up or down without losing detail or reducing image quality. These attributes make vector images ideal for creating architectural drawings. Programs such as Adobe Illustrator®, Autodesk AutoCAD, and Rhinoceros® handle vector objects.

Layer Management

Prior to exporting geometry, it is common practice to organize information through the use of *layers*. The use of layers is not exclusive to Rhino, rather, it is a standard method for organizing information that is utilized across various types of CAD, vector graphics, and image editing software. Within Rhino, the Layers tab can be selected to view the layer settings. (See Figure 9.4.) By clicking on the lightbulb icon, layers can be toggled on or off to view or hide objects. By clicking on the lock icon, Layers can be *locked*, which allows objects to remain visible but prevents them from being selectable. Double-clicking on a layer sets the layer to Current, which is indicated by the check mark under the Current label and the text appearing in bold. Colors can be assigned to layers and changed by left-clicking on the color swatch. This prompts the Select Layer Color dialog box, with preset color swatches and a color wheel to set custom colors. (See Figure 9.5.)

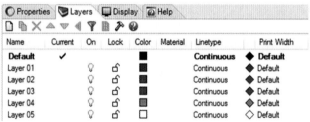

Figure 9.4. The Layers tab and settings in Rhino.

Figure 9.5. The Select Layer Color dialog box in Rhino.

By right-clicking on the layer, other options appear for working with layers, such as Create New Layer, Rename Layer, Delete Layer, and Selecte Object on the layer. Modeled objects can be moved to other layers by selecting the object, right-clicking on the layer that you want to move the object to, and selecting Change Object Layer.

Alternatively, the objects can be moved to a different layer by selecting the objects in Rhino, clicking on the Properties tab, and selecting the desired layer in which to place the objects from the Layer drop-down list.

Within architectural models and drawings, it is useful to organize information within separate layers by creating and renaming layers to reflect architectural naming conventions of elements and/or materials, such as walls, columns, glass, and so on. This is useful not only for organizing geometry and objects within the 3D model but also for organizing linework when generating two-dimensional projections. When the Make2D command is prompted, the *2D Drawing Options* dialog box appears and includes an option to Maintain Source Layers. When this option is selected, the two-dimensional *visible* geometry that is created will be placed in a new layer and sublayers, which maintain the names of the source layers. When the Hidden Lines option is checked, the two-dimensional geometry for *hidden* objects will be created and placed in a new layer and sublayers, which maintain the names of the source layers. (See Figure 9.6.) This is very efficient when working with the linework in Autodesk AutoCAD or Adobe Illustrator, allowing groups of lines on layers to be easily selected and modified.

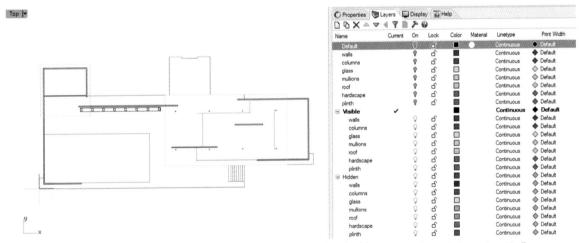

Figure 9.6. Example of using Layers to organize modeled objects, and the Visible and Hidden geometry layers that are automatically creating when the Make2D command is executed. *Courtesy of the author.*

Exporting to Adobe Illustrator

There are multiple workflows for exporting linework from Rhino to various graphic illustration and computer-aided drafting software. After generating the initial linework for floor plans, sections, axonometrics, perspectives, and other architectural projections in Rhino, these curve objects can be exported directly to Adobe Illustrator to develop with line weights, line types, color, and other drawing enhancing features. Adobe Illustrator is an industry standard vector graphics application software, and is ideal for creating shapes, color, effects, and typography.[4] The software is used in many design-related industries, primarily graphic design, where logos, text, and drawings can be scaled up or down and printed at various sizes from business cards to billboards without compromising image quality. These features make the software popular in architectural design, because it allows architectural design drawings and graphics to be scaled and plotted out at different scales without compromising image quality.

After two-dimensional projections are generated in Rhino through the Make2D command, the resulting curve objects are positioned on the XY CPlane, on or close to the origin. To export the two-dimensional curve objects from Rhino to Adobe Illustrator, open the File tab and click Export Selected. Select the curve objects from the Top viewport (if the curve objects are projected on the XY CPlane), and press the Enter key. (See Figure 9.7.) The Export dialogue box will appear. Expand the "Save as type" drop-down menu, select Adobe Illustrator (*.ai), and provide a name for the file. (See Figure 9.8.) Click Save (or the Options tab) and the AI Export Options window will appear. (See Figure 9.9.) The primary setting in this window is the Scale of the exported geometry. There are two options; "Snapshot of the current view" and "Preserve model scale." To export the geometry at an architectural scale, select the "Preserve model scale" option. The units can be set to imperial or metric, and should be set to match the units of the model. Imperial units of measurement are primarily used in the United States, and metric units are the units of an international system of

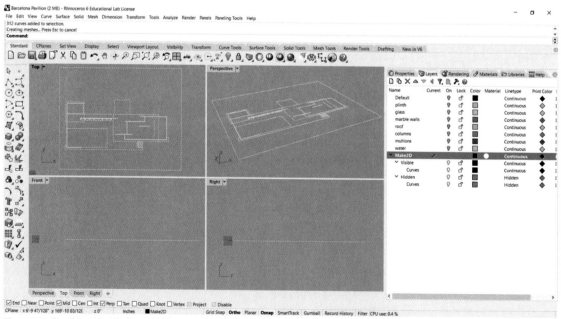

Figure 9.7. The Rhino 6 for Windows interface with exported objects selected and the Top viewport active. *Courtesy of the author.*

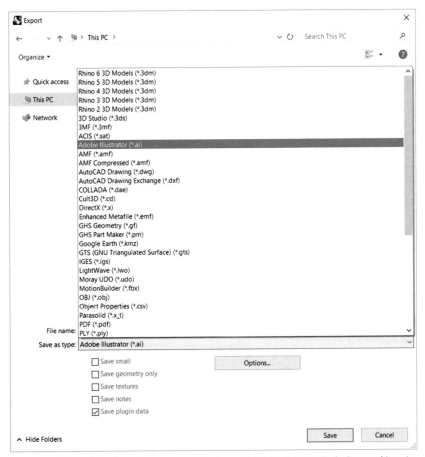

Figure 9.8. Export dialog box with "Save as type" option set to Adobe Illustrator (*.ai). *Courtesy of the author.*

measurement used in almost every country in the world. Imperial units for measuring length include inches and feet, while metric units for measuring length include millimeters, centimeters, and meters. Architectural drawings are typically measured in fractions of an inch per foot (for example, ¼" = 1'0", ⅛" = 1'0"). To set the numerical values in the "Preserve model scale" option, multiply the fraction denominator by 12 (the number of inches in a foot). For example, to export the drawing at the scale of ⅛" = 1'0", multiply 8 * 12, which results in 96. Therefore, the "Preserve model scale" values set to 96 inches in the model will equal 1 inch in the drawing. (See Figure 9.9.) Click OK to close the AI Export Options and Save the file (or it may save automatically) to complete the exporting process. The file is now saved and ready to be opened in Adobe Illustrator.

Figure 9.9. Adobe Illustrator Export Options dialog box. *Courtesy of the author.*

Exporting to Autodesk AutoCAD

Autodesk AutoCAD, first released in the early 1980s, is an industry standard computer-aided design (CAD) and drafting software application that is primarily used in the architectural and engineering industries. AutoCAD is designed to digitally draft and model geometry and objects at a one-to-one scale, such as a building, city, or landscape, while also providing a means to output drawings that are scaled down to fit and print on standard sheet sizes. AutoCAD provides two types of spaces: one for drafting and modeling, called *model space* and one for setting up sheets for plotting drawings, called *paper space*. This allows users to work at a one-to-one scale within the 2D drafting and 3D modeling environment (modeling space), while easily shifting to a proportionally scaled architectural drawing on standard and custom sized sheets of paper (paper space).

To export the two-dimensional curve objects from Rhino to Autodesk AutoCAD, open the File tab and click Export Selected. Select the curve objects from the Top viewport (if the curve objects are projected on the XY CPlane), and press Enter. The Export dialogue box will appear. Expand the "Save as type" drop-down menu, select AutoCAD Drawing (*.dwg), and provide a name for the file. (See Figure 9.10.) Click Save (or the Options tab) and the DWG/DXF Export Options dialog box will appear.

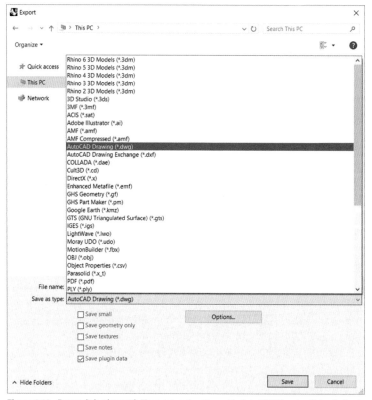

Figure 9.10. Export dialog box with "Save as type" option set to AutoCAD Drawing (*.dwg). *Courtesy of the author.*

(See Figure 9.11.) This setting can remain as default or a specific version of AutoCAD can be selected. Click OK to close the DWG/DXF Export Options and Save the file (or it may save automatically), to complete the exporting process. The file is now saved and ready to be opened in AutoCAD.

Figure 9.11. AutoCAD DWG/DXF Export Options dialog box. *Courtesy of the author.*

From the AutoCAD interface, click on the AutoCAD icon in the top left corner of the screen. From the drop-down menu, select Open, Drawing, and the Select File dialog box will appear. Select the file and click Open. The drawing will appear in the Top viewport of the AutoCAD modeling space. (See Figure 9.12.) AutoCAD is a very useful program for drafting architectural design drawings and construction documents. Once the .dwg file is opened, scaling the drawing in paper space and assigning various line weights and line types to the linework can be achieved in AutoCAD. Additional features typically found in architectural construction document drawings are also available, such as the ability to dimension drawings, add schedules, architectural symbols, and more. AutoCAD and Rhino share similar functionality, features, commands, and tools, and are very compatible programs that allow for streamlined interoperability between the two programs. AutoCAD drawings can be easily opened in Rhino, and the curve objects can be used to begin modeling three-dimensional geometry. Although AutoCAD is extremely useful in the production of architectural drawings, the ability to enhance architectural design drawings with imagery, color, and effects is typically easier to achieve in Adobe Illustrator. In this book, the focus will be on creating architectural design drawings; therefore, the following chapters will describe the process of setting up drawings in Adobe Illustrator.

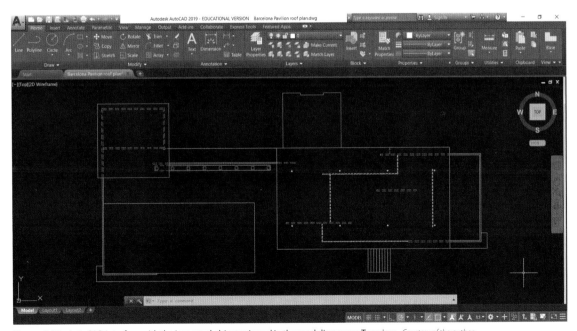

Figure 9.12. AutoCAD interface with the imported objects viewed in the modeling space Top view. *Courtesy of the author.*

Creating Adobe PDF files

Another workflow for exporting linework from Rhino involves creating Portable Document Format (PDF) files, which can be opened and edited in Adobe Illustrator, or imported and edited in AutoCAD, to create architectural drawings and diagrams. A PDF is a file format, invented by Adobe, that is used to present and exchange documents independent of software, hardware, or operating system.[5] Similar to a hard copy print on a printer, a PDF document is a digital print, in the form of an electronic file that can be viewed, printed, and edited. To create an Adobe PDF document from Rhino, select File from the Main Menu bar to view the drop-down menu, and then select Print. A Print Setup dialog box appears with various setting options and a print preview. (See Figure 9.13.) The Print Setup window provides six headings that can be expanded and contain various setting options for printing a document. These are Destination, View and Output Scale, Margins and Position, Linetypes and Line Widths, Visibility, and Printer Details.

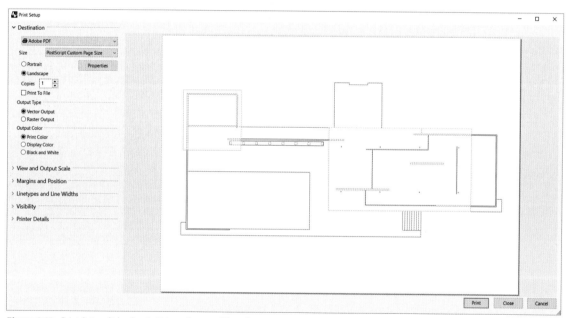

Figure 9.13. Print Setup dialog box in Rhino. *Courtesy of the author.*

Expand the Destination heading and select Adobe PDF. (See Figure 9.14.) The Size of the sheet can be selected from standard sheet sizes, or specified to custom dimensions. Select the sheet orientation, which can be set to Portrait or Landscape format. Set the Output Type to Vector, as the drawings will be edited in the vector-based software, Adobe Illustrator. Set the Output Color option to Print Color. This will be helpful for selecting objects based on their color when opened in Adobe Illustrator.

Figure 9.14. Destination settings. *Courtesy of the author.*

Figure 9.15. View and Output Scale settings. *Courtesy of the author.*

Figure 9.16. The list of standard architecture and engineering scale options in Rhino.

Under the View and Output Scale settings, select the *Top* view from the drop-down menu and select the Viewport option. (See Figure 9.15.) Set the *Scale* of the drawing. The scale of drawings varies, depending on the type of drawing and information that is represented, such as a floor plan of a building, a site plan of a landscape, or a detail of an architectural assembly. The sheet size can be adjusted and set after determining the correct scale of the drawing. Drawings can vary in scale; however, floor plans for residential projects, for example, are typically set to scales such as 1/8″ = 1′0″; site plans are represented at a much larger scale, such as 1:500; while detail drawings are much smaller, such as 1″ = 1′0″. Conventional options for architectural and engineering scales can be viewed and selected from the Scale drop-down menu. (See Figure 9.16.) Other settings can be adjusted to set up the drawing; however, these default settings should be sufficient for providing the necessary linework necessary to create the drawing in Illustrator. Linetypes and Line Widths, for example, will be edited in other software, so these settings will remain as default settings. The final step is to print the drawing by selecting the Print button on the lower right corner of the Print Setup window. Name the PDF file and select the folder in which it will be placed.

Figure 9.17. The New Layout command icon in Rhino.

Using Rhino Layouts to Create Adobe PDF files (Alternate Version)

An alternate method for creating a PDF document involves creating and setting up a Layout in Rhino. A Layout is an additional viewport that represents a sheet of paper that can be printed out on paper or as a PDF file. To create a sheet, type "Layout" in the command line or select the Layout icon located under the Viewport Layout tab. (See Figure 9.17.) This will prompt the New Layout dialog box to appear. (See Figure 9.18.) The default Name, or a unique name, can be specified for the layout. From the Printer drop-down menu, select Adobe PDF. From the Size drop-down menu, select a standard architectural sheet size or set a custom sheet size. Set the sheet orientation to Portrait or Landscape format. Click OK and the new sheet will appear as the viewport and a new layout tab will appear at the bottom of the Rhino interface. (See Figure 9.19.)

Figure 9.18. The New Layout dialog box in Rhino. *Courtesy of the author.*

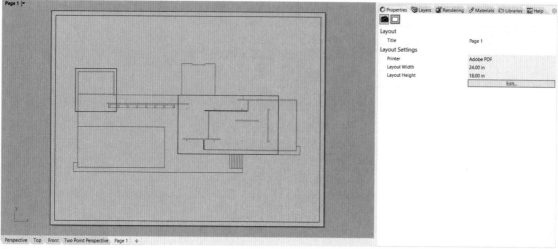

Figure 9.19. A new Page and its associated settings in the Properties tab. *Courtesy of the author.*

Once a sheet is created, it can be edited in the Properties tab. To resize the sheet, click Edit and the Modify Layout dialog box appears. (See Figure 9.20.) The view of the Layout sheet is known as Paper Space.

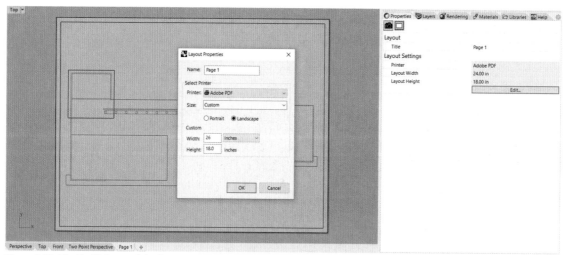

Figure 9.20. The Modify Layout dialog box Rhino. *Courtesy of the author.*

When the new layout is created, a boundary curve object appears. When the boundary curve is selected, the Scale option appears under the Properties tab. To set the drawing scale, specify the units on the layout in relation to the units on the model. For example, to create a ⅛″ = 1′0″ scale, multiply 8 * 12(in.) = 96. Therefore, specifying 1 inch on the layout and 96 inches on the model will set the drawing scale to ⅛″ = 1′0″. (See Figure 9.21.)

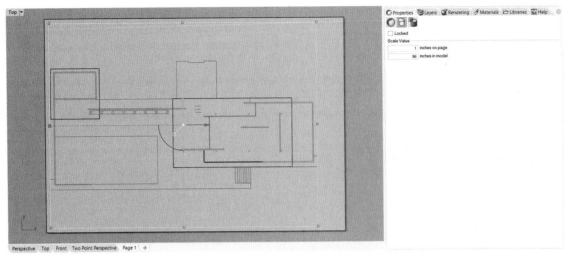

Figure 9.21. Specifying the drawing scale in the Properties tab. *Courtesy of the author.*

Similar to Autodesk AutoCAD, the Rhino Layout sheet provides a *paper space* and *model space* toggle. Paper space is the space and dimensions of the layout sheet. By zooming in and out while in paper space, the sheet moves forward and backward while the drawing stays set within the page. Model space is the space and dimensions of the model. By double-clicking within the boundary curve on the sheet, the sheet color changes and the layout changes to model space, also known as the Detail viewport in Rhino. (See Figure 9.22.) By zooming in and out while in detail view (model space), the sheet remains fixed, and the drawing moves forward and backward. This changes the scale of the drawing, which can be reset as described in the previous step.

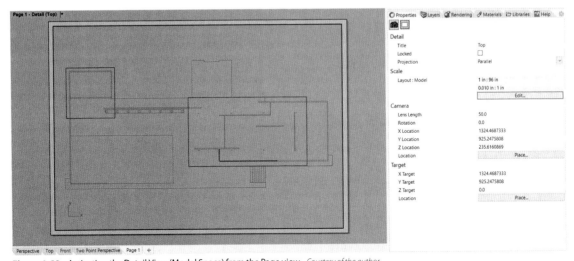

Figure 9.22. Activating the Detail View (Model Space) from the Page view. *Courtesy of the author.*

To create an Adobe PDF, select File from the Main Menu bar and Print from the drop-down menu. The Print Setup dialog box will appear. (See Figure 9.23.) Under the Destination heading, select Adobe PDF, and set the sheet size to a preset standard or custom size. (The custom size dimensions can be specified in Properties). Under the View and Output Scale heading, select the Layout name and set the Scale to 1:1. (See Figure 9.24.) Print the drawing by selecting the Print button on the lower right corner of the Print Setup dialog box. Name the PDF file and select the folder in which it will be placed.

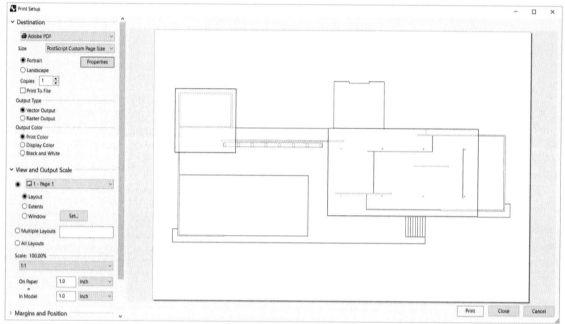

Figure 9.23. The Print Setup dialog box in Rhino. *Courtesy of the author.*

Figure 9.24. The View and Output Scale dialog box in Rhino. *Courtesy of the author.*

9.3 The Adobe Illustrator Interface

Adobe Illustrator CC is an industry standard vector graphics software. The main work-space within Illustrator is a two-dimensional *Artboard*, in which lines, shapes, text, graphics, and imagery can be created and edited. Commands are executed by click-ing on various tools within panels. The Adobe Illustrator CC Interface consists of the Application Bar, Control Panel, Document Window, Workspace Switcher, Tools Panel, Panel Tabs, Panel Groups, and the Artboard. (See Figure 9.25.)

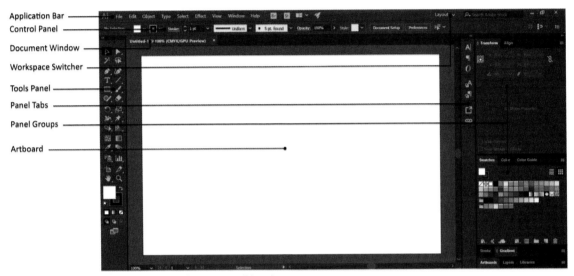

Figure 9.25. The Adobe Illustrator CC interface. *Courtesy of the author.*

Application Bar

The Application Bar (or Main Menus) consists of the titles that provide drop-down menus for many of the primary commands and tools that are available in Illustra-tor. For example, the File menu can be expanded to list commands that create New documents, Open files, and Save files. The Object menu can be expanded to list commands for working with objects, such as Transform. The small black arrows on the right side of the list indicate that submenus are available with additional commands. When the Transform submenu is expanded, other related commands appear, such as Scale. (See Figure 9.26.)

Figure 9.26. The Adobe Illustrator Interface: Application Bar (Main Menus). *Courtesy of the author.*

Figure 9.27. The Adobe Illustrator Interface: Control Panel.

Figure 9.28. The Adobe Illustrator interface: Workspace Switcher.

Control Panel

The Control Panel displays options for objects that are selected and changes to display the options that are available for the selected object, such as a Path object or a Text object. Options for a Path object include color and stroke width, while Text object options include color, font, and font sizes. (See Figure 9.27.)

Workspace Switcher

Within the Control Panel is the Workspace Switcher. This drop-down menu lists various types of workspaces that are available. The toolbars, panels, and windows can be reconfigured to set the interface workspace. (See Figure 9.28.)

Document Window

The Document Window displays the name of the document that is opened. Multiple documents can be opened at the same time and the Document Window tabs can be clicked to activate the selected tab as the current document.

Tools Panel

The Tools Panel provides tools for creating, editing, and assigning attributes to lines, shapes, and text. Tools for working with colors are also available, as well as navigation tools. (See Figure 9.29.)

Panel Tabs and Panel Groups

Panel tabs and groups provide additional features for working with objects. Panel tabs can be clicked on to view the panel features under each tab. For example, clicking on the Layers tab displays the layers in the document and provides options for creating new layers, viewing layers, locking layers, and so on. Panels are grouped together, such as Artboards, Layers, and Libraries, and can be stacked in various configurations. (See Figure 9.30.)

Figure 9.29. The Adobe Illustrator interface: Tools Panel.

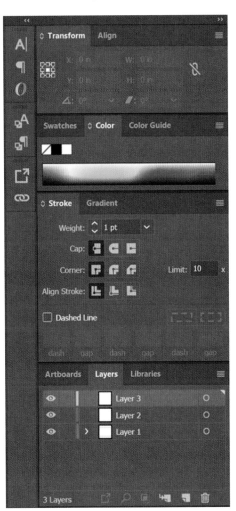

Figure 9.30. The Adobe Illustrator interface: Panel Tabs and Groups.

Artboards

The Artboard is the main two-dimensional workspace in which the drawing and graphics are placed. The Artboard is essentially a virtual sheet of paper for creating and editing lines, shapes, text, and graphics. Artboards can be resized, and multiple Artboards can be created within a single document.

Navigation

Navigation in Illustrator includes *panning* and *zooming* within the two-dimensional workspace. The Pan and Zoom tools can be found in the Tools Panel and are represented with the hand and magnifying lens icons, respectively. A more useful method for panning and zooming involves the use of keyboard shortcuts. To pan, hold the space bar down and click and hold the left mouse button down while moving the mouse. To zoom, hold the Alt key down while scrolling the middle mouse button back and forth to zoom in and out.

9.4 Setting Up the Page

To create a new Illustrator document, select File from the Main Menus, and select New from the drop-down menu. The New Document dialog box will appear, with various settings for setting up the page, including the file Name, the Artboard Size, displaying the Width and Height, Orientation options of Portrait and Landscape, and Color Mode options. (See Figure 9.31.) Clicking OK will create the document.

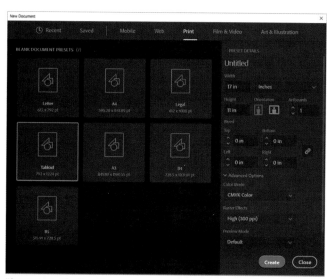

Figure 9.31. The New Document window in Adobe Illustrator.

To open an Illustrator file that was exported from Rhino, select File from the Main Menus, and select Open from the drop-down menu. Select the file and click Open. Continuing with the example file that was exported from Rhino at the architectural scale of ⅛" = 1'0", the linework appears in the Illustrator workspace, but falls off of the current Artboard. (See Figure 9.32.) The Artboard can be resized to the dimensions of a sheet that fits the scaled drawing, by clicking on the Artboard icon in the Tools Panel, or the Document Setup button in the Control Panel. When the Document Setup dialog box appears, click on the Edit Artboards button.

The Artboard settings will appear and can be modified in the Control Panel. The Origin of the Artboard can be set to the lower left corner of the sheet by specifying X and Y values of 0, and clicking on the lower left corner of the nine square Reference Point icon. The Artboard sheet size can be changed by dragging the square grippers on the edges of the Artboard, or by specifying a width (W) and height (H) value in the Control Panel. In this example, the Artboard size is set to W = 26 in. and H = 18 in. (See Figure 9.33.) After the Artboard dimensions are set, click the Esc key to exit the Artboard command. Rulers

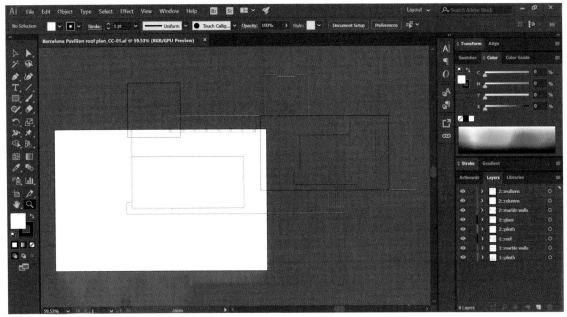

Figure 9.32. Example of a drawing extending beyond the limits of the Artboard. *Courtesy of the author.*

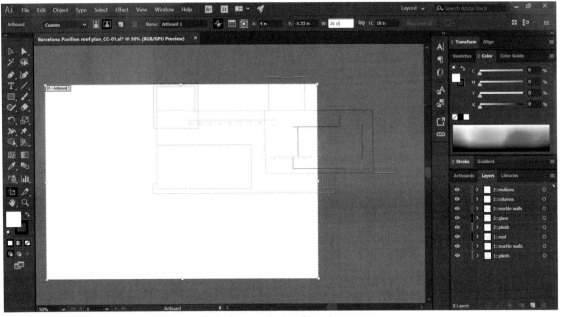

Figure 9.33. Example of resizing the Artboard to fit the drawing. *Courtesy of the author.*

Figure 9.34. The Selection Tool icon in Adobe Illustrator.

can also be turned on within the workspace, to see the dimensions of the Artboard, by selecting View from the Main Menus, selecting Rulers from the drop-down menu, and selecting Show Rulers.

To move the drawing to the center of the Artboard, click on the Selection tool, located in the Tools Panel. (See Figure 9.34.) All of the curve objects can be selected and moved by left-clicking and dragging from one corner of the workspace to the opposite corner to create a selection border, marquee, around all of the objects. Hover the mouse over one of the curve objects, and the Select tool icon will display a small white box next to it. Click and drag to relocate the linework so that it is centered on the page. (See Figure 9.35.) Left-click in a blank area of the workspace to deselect the curve objects.

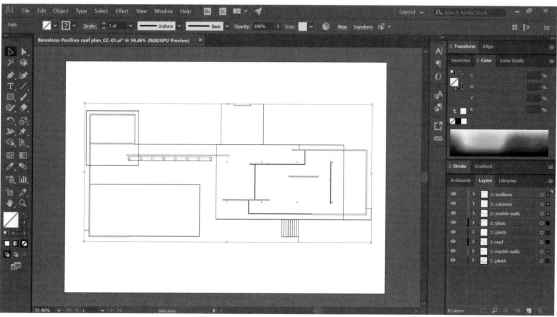

Figure 9.35. Selecting and moving the objects to center the drawing within the Artboard. *Courtesy of the author.*

9.5 Line Weights and Line Types

In Illustrator, lines, curves, and shapes are represented as Paths and Strokes. Paths are the sets of points and mathematical definitions that define lines, curves, and shapes. Strokes are Paths that have attributes such as width, color, and/or other properties that effect the appearance of the linework. The curve objects, Strokes, that are imported into Illustrator can be edited in various ways to create architectural drawings.

Selection

Curve objects that are organized by Layers will retain the same Layer organization in Illustrator when exported directly from Rhino. The curve objects, Strokes, can be selected as individual objects. However, to take advantage of the Layer organization, all of the Strokes on a Layer (or multiple Layers) can be selected simultaneously to edit their attributes, and change the linework to reflect architectural drawing conventions, through the use of color, line weights, and line types. To select all of the objects on one Layer, click on the small circle to the right of the Layer name. (See Figure 9.36.) Similar to other programs, Layers can be turned on or off (eye icon) to view or hide objects, and locked or unlocked (lock icon) to disable and enable selection.

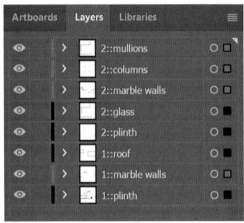

Figure 9.36. The Layers panel in Adobe Illustrator. *Courtesy of the author.*

Stroke Color

To change the color of all of the Stroke objects on a Layer, double-click with the left mouse button on the Stroke color icon. (See Figure 9.37.) The Color Picker dialog box will open. Select the preferred color, which will be assigned to the Strokes and will remain as the current Stroke color. (See Figure 9.38.) In this example drawing, the Strokes are assigned various black and grayscale values. (See Figure 9.39.)

Figure 9.37. The Stroke and Fill color icons in Adobe Illustrator.

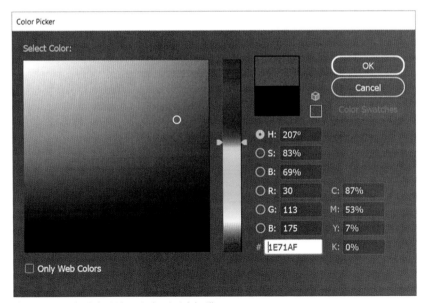

Figure 9.38. The Color Picker window in Adobe Illustrator.

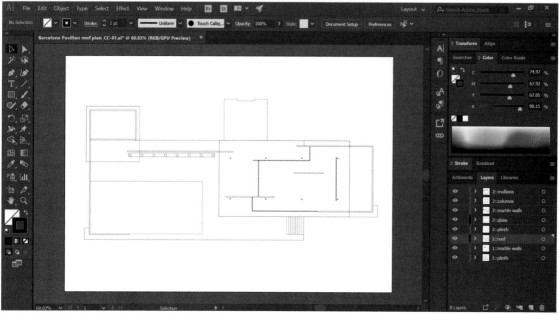

Figure 9.39. Linework objects selected and assigned black and grayscale colors to strokes, and no color (transparent) fills. *Courtesy of the author.*

Figure 9.40. The Stroke panel in Adobe Illustrator.

Stroke Panel (Line Weights and Line Types)

In Illustrator, various thicknesses can be assigned to linework by specifying the Stroke Weight. In architectural drawings, the various thicknesses of lines are known as *line weights*. The Stroke Weight can be found in the Control Panel, when a Path or Stroke is selected, or in the Stroke Panel. (See Figure 9.40.) The Stroke Weight is measured in points (pt), which is a unit of measurement used in typography, where one inch is equal to 72 points. Strokes can be assigned a pt Weight value from the drop-down menu or the value can be typed in. The first eight preset values—.25 pt through 5 pt—are illustrated in Figure 9.41.

Figure 9.41. Stroke Weights ranging from .25 pt (top) to 5 pt (bottom) values. *Courtesy of the author.*

Architectural drawings utilize various "line types," which include Continuous lines, Hidden lines, Center lines, and other conventional line types. Many of these various line types can by created within the Stroke Panel by checking the Dashed Line Stroke

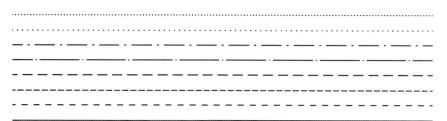

Figure 9.42. Various line types created with the Stroke Dashed Line option checked, and by using various combinations of dash and gap values. *Courtesy of the author.*

option. Strokes are continuous lines by default, meaning that they are solid, uninterrupted lines. Hidden, or Dashed, lines contain even alternating dashes and gaps. Center Lines can be created by adding extra dashes and gaps. By changing these values, many different line types can be created. (See Figure 9.42.) Additional settings to line types that are not continuous, include *preserving* dash and gap lengths, or *adjusting* them to fit evenly within the line. In architectural drawing, it is typically preferable to select the adjusted to fit option, as it allows the corners to remain legible. (See Figure 9.43.)

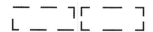

Figure 9.43. Dash options: Preserve (left) and Adjust (right). *Courtesy of the author.*

The Cap and Corner options within the Stroke Panel provide options for creating sharp or rounded edges. The three options for Caps are Butt Cap, Round Cap, and Projecting Cap. The Butt Cap option works well with architectural drawings, as it keeps edges sharp and allows the Stroke to end at the endpoint of the Path, as opposed to being rounded off or extending beyond. The three options for Corners are Miter Joins, Round Joins, and Bevel Joins. Miter Joins work well with architectural drawings, as they also keep corners sharp. Figure 9.44 shows a polygon shape with thick Stroke Weights to demonstrate the three corner conditions of Miter, Round, and Bevel corners.

Figure 9.44. The Stroke Corner options (left to right): Miter Join, Round Join, and Bevel Join. *Courtesy of the author.*

Additionally, individual paths can be joined together to create a continuous polyline. To join a series of connected paths, select Object from the Main Menus, Path from the drop-down menu, and Join. When paths that form corners are not joined, and connected as a polyline, the Cap options can be modified; however, the Corner options do not apply to individual line segments. (See Figure 9.45.) Through the use of various line weights and line types, projected geometry from the 3D digital model can be edited to create various architectural drawings such as floor plans, sections, and elevations. This linework communicates information, such as hidden elements, hierarchy, and materiality, through the use of conventional architectural graphics. The

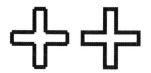

Figure 9.45. Strokes with Butt Cap and Bevel corners applied to segmented paths (left) and joined paths (right). *Courtesy of the author.*

architectural drawings in Figures 9.46 and 9.47 utilized various stroke editing tools and techniques to recreate drawings of the Marika-Alderton House, designed by the architect Glenn Murcutt.

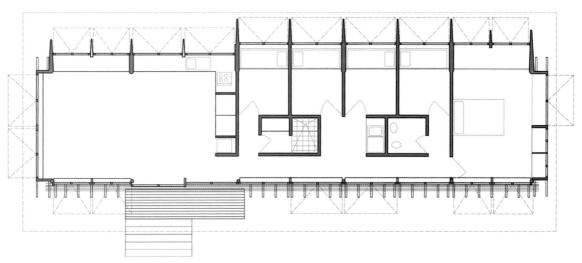

Figure 9.46. Glenn Murcutt, Marika-Alderton House, floor plan. Digital drawing reproduced by Margaret Li and Cindy Santamaria. Instructor, Frank Melendez. The Bernard and Anne Spitzer School of Architecture, City College of New York. *Courtesy of the author.*

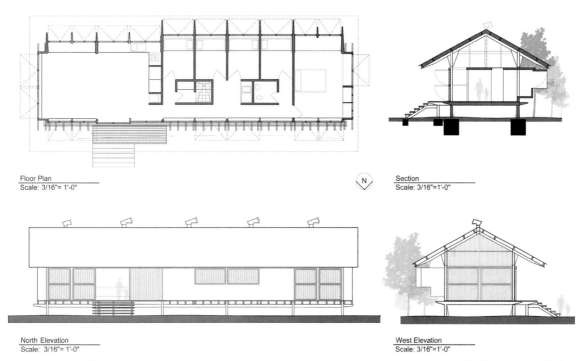

Floor Plan
Scale: 3/16"= 1'-0"

N

Section
Scale: 3/16"=1'-0"

North Elevation
Scale: 3/16"= 1'-0"

West Elevation
Scale: 3/16"=1'-0"

Figure 9.47. Glenn Murcutt, Marika-Alderton House, floor plan, section, and elevations. Digital drawings reproduced by Margaret Li and Cindy Santamaria. Instructor, Frank Melendez. The Bernard and Anne Spitzer School of Architecture, City College of New York. *Courtesy of the author.*

9.6 Lines, Curves, and Shapes

There are many tools available within Illustrator for creating Paths. The *Line Segment* and *Pen* tools are very useful for creating line segments, polylines, curves and shapes. (See Figure 9.48.) In the workflows described in this book, the majority of the linework has been drafted in Rhino, which provides more tools and options for computer-aided drafting. However, it is useful to understand how linework imported into Illustrator, which is converted to *Path* and *Stroke* objects, can be created and edited. Similar to the control points of curve objects in Rhino, Illustrator provides anchor points for Path objects. Anchor points are created and defined by the input points that are specified when creating a line segment, curve, or shape.

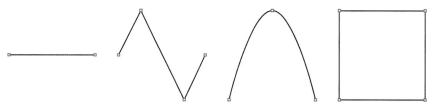

Figure 9.48. Paths created with the Line Segment and Pen tools in Adobe Illustrator (left to right): line segment, polyline, curve, and square shape. *Courtesy of the author.*

The Line Segment Tool

The Line Segment Tool is located in the Tools Panel. It can be expanded to view other options for creating linework. (See Figure 9.49.) After selecting the Line Segment Tool, left-click on the Artboard to display the Line Segment Tool Options dialog box (See Figure 9.50.) The Length and Angle of the line can be specified with numerical values. Alternatively, line segments can be created by holding down the left mouse button and moving the cursor in the workspace. Holding down the Shift key on the keyboard constrains the line segment to remain orthogonal to the X and Y axis, or at diagonals in 45° increments.

Figure 9.49. The Line Segment Tool icon and expanded tool options in Adobe Illustrator.

The Pen Tool

The Pen Tool is much more useful for creating a range of linework. It can be used to create line segments, polylines, curves, and shapes. Additional tools for working with Paths are also available when the Pen Tool is expanded that allow for adding, deleting, and converting Anchor Points. (See Figure 9.51.)

Figure 9.50. The Line Segment Tool Options window in Adobe Illustrator.

Figure 9.51. The Pen Tool icon and expanded tool options in Adobe Illustrator.

To create a line segment, select the Pen Tool from the Tools Panel. Left-click in the Artboard to define the start and end points of the line, and press the letter P on the keyboard to end the command. Polylines can be created using the same method, by adding additional points that define the polyline, by continuing to left-click prior to ending the command. Shapes can be created by creating closed polylines and curves. Create the shape by returning to the starting anchor point to define the final anchor point and close the polyline. (See Figure 9.52.)

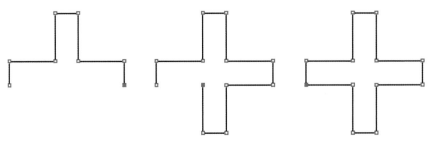

Figure 9.52. Sequence for creating and closing a polygon shape created with the Pen tool. *Courtesy of the author.*

Select Tool and Direct Select Tool

Figure 9.53. The Select Tool (left) and Direct Select Tool (right) icons in Adobe Illustrator.

Path objects and anchor points can be selected and moved using the Select tool and Direct Select tool located in the Tools panel (See Figure 9.53.) The Select tool can be used to select individual or multiple Path objects, which can be moved by holding down the left mouse button and dragging. The Select tool can also be used to transform geometry, by clicking on the Path and dragging the square grippers that appear when an object is selected. The Direct Select tool can be used to display and select individual or multiple Path anchor points, which can also be moved by clicking and dragging.

Anchor Points

Anchor points can be added to, or deleted from, Paths, using the Add Anchor Point tool and the Delete Anchor Point tool. To add anchor points, select the tool and left-click on the Path. An anchor point will be added at the same location of the cursor when clicked. Anchor points can also be converted from corner anchor points to smooth anchor points using the Convert Anchor Point tool. *Corner anchor points* result in sharp corners. *Smooth anchor points* are useful for creating curved geometry, and have additional handles and grips that appear to control the curvature. To create smooth anchor points, select the Convert Anchor Point tool and click and hold down the left button while dragging the mouse. The handles and grips will appear and their size will be based on when the button is released. These grips can be selected and edited to refine the shape of the curve. (See Figure 9.54.)

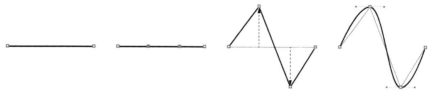

Figure 9.54. Example of transforming a line segment into a curve by adding, moving, and converting anchor points. *Courtesy of the author.*

Additional Path Tools

Additional tools available to create line segments, polylines, curves, and shapes include the Rectangle, Ellipse, Shaper, Pencil, and Paintbrush tools. (See Figure 9.55.) Similar to the Line Segment tool and Pen tool, all of these tools essentially provide alternative methods for creating geometry with Paths and anchor points that can be modified and edited in multiple ways to create various simple and complex shapes. This can be useful for creating additional linework and graphics that enhance architectural drawings.

Figure 9.55. The Rectangle Tool icon and expanded tool options in Adobe Illustrator.

Blending Curves

Lines, curves, and shapes can be *blended* to transition from one path to another using the Blend tool. (See Figure 9.56.) Select the Blend tool and the two Path objects to blend. A preview of the additional paths that are created appears. (See Figure 9.57.) To edit the Blend attributes, select the Blend object in the Artboard, and select Object from the Main menu, Blend from the drop-down menu, and Blend Options. (See Figure 9.58.)

Figure 9.56. The Blend Tool icon in Adobe Illustrator.

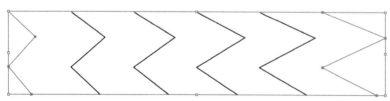

Figure 9.57. A previewed collection of new paths generated in between two select paths using the Blend Tool in Adobe Illustrator. *Courtesy of the author.*

Figure 9.58. The Blend Options window in Adobe Illustrator.

The Blend Options dialog box provides options for spacing the new paths that are generated between the two selected paths. The spacing can be set by a specified number of steps, distance, or color. In Figure 9.59, the Spacing is set to a Specified Steps value of 25. These values can be changed to increase or decrease the number of path objects that are created. Once the Blend is created, these values and the original input curves can be edited, and are parametric, meaning that the original curves can be modified and edited, and the changes to the Blend will automatically update. For example, if one of the original Path's anchor points are converted to create a curve, the Blend will update the transitional steps in between the polyline and the curve. (See Figure 9.60.) Also, if the Stroke color of the polyline and curve are modified, each with a unique color, the Smooth Color spacing option can be applied to create a gradual transition in between the two colors. (See Figure 9.61.)

Figure 9.59. A Blend between two polylines. *Courtesy of the author.*

Figure 9.60. A Blend that is modified by converting anchor points to transform the polyline into a sinuous curve. *Courtesy of the author.*

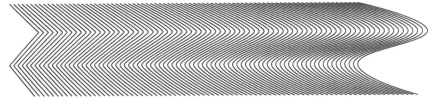

Figure 9.61. A Blend that is modified by changing the Stroke colors of the polyline and curve, applying the Smooth Color spacing, and increasing the Specified Step value. *Courtesy of the author.*

Variable Stroke Widths

Figure 9.62. The Stroke Width tool in Adobe Illustrator.

The weight of a stroke can vary throughout the length of the Path by using the Width tool in the Tools panel. (See Figure 9.62.) The Stroke width can vary at any point along the Path and multiple widths can be applied to one Stroke. To vary the width, click and drag on any point along the path, and release to set the new width with anchor points. The width anchor points can be reactivated to modify the distance of the width by selecting the Stroke Width tool and hovering over the path. (See Figure 9.63.)

Figure 9.63. A Stroke line segment with a variable width from one endpoint to the other (top), and a stroke curve with a variable width increasing at the center and decreasing at the endpoints (bottom). *Courtesy of the author.*

Arrows

Various types of arrowheads can be assigned to Strokes. To assign an arrowhead to a Stroke, select the Path, and drop down the arrowhead options from the Stroke panel, which displays various arrowhead types and shapes. (See Figure 9.64.) Arrowheads can be applied to either end of a line or curve, as indicated by the two arrowhead options in the panel that face left or right. The size of the arrowhead can be increased or decreased by changing the percentage values of the arrowhead Scale. In addition to using arrows to point to specific elements in a drawing, arrows can be used to indicate directionality. By combining arrows with other techniques, such as blends and variable stroke widths, linework can be used to produce other effects. For example, linework effects can suggest movements and flows, that represent information and enhance drawings. (See Figure 9.65.)

Figure 9.64. Stroke panel Arrowhead options and settings.

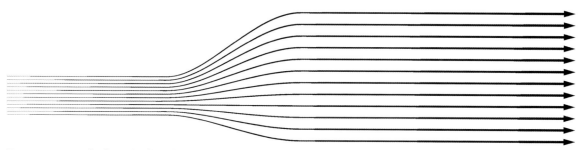

Figure 9.65. Example of arrowheads applied to blended strokes with variable widths. *Courtesy of the author.*

9.7 Color

Color can be used to enhance architectural drawings, diagrams, and graphics, and utilized for various reasons, such as aesthetics and communicating information. Principles of color theory can be applied systematically to create visual effects such as harmony, spatial depth, and vibration.[6] Colors can highlight specific moments in a drawing and/or draw the eye to a particular point on a page. Colors can be used to indicate temperature, such as hues of blue and red to indicate cool and warm temperatures. Color can be subtle, by using various tones to create a monochromatic drawing or image. There are many ways in which color can be used strategically to create specific effects and communicate information in architectural design drawings and imagery.

RGB Color Model

In light-emitting sources, such as computer and television screens, colors are creating by *adding* combinations of red, green, and blue (RGB). This *additive* system is known as the RGB color model. This color model uses numerical values ranging from 0 to 255, for a total of 256 values (counting 0) that represent each color, which is the maximum number of combinations that can be created with an eight-digit binary number. In an RGB color model, combining the maximum 255 value of red, green, and blue produces white. The combination of green and blue produces cyan, combining blue and red produces magenta, and combining red and green produces yellow. (See Figure 9.66.) Combining the minimum 0 value of red, green, and blue produces black. Through the various combinations ranging from 0 to 255 values of red, green, and blue, a spectrum of over 16 million color values is possible. In light-absorbing sources, such as ink on paper, colors are creating by subtracting combinations of cyan, magenta, and yellow. Combining the maximum value of cyan, magenta, and yellow, produces black. This *subtractive* system makes up the CMYK color model, which is used in printing. The K stands for black, which is added for better shadow density.[7]

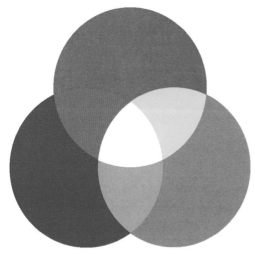

Figure 9.66. RGB color model.

Stroke and Fill Colors

In Illustrator, colors can be assigned as Stroke and Fill colors. A Path, whether open or closed, straight or curved, has a Stroke and Fill color. The Stroke color follows the Path, and the Fill color occupies the area in between the path. RGB values can be set in the Color Picker dialog box, which can be activated by double-clicking the left mouse button on the Stroke or Fill color icon. (See Figure 9.37.) The color can be selected by clicking on the color spectrum or by specifying the numerical R, G, and B values. When the RGB values are all set to 255, the result is white (See Figure 9.67.) RGB values that are all set to 0 result in black. When the RGB values are between 0 and 255 and are the same value, the result is various shades of gray, ranging from black to white. Color can be removed from a Stroke or Fill by selecting the None option, represented

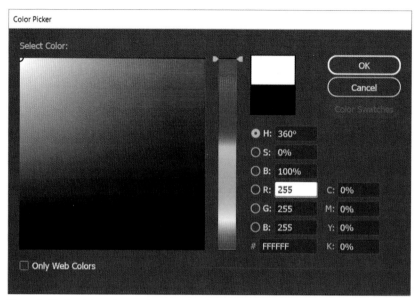

Figure 9.67. The Color Picker window in Adobe Illustrator.

by a red diagonal line through the Stroke and Fill frames. (See Figure 9.68.) Through various combinations of using color, or removing color, with the Stroke and Fill color options, linework and shapes can be represented in different ways. (See Figure 9.69.) Additional tools, such as the Paint Bucket tool in the Tools panel, provide other methods for applying Fills to overlapping geometry. Fills can be used to apply poché to represent architectural elements that are cut, such as walls in a floor plan or section. Fills are also useful for creating figure-ground drawings, such as analytical drawings that show solid-void relationships. (See Figure 9.70.)

Figure 9.68. Apply the None (transparent) option to remove a color value from the Stroke and Fill.

Figure 9.69. Various combinations of Stroke and Fill colors (and transparent) applied to open and closed paths. *Courtesy of the author.*

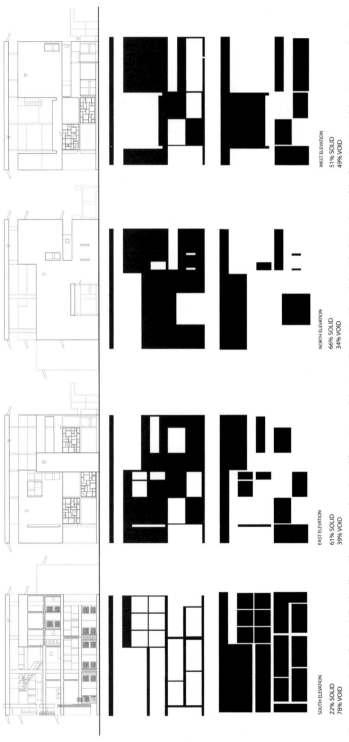

SOUTH ELEVATION
22% SOLID
78% VOID

EAST ELEVATION
61% SOLID
39% VOID

NORTH ELEVATION
66% SOLID
34% VOID

WEST ELEVATION
51% SOLID
49% VOID

Figure 9.70. Le Corbusier, Villa Shodhan. Elevations and analytical figure/ground drawings illustrating the solid/void relationships of the facades. Digital drawings reproduced and analytical diagrams created by Renee Thomas. Instructor, Frank Melendez. The Bernard and Anne Spitzer School of Architecture, City College of New York. *Courtesy of the author.*

Gradients

In terms of color graphics, *gradients* are gradual changes between two or more colors. Gradients can be useful for creating visual effects that enhance architectural drawings and diagrams, such as to represent surface lighting gradations, surface inclines, backgrounds, and other effects that add depth and visual interest to two-dimensional drawings. To create a gradient, select the Path object, and click on the default Gradient symbol below the Stroke and Fill color options. With the Path selected, click on the Gradient Tool in the Tools panel. An interactive gradient tool will appear in the object, which can be edited to change colors and the start and end points of the gradients. From the Main Menus panel, select Window and from the drop-down menu, select Gradient. The Gradient panel will open, displaying the current settings. (See Figure 9.71.) Additional parameters can be specified, such as changing the gradient type from *linear* to *radial*, changing colors, adding additional gradient points, and rotating the gradient. (See Figure 9.72.) Custom gradients can be saved to the Swatch panel

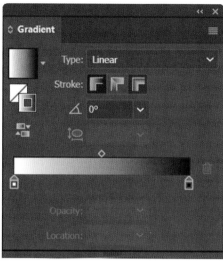

Figure 9.71. The Gradient panel.

for future reference and use. (See Figure 9.73.) There are many different possibilities for using gradients with Strokes and Fills and exploring their effects. (See Figure 9.74.) Combining gradients with other linework graphics can be used to communicate various information. For example, a series of Strokes with gradients that range from a cool blue to a warm orange might be useful in representing invisible environmental phenomena, such as air currents and flows that vary in temperature. (See Figure 9.75.)

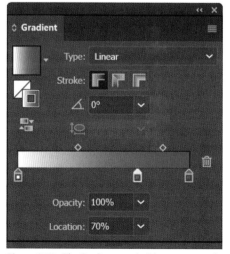

Figure 9.72. The Gradient panel with a custom gradient.

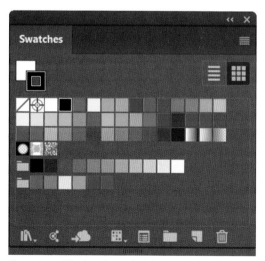

Figure 9.73. The Swatch panel in Adobe Illustrator.

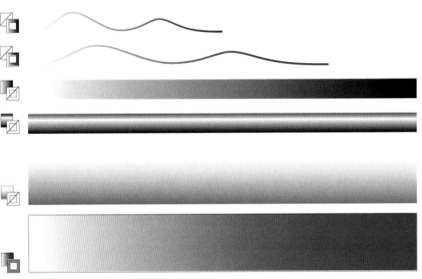

Figure 9.74. Examples of default and custom gradients applied to Strokes and Fills. *Courtesy of the author.*

Figure 9.75. A custom gradient applied to a blend of Strokes with arrowheads. *Courtesy of the author.*

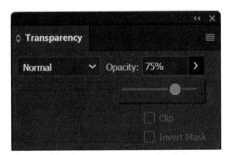

Figure 9.76. The Transparency panel with the drop-down menu of preset Opacity percentage options in Adobe Illustrator.

Transparency

Path objects that have Stroke, Fill, or Gradient colors can be assigned various levels of transparency. By default, colors have an opacity value of 100%. These values can be edited within the Transparency panel by sliding the transparency scale, or specifying a percentage value. (See Figure 9.76.)

By using a combination of various tools and techniques, many different types of graphics can be produced and used to enhance architectural drawings and create architectural diagrams. For example, in the recreated architectural drawings of the Marika-Alderton House designed by Glenn Murcutt, new linework and graphics were generated, such as arrowheads, color, gradients, and transparencies, to represent and speculate on temperatures and wind flow through the building at different times of the year. (See Figures 9.77 and 9.88.)

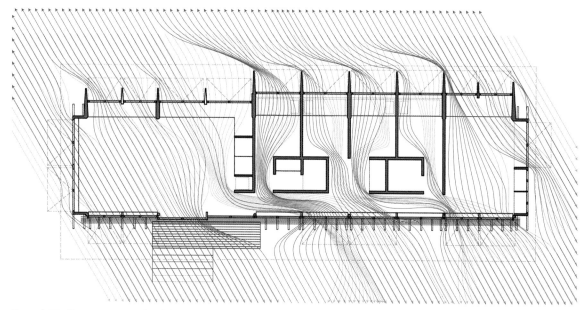

Figure 9.77. Glenn Murcutt, Marika-Alderton House. Speculative analysis drawings of summer (red) and winter (blue) wind flows through the house. Digital drawing reproduced and speculative analysis created by Margaret Li and Cindy Santamaria. Instructor, Frank Melendez. The Bernard and Anne Spitzer School of Architecture, City College of New York. *Courtesy of the author.*

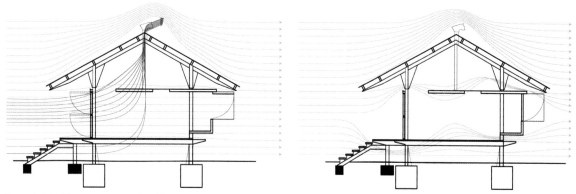

Figure 9.78. Glenn Murcutt, Marika-Alderton House. Speculative analysis drawings of wind flows through the house with wall panels open (left) and wall panels closed (right). Digital drawing reproduced and speculative analysis created by Margaret Li and Cindy Santamaria. Instructor, Frank Melendez. The Bernard and Anne Spitzer School of Architecture, City College of New York. *Courtesy of the author.*

9.8 Text

Architectural drawings communicate information about forms and spaces through linework and graphics; however, they typically require text to communicate other information, such as the title of a drawing, the scale of the drawing, programmatic spaces, detail information, material information, and so on. There are many different types of texts, and the subject of typography—the art and style of creating and working with type—is a broad subject with a vast history. As graphic design software in which typography plays a major role, Illustrator provides many tools for working with text that are beyond the scope of this book. However, it is useful for architects to have a basic understanding of tools and concepts for working with text in the context of architectural drawings.

Area and Point Type

Figure 9.79. The Type Tool icon and expanded tool options in Adobe Illustrator.

To create text in Illustrator, select the Type Tool in the Tools panel. The Type Tool can also be expanded to view and access additional tools that are available for working with type. (See Figure 9.79.) There are two methods for creating text with the Type Tool: *area type* and *point type*. The area type method relies on a box to define the area of the text, and the font size remains the same if the box is modified. After selecting the Type Tool, left-click and drag to define an area box. The text will begin in the upper left corner of the area box as text is typed. When the scale of the area box is adjusted by selecting and moving the box grips, the text remains the same size and adjusts to the new limits of the box. (See Figure 9.80.) The point type method creates a boundary around the text, and the font size changes if the boundary is modified. After selecting the Type Tool, left-click and release. Text can be typed without the limitations of a box. When the text is selected, a boundary appears that is confined to the limits of the text. When the scale of the boundary is adjusted by selecting and moving the boundary grips, the text size changes and is stretched and/or compressed in either direction to adjust to the new limits of the boundary. (See Figure 9.81.)

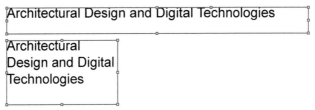

Figure 9.80. The Area Type method adjusts text to the limits of the specified area box. *Courtesy of the author.*

Figure 9.81. The Point Type method scales and stretches the text to the limits of the adjusted boundary. *Courtesy of the author.*

Serif and Sans Serif Fonts

There are two basic categories of fonts: *serif* and *sans serif*. Serif fonts contain additional decorative lines that extend beyond the main portion of the letter and are considered more traditional, such as Times New Roman and Garamond. Sans serif fonts do not have the additional lines and are considered cleaner and more modern, such as Arial and Helvetica. (See Figure 9.82.) Architectural drawings typically use sans serif fonts in order to omit any additional decorative elements that may distract from the linework of the drawing. Text can be edited from the Control Panel, or within the Type panels. Select Windows from the Main Menu, expand Type, and select the Character and Paragraph panels. The Character panel provides options for changing the font type, style, and size. The Paragraph panel provides options for aligning, justifying, and spacing text. (See Figure 9.83.)

Figure 9.82. Serif (left) and sans serif (right) fonts. *Courtesy of the author.*

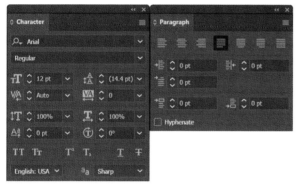

Figure 9.83. The Character and Paragraph panels in Adobe Illustrator.

Type Along Path

Text can be specified to flow along various path curves that are open or closed. The start position of the text is based on the location of the initial click when selecting the path. (See Figure 9.84.)

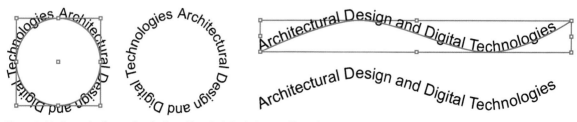

Figure 9.84. Example of text using the Type Along Path Tool. *Courtesy of the author.*

Color can be added to text through the use of Fill and Stroke colors. (See Figure 9.85.)

Figure 9.85. Examples of using various Stroke and Fill colors with text. *Courtesy of the author.*

Type and Clipping Masks

Creating outlines and clipping masks from a text allows other background graphics to be used as the fill color for a text. In this example, a rectangle shape with a gradient of colors is used as the background graphic which will be used to fill the text. (See Figure 9.86.)

Figure 9.86. Text placed over a rectangular shape with a gradient fill of various colors. *Courtesy of the author.*

Select the text, go to the Type heading in the Main Menu, and select Create Outlines. While the outlines are select, go to the Object heading in the Main Menu and select Compound Path and Make. (See Figure 9.87.)

Figure 9.87. Creating Outlines of the text. *Courtesy of the author.*

While selected, hold the Shift key down and click the background graphic to add it to the selection. Go to the Object heading in the Main Menus and select Clipping Mask and Make. The Clipping Mask will clip everything outside of the text outlines, leaving the background graphic within the type. (See Figure 9.88.)

FORM + SPACE

Figure 9.88. Creating a Clipping Mask to use the background gradient image as the text fill. *Courtesy of the author.*

9.9 Raster Graphics

As opposed to *vector* graphics, which use mathematical equations to define paths to create strokes and shapes, *raster* graphics utilize cells that are filled with color values, called *pixels*, which are arranged in a grid and collectively form an image. In a digital photograph, the grid of colored pixels can be seen by zooming into an image. (See

Figure 9.89.) While vector graphics are ideally suited for working with linework, *raster* graphics are ideal for working with photographic images. The dimensions and the number of pixels within an image determine the image *resolution*. The pixel count is measured as the number of *pixels per inch* (*ppi*). A high-resolution image consists of a high ppi count and results in a sharp, high-quality image. A low-resolution image consists of a low ppi count and decreased image quality, which results in the image looking *pixelated*. (See Figure 9.90.) Increasing the ppi count also requires more computing memory; therefore, it is often good practice to adjust the ppi count of the image based on the method of output. This is a balance of maintaining a quality image while keeping the file size (memory) to a minimum for efficiency. Images that are output as hardcopy prints generally require a minimum of 300 ppi to maintain image quality and avoid pixelation. Images viewed on monitors and screens require a minimum of 72 ppi to avoid image pixelation.

   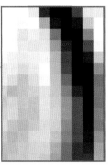

Figure 9.89. Louis Sullivan, Bayard-Condict Building. Photograph of the terra-cotta ornament. The pixels can be seen by zooming into the image. Original photograph by Solomon Oh. *Courtesy of the author.*

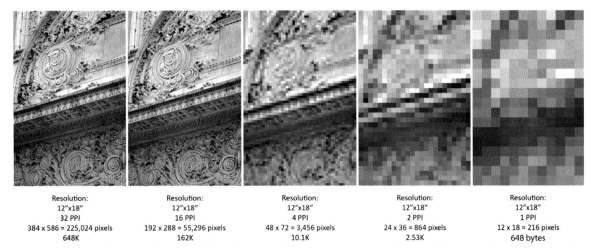

Resolution:	Resolution:	Resolution:	Resolution:	Resolution:
12"x18"	12"x18"	12"x18"	12"x18"	12"x18"
32 PPI	16 PPI	4 PPI	2 PPI	1 PPI
384 x 586 = 225,024 pixels	192 x 288 = 55,296 pixels	48 x 72 = 3,456 pixels	24 x 36 = 864 pixels	12 x 18 = 216 pixels
648K	162K	10.1K	2.53K	648 bytes

Figure 9.90. Louis Sullivan, Bayard-Condict Building. Photograph of the terra-cotta ornament. Image resolution comparisons of the image with various pixels per inch (ppi) settings. High to low resolution (left to right). Original photograph by Solomon Oh. *Courtesy of the author.*

Raster images can be edited in various ways in programs such as Adobe Photo-shop©, an industry standard, raster-based image-editing software. Many tools are available to manipulate, alter, and create imagery. For example, color photographic images can be converted into grayscale, or black-and-white images, by reducing the *saturation*, or creating a *threshold*. (See Figure 9.91.) The color of an image can also be modified by adjusting the *color balance* or *hue*. Additional color effects such as *inverting* an image changes the color value of each pixel to its opposite color on the color spectrum. (See Figure 9.92.)

Figure 9.91. Gian Lorenzo Bernini, Ecstasy of Saint Teresa. Comparisons of the original photographic image in color modified to grayscale, and black and white (left to right). Original photograph by the author. *Courtesy of the author.*

Figure 9.92. Gian Lorenzo Bernini, Ecstasy of Saint Teresa. Comparisons of the original photographic image in color modified by adjusting the color balance and by inverting (left to right). Original photograph by the author. *Courtesy of the author.*

There are various file formats for raster images that vary in compression. These include JPEG, TIFF, PNG, and PSD formats.

JPEG: One of the most commonly used raster image file formats that uses a lossy compression method, in which data is lost when compressed and irreversible. JPEG is an acronym for Joint Photographic Experts Group.

TIFF: A raster image file format that is standard for professional printing, with no image compression, resulting in larger file sizes. (TIFF is an acronym for tagged image file format.)

PNG: A raster image file format that is commonly used for transferring files on the internet. Similar to zipped files, this format uses lossless compression, meaning, data is restructured and is not lost when compressed. (PNG is an acronym for portable network graphics.)

PSD: A raster image file format that is used specifically for Adobe Photoshop. Images are stored with the software's imaging options such as layers, channels, and so on. (PSD stands for Photoshop document.)

Photographic images can be edited and adjusted in Adobe Photoshop, and imported into Adobe Illustrator in order to enhance drawings. This is useful for adding photographic imagery such as the image of a sky or vegetation to provide drawings with site specific information and context. The use of figures also enhances drawings by providing a sense of scale and an understanding of the programmatic use of an architectural design. (See Figure 9.93.)

Figure 9.93. Imagery used to enhance an architectural section drawing with site and landscape features. Drawing by Christopher Lin. Instructor, Martin Stigsgaard. The Bernard and Anne Spitzer School of Architecture, City College of New York. *Courtesy of the author.*

Endnotes

1. Lebbeus Wood, "Libeskind's Machines," November 24, 2009, https://lebbeuswoods.wordpress.com/2009/11/24/libeskinds-machines/.
2. Casey Reas and Chandler McWilliams, *Form + Code: In Design, Art, and Architecture* (New York: Princeton Architectural Press, 2010).
3. Ibid.
4. https://helpx.adobe.com/illustrator/how-to/what-is-illustrator.html.
5. https://acrobat.adobe.com/us/en/why-adobe/about-adobe-pdf.html.
6. Albers, Joseph, *Interaction of Color* (New Haven: Yale University Press, 1963).
7. https://helpx.adobe.com/illustrator/using/color.html.

Part 4
Computational Design

Part 4 provides an overview of computational design processes and their application toward architectural modeling, drawing, and representation. Through the use of parametric and algorithmic modeling, architects and designers can develop 3D models that update based on variable parameters and inputs as inputs. Algorithmic processes allow for rule-based approaches to design that utilize the agency of computation to automate tasks and procedures. Computational technologies have not only changed the way in which architects and designers work through drawings and models but also approaches to methods and processes of architectural design and representation. Through visual programming platforms, algorithmic and scripting procedures can be implemented to explore and develop architectural geometry, patterns, modular assemblies, emergent formations, and much more. Visual programming platforms for creating simulations based on environmental data and phenomena, and physics-based forces and material behaviors, bring real-world attributes into virtual environments. These simulations can be used to enhance design solutions that are performative and optimized, as well as to discover design solutions through experimental processes and emergent outcomes.

Robotic technologies are changing the methods in which architecture is fabricated and automated, while physical computing platforms are creating new possibilities for bridging physical and digital worlds by connecting sensed, real-time data to drive responsive systems and computationally controlled architectures. Robotic and physical computing technologies are also being explored as nascent instruments for experimental and novel approaches to creating architectural drawings, visualizations, and imagery. These methods open up new possibilities for teaching architectural drawing in a manner that builds on the history of drawing, while preparing future generations of architects for designing architectures that are based in computation, automation, responsive design, and robotics.

Chapter 10
Parameters and Algorithms

Chapter 10 provides a description of parametric modeling and algorithmic processes in architectural design and drawing. Working with parametric models has become a standard method of 3D modeling. This includes the use of variable inputs that control and drive geometric properties and relationships within the model. This allows for the ability to quickly update changes and create multiple iterations of a 3D model, which are based on topological variations. Algorithms are sets of instructions that are executed to complete a task. Algorithmic procedures allow for the design of rule-based systems, and logical operations that yield outcomes. This method of drawing and modeling allows for the repetition of procedures that are based on bottom-up design processes and concepts of emergence. Parametric and algorithmic modeling environments provide architects and designers with the ability to explore computational methods for drawing and modeling that go beyond the limitations of standard commands and tools within software.

10.1 Parameters and Constraints

Parameters are constant or variable values that are used to define a system. In traditional methods of drawing and modeling, a curve can be described by discrete points within Euclidean space. A series of continuous line segments and arcs can be used to describe a curve. NURBS curves, however, are defined by calculus, and use control points, control point weights, curve degrees, and knots vectors to define continuous numerical values based on the calculation of a Bezier curve. Curves have two endpoints and exist within a numeric interval called a domain. Curves are also defined by collections of functions. For example, the sine function, which results in a sine wave, is defined by the functions $x = t$ and $y = \sin(t)$. These functions describe a two-dimensional curve along the X and Y axes, where the variable t is the parameter. The parametric properties of a curve, or curve parameterization, also include the domain and the parameter density.[1] When curve control points are edited, by changing their location in space or changing their "weight," the curve's parameters are changed, and result in topological variations of the curve. (See Figure 10.1.) Topological curves and surfaces can be deformed by stretching, twisting, and bending, without tearing. As Greg Lynn states in his seminal book *Animate Form*, topological entities take the shape of a multiplicity, meaning they are not composed of discrete points but rather of a continuous stream of relative values.[2] Topological variations are utilized in the design of the Embryological House, providing multiple options and combinations for customization. (See Figure 10.2.)

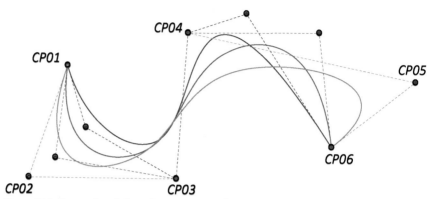

Figure 10.1. Parametric variations of a curve generated by moving the control points CP02 and CP05. *Courtesy of the author.*

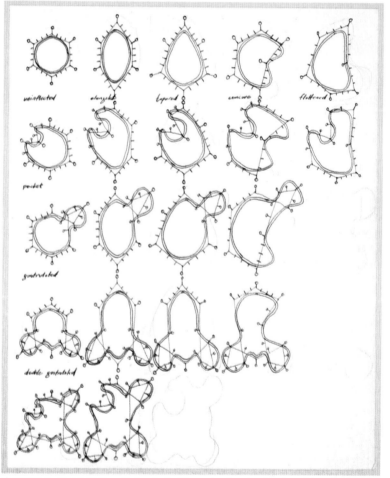

Figure 10.2. Greg Lynn Form, Embryological House, Los Angeles. Drawing of the spline matrix. *Courtesy of Greg Lynn FORM and the Canadian Center for Architecture.*

In parametric design, geometric values are used as input information to define a shape or form, and geometric relationships establish associative links between shapes and forms. By changing these geometric values and relationships, the parametric model is updated, reflecting the changes in the shape or form. This shift from modeling geometric forms to establishing topological relationships allows architects and designers to generate multiple self-similar variations of shapes and forms.[3] In the following example, two circles (C1 and C2) and a line (L1) are used to describe a lofted surface. By changing the parameters (input numerical values) of C1 and C2 (radii) and L1 (length), multiple versions of the lofted surface can be generated. (See Figure 10.3.)

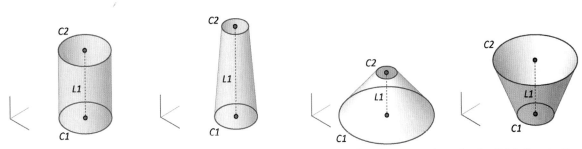

Figure 10.3. Parametric variations of a surface that is lofted between two circles (C1 and C2) that are spaced apart by a length (L1). Changing the numerical values of C1, C2, and L1 produces various forms. *Courtesy of the author.*

There are additional constraints within this simple example of a parametric model. C1 is dependent upon a center point (an XYZ coordinate), and a normal direction (the Z axis). L1 is dependent upon a start point (the C1 center point) and a tangent direction (the Z axis). C2 is dependent on a center point (the L1 end point) and a normal direction (the Z axis). These constraints result in a hierarchical chain of geometric dependencies, which flow "stream" (the top of the chain) and "downstream" (the bottom of the chain). Changes made to geometries upstream affect geometries downstream. For example, if the center point location of C1 is changed, the position of L1 is affected therefore, C2 is affected as well. If the length of L1 is changed, the center point location of C2 is affected. Therefore, C1 is at the top of the hierarchical chain, "upstream," and C2 is at the bottom of the hierarchical chain, "downstream."[4]

10.2 Algorithms

An algorithm is a sequence of steps and instructions that describes a procedure to solve a problem. In architectural design software, algorithms are used in many different ways, from the graphic interface to the generation of geometric objects. Initial development in CAD software allowed for designers to generate geometric entities without relying upon the computational algorithms in the "back end" of the software that were used to create graphics and geometries. As digital tools were adopted into architectural design processes, designers began to explore and integrate computational processes that allowed them to interface with scripting environments. This method of working "confronts the design of procedures themselves," allowing designers to grasp the agency of working with algorithms as a means of exploring emergent patterns and forms, replicating geometry, and automating tasks.[5] (See Figure 10.4).

Figure 10.4. Example of a cuboid form that is copied and incrementally rotated using an algorithm. *Courtesy of the author.*

Today, many platforms are available that allow designers to access and deploy algorithmic procedures in design without having an extensive knowledge of computer science and programming languages. These relatively recent developments in CAD software provide opportunities for users to design and work with algorithms. Visual programming interfaces are one method in which designers with little to no coding experience can begin to work with algorithmic procedures within a user-friendly interface.

Endnotes

1. David Rutten, "Curve Parameter Space," *I Eat Bugs for Breakfast* (blog), September 27, 2013, https://ieatbugsforbreakfast.wordpress.com/2013/09/27/curve-parameter-space/#more-873.
2. Greg Lynn, *Animate Form* (New York: Princeton Architectural Press, 1999).
3. Branko Kolarevic, *Architecture in the Digital Age: Design and Manufacturing* (New York and London: Routledge, Taylor & Francis, 2005).
4. Dennis Sheldon, "Information Modelling as a Paradigm Shift," *AD: Closing the Gap-Information Models in Contemporary Design Practice,* Richard Garber, guest ed. (London: John Wiley & Sons, March/April 2009).
5. Benjamin Aranda and Chris Lasch, *Pamphlet Architecture 27: Tooling* (New York: Princeton Architectural Press, 2006).

Chapter 11
Visual Programming

Chapter 11 introduces concepts and methods for working with parameters, constraints, and algorithms through the use of the visual programming language and environment, Grasshopper. This includes an overview of the Grasshopper interface and visual programming workflows for generating geometry within the Rhino 3D modeling space. This chapter describes components, the component structure, component types, and connecting components to provide input and output data. It also introduces basic visual programming syntax and methods for working with data through the use of lists, domains, series, range, math, and cull operations. Scripting and algorithmic processes expand the possibilities for architectural drawing and modeling, through the use of rule-based systems, and bottom-up approaches to design that yield emergent patterns and formations.

11.1 The Grasshopper Interface

An integrated development environment (IDE) is a software application that allows computer programmers to write and edit source code. Learning how to write and work with computer code, or scripting, is becoming an increasingly useful skill for architects and designers, because proficiency with computer programming extends beyond the limitations of standard tools and opens up more possibilities for digital drawing, modeling, and fabrication. Grasshopper is a visual programming language and environment within Rhino 6 for Windows (and a plug-in for previous versions), developed by David Rutten, which provides a graphical user interface (GUI) for designing algorithms.[1] Users can work with "components" that can be connected in various ways to create programs that define parametric models. Grasshopper is a node-based algorithmic editor, which allows users to program without requiring extensive knowledge of text-based programming languages or scripting syntax.

Grasshopper can be launched by typing the word Grasshopper in the Rhino command line and pressing the Enter key or clicking on the Grasshopper icon in the Standard tab. (See Figure 11.1.) This will prompt the Grasshopper program to run and display the interface on the screen. The interface is a two-dimensional environment with Main Menus, Component Tabs, Component Panels, a Canvas, and Canvas Toolbars. (See Figure 11.2.)

Figure 11.1. The Grasshopper command icon in Rhino.

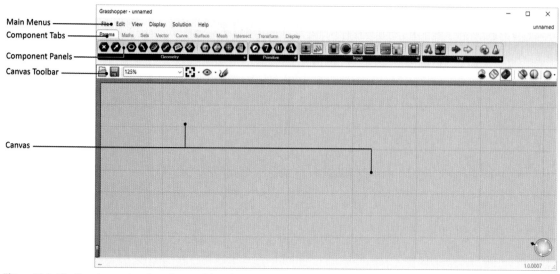

Figure 11.2. The Grasshopper interface. *Courtesy of the author.*

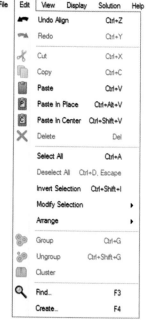

Figure 11.3. The Grasshopper Main Menu and expanded Edit menu. *Courtesy of the author.*

Main Menus

The Main Menus provide commands and features that are organized according to the menu title. The Main Menus tabs provide drop-down menus of all of the command and features associated within that menu. For example, clicking on the Edit menu lists options for editing the document, such as undo, copy, paste, and so on. (See Figure 11.3.) The File drop-down menu lists commands for creating, opening, and saving files. The Grasshopper file format, Grasshopper document (.gh), is separate from the Rhino file format, Rhino 3D Model (.3dm), and can be saved by selecting Save Document, from the Grasshopper Main Menus, File drop-down menu.

Component Tabs and Panels

Components are the primary elements in Grasshopper that contain geometry, operations, and functions. They can be connected in various ways to create programs. The Component tabs are used to categorize the various components that are available in Grasshopper. The Component panels are subcategories within each tab. Each Component panel displays commonly used components, and can be expanded to display the entire list of components that are available in that panel, by clicking on the black colored bar underlining each panel. (See Figure 11.4.)

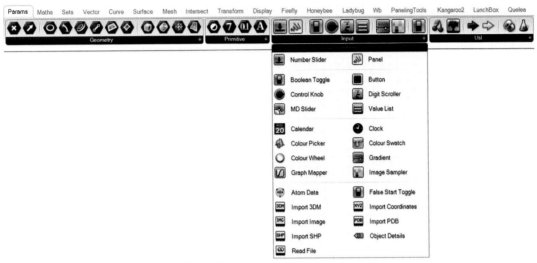

Figure 11.4. The Grasshopper Component Tabs and Panels. *Courtesy of the author..*

Canvas and Canvas Toolbar

The Canvas is a two-dimensional environment that serves as the primary workspace for placing, arranging, and connecting components to create programs. Components can be selected, dragged and dropped into the canvas, and connected in various ways to create algorithms. The Canvas toolbar provides tools for opening and saving files, zooming in and out of the canvas with a zoom factor, and sketching in the canvas. (See Figure 11.5.)

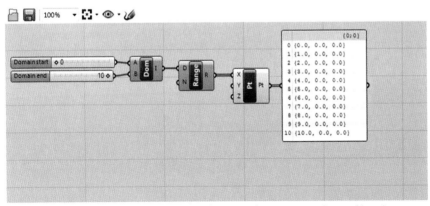

Figure 11.5. The Grasshopper Canvas toolbars and Canvas with components. *Courtesy of the author.*

Navigation

Navigation occurs within the two-dimensional environment of Grasshopper Canvas by zooming and panning. Zooming in and out of the canvas can be achieved by scrolling with the middle mouse button. The focal point of the area on the canvas in which to zoom can be targeted by placing the cursor in that area while zooming. Panning is achieved by holding down the right mouse button while moving the mouse.

11.2 Visualization Methods

Various options and settings for displaying and visualizing components and geometry can be found in the Main Menu Display tab. (See Figure 11.6.) When components that contain geometry are placed in the Grasshopper Canvas, they are visualized in the Rhino 3D modeling space. This visualization is a "preview" of the geometry, but the geometric "objects" do not exist in the Rhino 3D modeling space until the definition in Grasshopper is turned into an object. This is achieved by "baking" components in Grasshopper. Until components are baked, they remain as previewed geometry in the Rhino 3D modeling space. The Preview settings can be changed from wireframe to shaded, and the quality of the display can be set. The colors of previewed and selected objects are set to faint red and green, respectively, by default, but can be changed in the Document Preview Settings dialog box. (See Figure 11.7.)

Figure 11.6. The Grasshopper Display menu. *Courtesy of the author.*

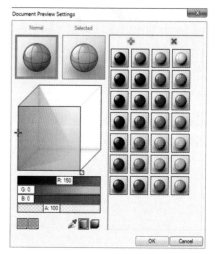

Figure 11.7. The Grasshopper Document Preview Settings dialog box.

The visual display of components in the canvas can be modified so that the middle portion displays the icon graphic or the text graphic of the component by toggling the Draw Icons option on or off. (See Figure 11.8.)

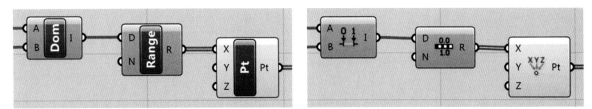

Figure 11.8. The component text and icon graphic options can be changed in the Display menu: Draw Icons option toggled off (left) to display text, and toggled on (right) to display icons. *Courtesy of the author.*

11.3 Components

Components are the primary elements in Grasshopper that contain geometry, operations, and functions. They can be connected in various ways to create programs. Although components vary depending on their function, the general structure of a component is divided vertically into three columns, and data flows from left to right. The left column of a component is dedicated to receiving input data, the middle column of a component describes the component type, and the right column of a component provides output data.[2] (See Figure 11.9.)

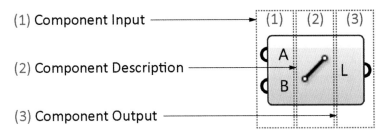

(1) Component Input

(2) Component Description

(3) Component Output

Figure 11.9. The structure of a Grasshopper component. *Courtesy of the author.*

Component Colors

Grasshopper utilizes a color-coding system to indicate the current state of a component. When components have the input data that is required for them to operate, they are gray. Some components have default input values and are therefore gray when they are placed into the canvas. When components do not have the data that is required for them to operate they are orange. Components have an Enable function that can be toggled on or off. When the Enable function is toggled off, or disabled, the component is dark gray and the text appears faint. Disabling the component affects the other elements in the program that are dependent on this object. When a component is selected, it is green and the associated geometry in the Rhino 3D modeling space also previews in green. When a component does not have the correct input data that it needs to complete a command, a warning appears. Components that contain warnings, which are potentially but not always an error, will turn red.[3] (See Figure 11.10.)

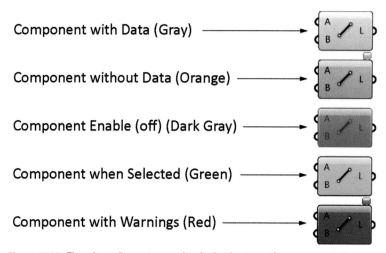

Component with Data (Gray)

Component without Data (Orange)

Component Enable (off) (Dark Gray)

Component when Selected (Green)

Component with Warnings (Red)

Figure 11.10. The color-coding system used to display the status of a component in Grasshopper. *Courtesy of the author.*

Connecting Components

Components can be connected and "wired" together to create programs. The black and white semicircles on the left and right sides of a component serve as the connection nodes for receiving input and providing output wires. The workflow for connecting components runs from left to right, which is referred to as upstream and downstream, respectively. Elements that are upstream are used as input data to define the elements that are downstream. By clicking and holding down the left mouse button over the upstream element's output node, a wire can be dragged and plugged in to the downstream element's input node. (See Figure 11.11.) Elements can be disconnected by repeating the same procedure while holding down the Ctrl key. Additional input wires can be added to the input node by holding down the Shift key.

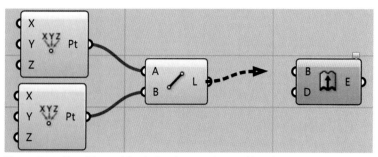

Figure 11.11. The wiring workflow in Grasshopper. *Courtesy of the author.*

11.4 Component Types

Geometric, Transformation, and Replication Components

Many of the geometric object, transformation, and replication modeling commands and tools that are available within the Rhino 3D modeling environment are also available as components within the Grasshopper visual programming environment. This includes point and curve geometric components, such as Construct Point, Line, Rectangle, Circle, and Interpolate (curve). (See Figure 11.12.) Surface and volumetric geometric components include Extrude, Loft, Sweeps, Pipe, and Box. (See Figure 11.13.) Transformation components include Move, Rotate, and Scale. (See Figure 11.14.) Replication components include Mirror, Offset, Array, and Tween Curve. (See Figure 11.15.) These various components can be used to generate geometry, transformations, and replications within a Grasshopper algorithmic definition.

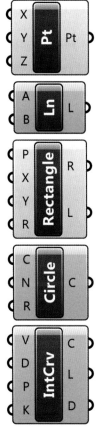

Figure 11.12. Various Point and Curve components in Grasshopper.

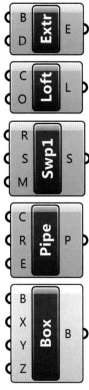

Figure 11.13. Various Surface and Solid Model components in Grasshopper.

Figure 11.14. Various Transformation components in Grasshopper.

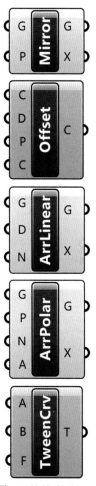

Figure 11.15. Various Replication components in Grasshopper.

Geometric Parameter Components

A series of components are available within the Params tab, Geometry panel, which allow geometric objects from Rhino to be linked to parametric components in Grasshopper. (See Figure 11.16.) These components can be thought of as empty containers that can hold geometric objects from a Rhino 3D model, such as points, lines, curves, and surfaces. For example, to assign a single point object in the Rhino 3D modeling space to a geometric parameter component in Grasshopper, create a point object in Rhino, and place a Point parameter component in the Grasshopper canvas. Components can be placed into the Grasshopper canvas by clicking the component, and then clicking in the canvas. Right-click over the Point parameter component and select the Set one Point option. (See Figure 11.17.) The Grasshopper interface will momentarily disappear. Select the point object in Rhino, and the Grasshopper interface will reappear. The Point parameter component will appear gray because it contains data, and the point will preview in the Rhino 3D modeling space as a red "x" graphic that is associated with the point object.

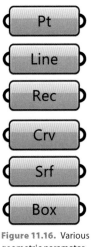

Figure 11.16. Various geometric parameter components in Grasshopper.

Figure 11.17. The point parameter component options.

To create a parametrically defined line, create a second point object in Rhino, a second Point parameter component in Grasshopper, and repeat the process to set the second point. Place a Line component, which can be found in the Curve tab, Primitive panel, in the Grasshopper canvas. Connect one Point parameter component to the Line component's input A parameter, and the second Point parameter component to the Line component's input B parameter. Both points are previewed with a red "x" and the parametrically defined line appears in Rhino in red as previewed geometry.

When the point objects in the Rhino 3D modeling space are moved, the previewed line updates. (See Figure 11.18.) This demonstrates the basic concept of parametric modeling. The Line component is dependent on and is associated with the Point parameters.

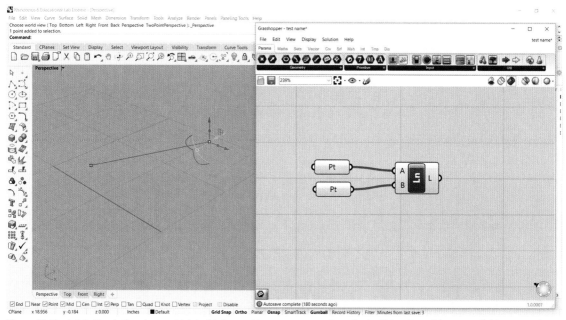

Figure 11.18. A definition in Grasshopper (right) with the resulting geometry previewed in the Rhino 3D modeling space (left). *Courtesy of the author.*

Baking Components

To convert the previewed geometry from the Grasshopper environment into an object in the Rhino 3D model, the Grasshopper component has to be "baked." To "bake" a component, right-click on the middle column of the component, in this case, the Line component, and select Bake from the pop-up window. (See Figure 11.19.) The line will appear as a curve object in the Rhino 3D modeling space, which can be selected and edited.

Figure 11.19. The Bake command in Grasshopper.

Number Sliders

Number sliders are commonly used components for defining input parameters and are located in the Params tab, Input panel. They provide numerical data that can be used as input values with other components. The numerical value of a number slider is *variable* and can be modified, which will result in a change to the downstream components.

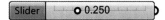

Figure 11.20. The Number Slider component in Grasshopper.

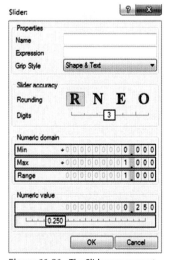

Figure 11.21. The Slider component window and settings.

Number slider values can be set as *integer numbers* or *floating point numbers*, which are two different types of numerical data.[4] An integer number (commonly known as an *int*) is a whole number without a decimal point, while a floating point number (commonly known as a *float*) is a real number that has a decimal point. By default, number sliders are set to a floating point number with a numerical value of 0.250, within a numeric domain ranging of 0.000 to 1.000. A numeric domain is a numerical range between a low value and high value. By clicking and sliding the white circle in the Number Slider, the numerical value can be redefined and set within the numeric domain, at numerical intervals of 0.001. (See Figure 11.20.)

The default settings of a number slider can be redefined by right-clicking on the title "Slider" within the component and selecting the Edit option. The Slider Dialog Box will appear with current settings and allows for changes to the numerical value, the numerical data type, and the numeric domain. (See Figure 11.21.)

Domains

Domains can be defined as the low and high values of a numerical range. There are various options for domain components located in the Maths tab, Domain panel. The default Construct Domain component requires numerical input parameters. By default, the Construct Domain component has a numerical domain from 0.0 to 1.0. The output information, or data, from most components can be viewed by connecting the output node to a Panel component, which can be found in the Params tab, Input panel. Panel components can also be used as input parameters. (See Figure 11.22.)

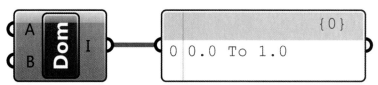

Figure 11.22. A Domain component with its output values displayed in a Panel component. *Courtesy of the author.*

Series and Range

A repetition statement in a computational algorithm is referred to as a *loop*. For example, when a loop is initiated with the variable $t = 0.0$, stepping in increments of 1.0, and terminating when $t = 10.0$, the resulting output list of values is 0.0, 1.0, 2.0, 3.0, 4.0, 5.0, 6.0, 7.0, 8.0, 9.0. The Series and Range components in Grasshopper operate as loop functions and are located under the Set tab, Sequence palette. By default, both the Series and Range components have specified input parameters. The Series component has the following input parameters: the start number of the series (S), the step size for each successive number (N), and the total number of values in the series

(C). Connecting a Panel component to the output series of numbers (S), displays see the list of values from 0.0 to 9.0 in increments of 1.0. (See Figure 11.23.) The Range component works in a similar way but divides a specified range of numeric values, known as a domain (D), by a total number of steps (N). Connecting a Panel component to the output range of numbers (R), displays the list of values from 0.0 to 1.0 in increments of 0.1. (See Figure 11.24.)

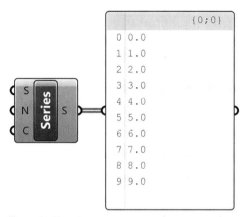

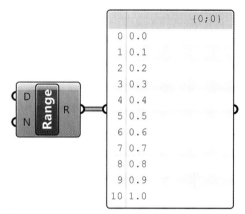

Figure 11.23. A Series component with its output values displayed in Panel component. *Courtesy of the author.*

Figure 11.24. A Range component with its output values displayed in a Panel component. *Courtesy of the author.*

When the Series component (with the default settings) output data is input as the parameter for the X value of a Construct Point component, a series of points is generated in the X direction. The list of point coordinates can be displayed when the Construct Point output (Pt) is connected to a Panel component. (See Figure 11.25.) The point is previewed in the Rhino 3D modeling space and results in a linear series of 10 points. (See Figure 11.26.)

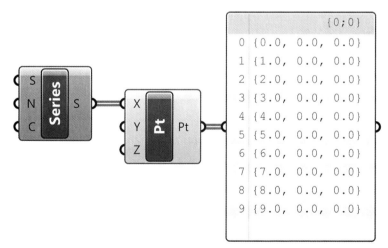

Figure 11.25. A Construct Point component with an X value that is defined by the default values of a Series component. *Courtesy of the author.*

Figure 11.26. A Construct Point defined by a series of X values previewed in the Rhino 3D modeling space. *Courtesy of the author.*

When the same Series component output data is input as the parameters for the Y value of the Construct Point component, a series of points are generated with X and Y. The list of point coordinates can be displayed when the Construct Point output (Pt) is connected to a Panel component. (See Figure 11.27.) The point is previewed in the Rhino 3D modeling space and results in a diagonal series of 10 points. (See Figure 11.28.)

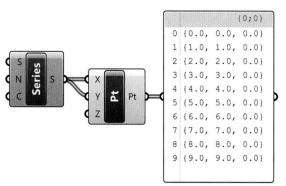

Figure 11.27. A Construct Point component with X and Y values that are defined by the default values of a Series component. *Courtesy of the author.*

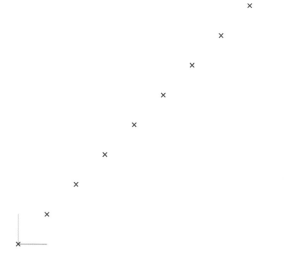

Figure 11.28. A Construct Point defined by a series of X and Y values previewed in the Rhino 3D modeling space. *Courtesy of the author.*

Lists

Lists of data can be organized and referenced in various ways. List components can be found under the Sets tab, List panel. List components can be used to sort, reverse, and partition lists, to name a few organizational options. Specific items from a list can also be retrieved. Short List components can be used to shrink a collection of lists to the shortest list in the collection, and Long List components can be used to grow a collection of lists to the longest list in the collection. The Cross Reference component creates lists that are based on all of the possible combinations for matching items in each list. For example, if the default Series component output data, a list containing 10 values, is cross-referenced as two lists, the resulting cross-referenced list consists of 100 values. (See Figure 11.29.) These values are sorted in two different ways, which are output as adjusted list (A) and adjusted list (B). When these values are used to define the X and Y values of a Construct Point, the result is 100 points that are arranged in a grid. (See Figure 11.30.)

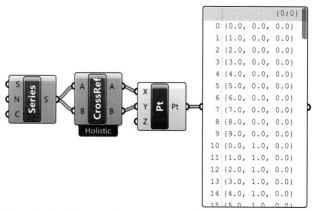

Figure 11.29. A Construct Point component with X and Y values that are defined by the cross-referenced series of values. *Courtesy of the author.*

Figure 11.30. A Construct Point defined by a cross-referenced series of X and Y values, previewed in the Rhino 3D modeling space. *Courtesy of the author.*

Culling

Items in a list can be culled, or selected, as items to be kept or removed from a list. There are various components for culling items in a list, which are located in the Set tab, Sequence palette. A Cull Pattern component, for example, can be used to specify a pattern for keeping and removing items in a list using *logical operations*, which are operations that involve the comparison of two variables. A *Boolean* function is a logic operation that is either true or false, which can also be expressed as 1 or 0, respectively.[5] The default Cull Pattern component requires two input parameters, the list to cull (L) and the cull pattern (P), which is specified as a Boolean logic operation. By default, the pattern is false, false, true, true, which results in removing the first two items in the list, and keeping the following two items. (See Figure 11.31.) This pattern, which can also be expressed as 0,0,1,1, repeats throughout the entire list. When using the default Cull Pattern component with the output list of the previous cross referenced point example, the Boolean logic operation results in a repeating pattern of two removed points and two remaining points, starting at the origin and moving left to right along the X axis, and continuing to the row above in the Y axis. (See Figure 11.32.) Various sequences of true/false (or 0/1) values can be specified as the cull pattern (P) input parameter, to create various culled patterns.

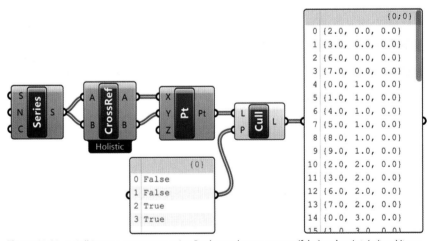

Figure 11.31. A Cull Pattern component using Boolean values to remove (false) and maintain (true) items from a list. *Courtesy of the author.*

Figure 11.32. A Construct Point defined by a cross-referenced series with a Cull Pattern to create a pattern of points using the following Boolean sequence: False, False, True, True.
Courtesy of the author.

Maths

Various mathematical operations such as addition, subtraction, multiplication, and division can be used to calculate values for input parameters. These components can be found in the Maths tab, Operators panel. Other mathematical components, such as the Pi component, can be found in the Maths tab, Util panel. Additionally, mathematical expressions with variable parameters can be used to calculate a value. The Expression component is located in the Maths tab, Script panel. The following definition, by Daniel Christev of The Christev Creative, is used to generate a sine wave.[6] (See Figure 11.33.) The expression A*sin(t) can be defined within the Expression Designer dialog box, which appears when double-clicking on the Expression component. (See Figure 11.34.) The sine wave curve is generated when the output list of point coordinates is input as a parameter to define the vertices of a curve (V) using the Interpolate Curve component. By changing the Variable A parameter in the definition, sine waves with various amplitudes can be generated. (See Figure 11.35.)

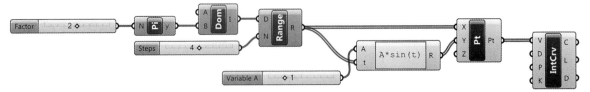

Figure 11.33. A Grasshopper definition for a sine wave based on a Grasshopper definition by Daniel Christev. *Courtesy of the author.*

Figure 11.34. The Expression Designer window in Grasshopper.

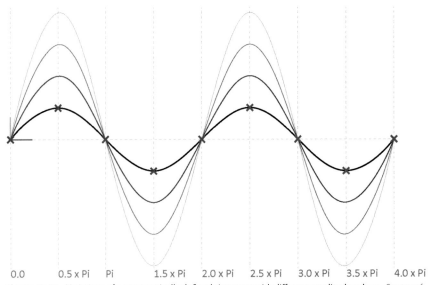

Figure 11.35. Variations of a parametrically defined sine wave with different amplitude values. *Courtesy of the author.*

Graph Mappers

The Graph Mapper component provides an interface that allows users to interact with various graph types (numeric mapping functions), such as Bézier, Conic, Parabola, Sine, and more. The Graph Mapper, located in the Params tab, Utility panel, can be used in various ways, such as mapping point values that can be used as the input parameter for a point. (See Figure 11.36.) The *Graph type* can be selected by right clicking on the Graph Mapper component. Double-clicking on the Graph Mapper component opens up the Graph Editor dialog box. Within the dialog box, a visual graph curve appears, which can be edited by selecting and dragging the grippers, and X and Y domain values can be specified. In this example, the X and Y domain values are set to the following: X(0) = 0, X(1) = 10, Y(0) = 0, Y(1) = 5. (See Figure 11.37.) The list of points is previewed in the Rhino 3D modeling space and updated in real-time when the Graph Mapper is modified by selecting and dragging the grippers in the Graph Mapper component or the Graph Editor dialog box. (See Figure 11.38.)

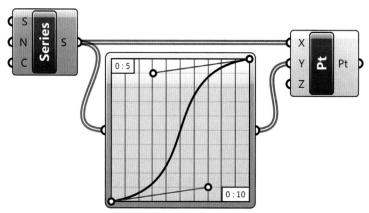

Figure 11.36. The Graph Mapper component in Grasshopper. *Courtesy of the author.*

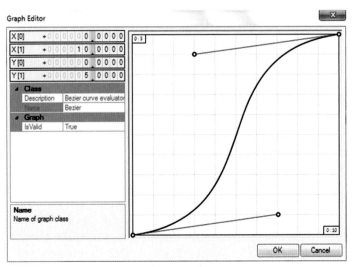

Figure 11.37. The Graph Editor window in Grasshopper.

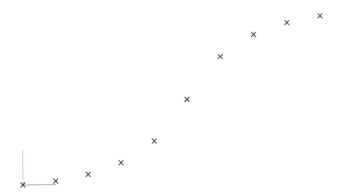

Figure 11.38. A Construct Point defined by a Graph Mapper previewed in the Rhino 3D modeling space. *Courtesy of the author.*

Endnotes

1. Gil Akos and Ronnie Parsons, *The Grasshopper Primer*: Foundations (3rd ed.), http://grasshopperprimer.com/en/index.html?index.html.
2. Andrew Payne, *The* Grasshopper Primer (1st ed.).
3. Ibid.
4. Casey Reas and Ben Frye, "Integers Floats," Processing.org, https://processing.org/examples/integersfloats.html, accessed October 15, 2017.
5. Nathan Emberton, "Boolean," Computerhope.com, June 16, 2017, https://www.computerhope.com/jargon/b/boolean.htm.
6. Daniel Christev, "Grasshopper 10: Sine Functions," January 2016, https://www.youtube.com/watch?time_continue=4&v=PKuZQhJhbbE.

Chapter 12
Geometric Patterns

Chapter 12 presents types of patterns and methods for working with patterns using computational tools. Our human sense of vision provides us with the ability to recognize patterns. Patterns can be found all around us in nature, ranging in scale from the micro to the macro, from nano cellular structures to cosmic spiraling galaxies.[1] Other patterns are created by humans for various reasons, such as organizing information and communicating symbolic meaning. Throughout the day, we (humans) are constantly processing color, light, texture, and pattern, both consciously and subconsciously. Patterns can change our experience of a space, by providing cultural associations, as well as triggering psychological and neurological effects. For example, the perception of motion experienced by viewing some patterns, known as acuity patterns, can result in physiological effects on an observer.[2] Although the topic of "pattern" is broad, this chapter will focus on the use of geometric patterns in architecture and design, as a method for spatial organization and effects, and the use of computational design tools for creating patterns. Through the generation of architectural patterns using algorithmic procedures, variations and discoveries of patterns can be achieved in the drawing process.

12.1 Tessellations

Patterns are often formed by the repetition of geometric elements. Tessellations, also known as tilings, are created when geometric shapes are repeated to cover a plane without overlapping or leaving any gaps. Tiling patterns that repeat are known as *periodic* tilings, while patterns that can be adjusted to allow for variation, or nonrepeating patterns, are known as *nonperiodic* tilings. *Aperiodic* tilings are a subset of nonperiodic tilings, in which every tiling is necessarily nonperiodic.[3] The use of geometric patterns in architecture and design can be traced back thousands of years. Historically, architects and designers have utilized tiling patterns in many different ways, for example, the parceling of land to organize a city, the assembly of modular systems to form a façade, and the arrangement of elements to form interiors, as a means of achieving organization, structure, symbolic meaning, visual interest, and aesthetic beauty. The characteristics of repetition, modularity, and adjacency allow tiling systems to inspire architectural tectonics and assemblies.[4] Physical tessellations consist of geometric modules with material properties, for example, metal panels that clad a surface, or bricks that can be stacked and arranged to form a wall. The method in which the modules are arranged, their dimensions, and the the overall shape or form in which they are assembled, are all parameters that effect the design of the tiling system and pattern. Architectural patterns can play a critical role in creating spatial experiences and effects, as evident in the design of the Sky Reflector Net at Fulton Center, New York, a project designed through the collaboration of Grimshaw, Arup, and James Carpenter Design Associates. (See Figure 12.1.)

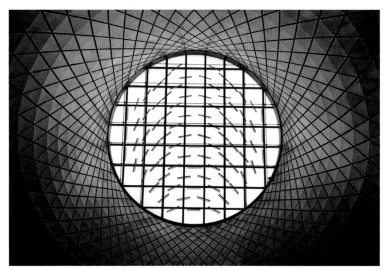

Figure 12.1. Grimshaw, Arup, and James Carpenter Design Associates, Sky Reflector Net, Fulton Center, New York. Photo by the author. *Courtesy of the author.*

Various periodic tiling patterns, including hexagonal, radial, square, rectangular, and triangular patterns, can be quickly generated in the Rhino 3D modeling space by using Grid components in Grasshopper, which are located under the Vector tab, Grid panel, and listed as preset pattern options. (See Figure 12.2.)

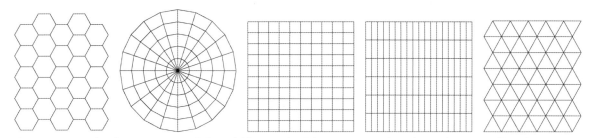

Figure 12.2. Examples of geometric patterns (left to right): hexagonal, radial, square, rectangular, and triangular. *Courtesy of the author.*

After placing a grid component in the canvas, it can be defined and modified with input parameters. Modifying geometry with *parameters* and *constraints* is the basis of parametric modeling. For example, the Rectangular Grid component can be defined by providing the input parameters of a base plane (P), the numerical values for the size of each cell (Sx, Sy), and the number of cells in each direction of the plane's axes (Ex, Ey). (See Figure 12.3.) By using Number Slider components, the amount of grid cells and their sizes can be easily modified to create multiple variations of the rectangular pattern using the same Grasshopper definition. (See Figure 12.4.)

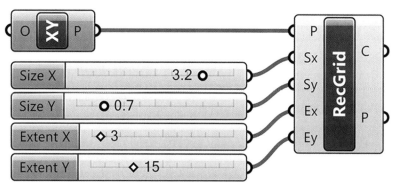

Figure 12.3. The Rectangular Grid component with various input parameters. *Courtesy of the author.*

Figure 12.4. Parametric variations of a Rectangular Grid pattern. *Courtesy of the author.*

Some periodic tilings, such as those produced by equilateral triangles, can shift to produce variation. This creates nonperiodic tilings, which have variation, or non-repeating patterns. Tiling patterns in which nonperiodic tilings are necessary are known as aperiodic tilings. The Penrose pattern is an example of an aperiodic tiling, in which an infinite variety of tilings can be created, in which no such tiling has a trans-lation, such as symmetry.[5] Aperiodic tilings are utilized in the design of the "prosolve 370e" system developed by the architecture and design firm Elegant Embellishments, based in Berlin, Germany. The decorative architectural modules are coated in titanium dioxide (TiO_2), a pollution-fighting technology, and arranged to form a nonrepeating pattern, resulting in an ornamental, modular, facade system that is both performative and decorative. (See Figures 12.5 and 12.6).

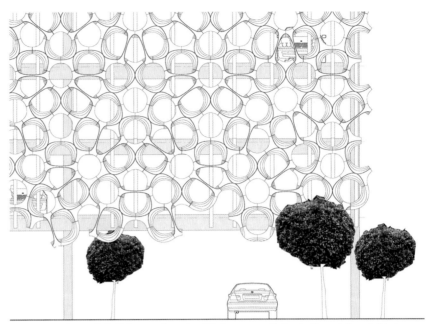

Figure 12.5. Elegant Embellishments, "prosolve 370e" system applied to the Torre de Especialidades, Mexico City, Mexico. Elevation drawing of the facade modules. *Courtesy of Elegant Embellishments.*

Figure 12.6. Elegant Embellishments, "prosolve 370e" system applied to the Torre de Especialidades, Mexico City, Mexico. Photograph of the facade modules. Photo by Alejandro Cartagena. *Courtesy of Elegant Embellishments.*

Tessellated patterns can also comprise elements that are not repeated. The Voronoi tessellation is a pattern found in various natural systems, such as the pattern of veins on a leaf or of a dragonfly wing. (See Figure 12.7.) This tessellation is the subdivision of space into polygons, known as *cells*, based on sets of points, known as *seeds*. The polygonal cell regions consist of all points that are closer to its corresponding seed than any other. The Voronoi tessellation is dual to the Delaunay triangulation, in which the triangles do not have any additional points that lie within the boundary of their circumcircle. When the lines of the triangles are bisected at their midpoint with perpendicular lines, they meet to form the Voronoi tessellation. (See Figure 12.8.)

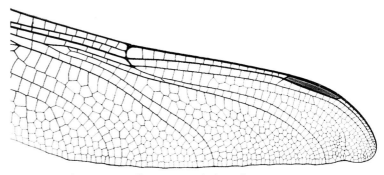

Figure 12.7. The Voronoi tessellation pattern of a dragonfly wing.

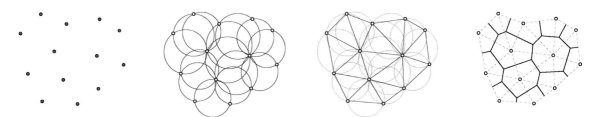

Figure 12.8. A diagram of the geometry of the Voronoi pattern (left to right): a collection of points, circumcircles of triangles, Delaunay triangulation, Voronoi pattern. *Courtesy of the author.*

A Voronoi tessellation can be created in Grasshopper by using the Voronoi component, which is located under the Mesh tab, Triangulation panel. Create a set of point objects in the Rhino 3D modeling space. Bring this set of points into Grasshopper by creating a Point component in the canvas, and right-clicking on the component to Set Multiple Points from the Rhino 3D modeling space. Use this Point component (collection) as the input parameter (P) on the Voronoi component, which will create the Voronoi pattern. (See Figure 12.9.) Additional optional input parameters are available, such as cell size, boundary, and base plane. (See Figure 12.10.)

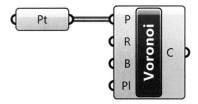

Figure 12.9. The Voronoi component in Grasshopper. *Courtesy of the author.*

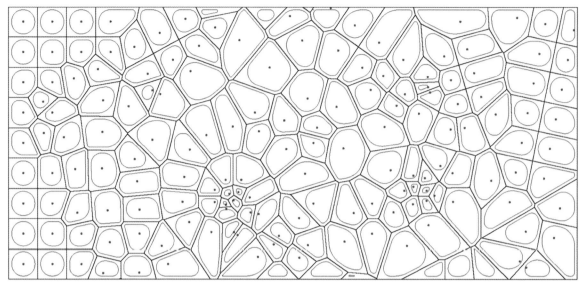

Figure 12.10. A Voronoi tessellation pattern generated with Rhino and Grasshopper. *Courtesy of the author.*

Figure 12.11. Visible light image of Tropical Cyclone Joalane captured by the MODIS instrument aboard NASA's Terra satellite, 2015. *Courtesy of NASA Goddard MODIS Rapid Response Team.*

12.2 Spirals

Spiral patterns can be observed in many natural formations as the result of energy distributions, matter, and growth, such as the arrangement of petals on a plant or the formation of storm clouds. (See Figure 12.11.) Perhaps due to the observation and influence of spiral patterns in nature, the use of spiral patterns in design appears within many cultures, and can be traced back thousands of years. The triskelion motif, which consists of three interlocking spirals, appears on various artifacts from the Neolithic period. This motif utilizes the Archimedean spiral, which is a spiral generated by a point moving away from a fixed point at a constant speed. In Greek architecture, spiral patterns appear as architectural ornament in the scroll-like forms found in the capitals of Ionic columns. (See Figure 12.12.) This use of ornament appears to serve as a visual figuration that reveals cycles and acts as a force that unites elements.[6]

Figure 12.12. Archimedean spiral patterns on the Ionic capital of a Greek column.

The Fibonacci series is a pattern based on a sequence of numbers in which each consecutive number is based on the addition of the previous two: 1-1-2-3-5-8-13-21-etc. (See Figure 12.13.) This pattern, introduced by the Italian mathematician Leonardo Fibonacci around 1200, can also be found in natural formations, such as the arrangement of petals and florets in plants and flowers. This model is typically used to describe phyllotaxis, the naturally occurring plant growth pattern that governs the arrangement of leaves, flower petals, pine cones, and the like. (See Figure 12.14.) These patterns tend to be arranged as spirals that run in opposite directions, clockwise and counterclockwise. The number of spirals in each direction is asymmetrical and consecutive with the Fibonacci series; for example, eight spirals run in one direction and thirteen in the other direction. (See Figure 12.15.) This example of a Fibonacci spiral, based on a Grashopper definition by Anastasia Globa, is generated using a Fibonacci component found in the Sets tab, Sequence panel.[7] (See Figure 12.16.)

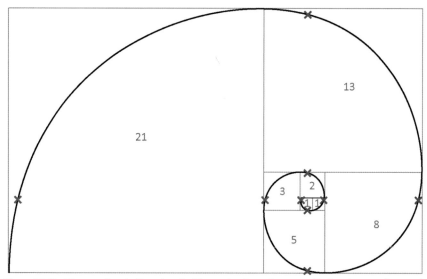

Figure 12.13. Diagram of a spiral based on the Fibonacci series and generated in Grasshopper. *Courtesy of the author.*

Figure 12.14. The phyllotaxis spiral pattern of the *Aloe polyphylla*.

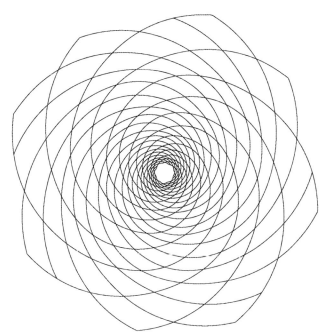

Figure 12.15. A phyllotaxis spiral pattern based on the Fibonacci spiral sequence. *Courtesy of the author.*

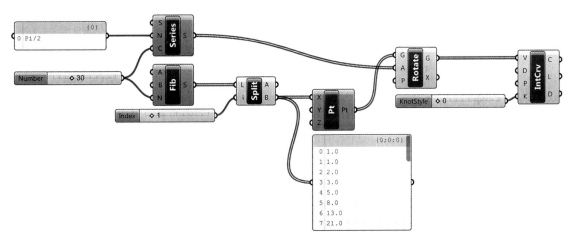

Figure 12.16. A Grasshopper definition for generating a spiral using the Fibonacci sequence. *Courtesy of the author.*

Other spiral formations can be created through the use of mathematical functions. The Archimedean spiral in Figure 12.17 was generated by defining a curve through cosine and sine values that are used to define the X and Y input parameters.

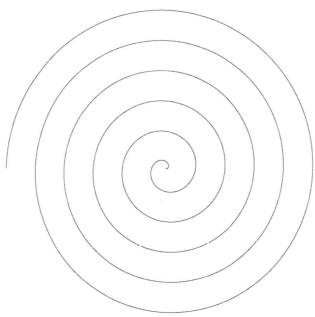

Figure 12.17. The Archimedean spiral. *Courtesy of the author.*

The following version of a Grasshopper definition, by Gil Akos and Ronnie Parsons of Mode Lab, uses an algorithm that combines a spiral pattern defined by mathematical functions and a Voronoi tessellation pattern to generate a phyllotaxis pattern that can be controlled parametrically.[8] (See Figure 12.18.) By modifying the input variables, multiple versions of phyllotaxis patterns can be quickly generated. (See Figure 12.19.)

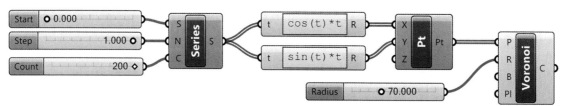

Figure 12.18. A Grasshopper definition for generating a spiral pattern that is combined with a Voronoi tessellation. *Courtesy of the author.*

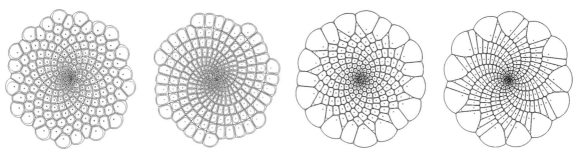

Figure 12.19. Multiple versions of a phyllotaxis spiral pattern generated by combining a Fibonacci spiral pattern with the Voronoi tessellation. *Courtesy of the author.*

12.3 Pattern Effects

Various architectural effects can be generated through patterns that utilize geometries that incrementally vary. Through the use of subtle, incremental changes in geometric transformations, such as scale, rotation, and translation, patterns can convey visual effects, such as depth and motion. The complexity of this type of pattern and its effects can be seen in the design of the dome of the church of San Carlo alle Quattro Fontane by the Italian architect Francesco Borromini. The ornamental geometric pattern of the dome consists of interlocking octagons, crosses, and hexagons that gradually diminish in scale as they reach the top of the dome, maintaining a consistent number of geometrical components from the lower perimeter to the upper perimeter of the elliptical dome. (See Figure 12.20.) The effect of depth is exaggerated, producing an illusion of the dome reaching further and higher in elevation.

Figure 12.20. Francesco Borromini, San Carlo alle Quattro Fontane, Rome, Italy, 1638–1641. Photograph of the dome interior.

In addition to visual perception, patterns can trigger physiological effects. The research presented by Patricia Rodeman, in her journal article "Psychology and Perception of Patterns in Architecture," describes acuity patterns, which she describes as designs that exhibit perceptions of movement through the use of high-contrasting stripes, checkerboards, and highly regimented geometric, graphic, and dot patterns.[9] The work of the English painter Bridget Riley often conveys visual effects of movement that engaged the mind and body of the viewer. Her painting *Fall* (1963) creates a "visual energy" through the repetition of a curve that produces a field of optical frequencies.[10] (See Figure 12.21.) Pattern effects are typically achieved through the repetition of lines, curves, and components that gradually change and/or transform through incremental variations.

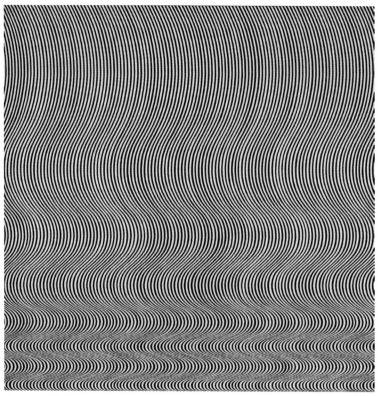

Figure 12.21. Bridget Riley, *Fall,* 1963. Polyvinyl acetate paint on hardboard. © Bridget Riley 2018. All rights reserved. Photograph: © Tate Gallery, London, 2018.

Replication

In a computational algorithm, a repetition statement, referred to as a *loop*, can be defined and executed with a Series component in Grasshopper. The Range component can be used to specify changes to geometry within the loop to produce transformations that incrementally vary, such as rotation and scaling. In the following example, a series of boxes are replicated along the X axis. The definition starts by using the Series component to define the X value of a Construct Point component. (See Figure 12.22.) The output list of point coordinates (Pt) is used as the input parameter for the base (B) of a Center Box component. A Number Slider set to an integer number provides the input parameter for the series count (C) to define the total number of boxes, and a single Number Slider set to a float number is used as the input parameter for the X, Y, and Z values of the boxes, which results in a linear series of cubes. (See Figure 12.23.)

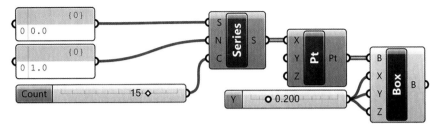

Figure 12.22. A Grasshopper definition producing a series of boxes along the X axis. *Courtesy of the author.*

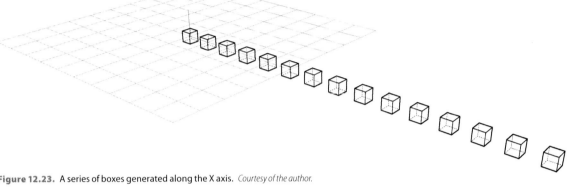

Figure 12.23. A series of boxes generated along the X axis. *Courtesy of the author.*

Incremental Rotation

Building off the previous definition, the Rotate and Range components can be used to rotate the boxes incrementally within a *range* of values. (See Figure 12.24.) The Rotate component, located in the Transform tab, Euclidean panel, can be used to rotate the boxes to a specified angle, and requires three input parameters: the base geometry (G), rotation angle (A), and the base plane (P). The output list of boxes can be used as the input for the base geometry (G) of the Rotate component. Using the Range component, located in the Sets tab, Sequence panel, the total number of boxes in the series can be rotated in equal increments within a range of specified angles. A Range component requires two inputs; a domain (D) and a value for the number of steps (N). A Construct Domain component can be used with Number Sliders to define the domain, and its output (I), with a start value of 0 and an end value of 180. This will establish the rotational range of the boxes to begin at 0 degrees and end at 180 degrees.

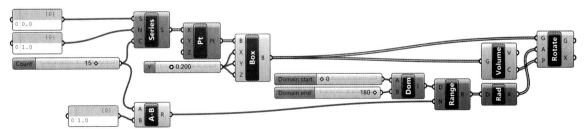

Figure 12.24. A Grasshopper definition producing a series of boxes along the X axis that rotate incrementally from their centroids. *Courtesy of the author.*

By default, the Rotate component's input rotation angle (A) parameter is measured in radians. A Radians component can be used to convert the 0 to 180 values of the domain from degrees into radians, which is then used as the input parameter for the Rotate component's input rotation angle (A). The same input number slider that was used to define the count in the Series component (minus 1) can be used as the value for the number of steps (N) in the Range component. This allows the total number in the range to equal the total number in the series. The base plane (P), by default, is centered at the World Coordinates origin (0, 0, 0), and rotates geometry around this origin. In order to rotate the boxes around their individual centroids, the Volume component, located in Surface tab, Analysis palette, can be used to generate and output the centroids of the boxes (C). This list of centroid coordinates can be used as the input parameter for the Rotate component's rotation plane (P). The resulting preview of the incrementally rotating boxes can be modified by adjusting the various, variable parameters in the Grasshopper definition. (See Figure 12.25.)

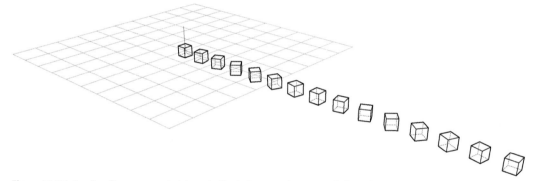

Figure 12.25. A series of boxes generated along the X axis that rotate incrementally from their centroids. *Courtesy of the author.*

Incremental Scaling

Continuing with the previous definition, the Scale and Range components can be added to scale the boxes incrementally. (See Figure 12.26.) The Scale component, located in the Transform tab, Affine panel, requires three input parameters: the base geometry (G), the center of scale (C), and the scaling factor (F). The Rotate component's output rotated geometry (G) can be used as the Scale component's input base geometry (G). The Volume component can be used again, this time to determine the centroids of the rotated geometry. The Volume component's output list of centroids (C), can be used as the input parameter for the Scale component's center of scale (C). The Range component is used to establish a scale factor that decreases and increases the scale of the current boxes. Creating a Construct Domain component that is set with float values ranging from 0.000 to 2.000, the Range component's output range of numbers (R) is used as the Scale component's input scaling factor (F). (See Figure 12.27.)

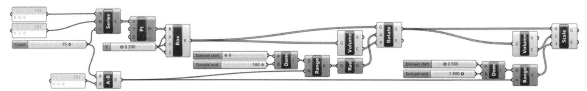

Figure 12.26. A Grasshopper definition producing a series of boxes along the X axis that rotate and scale incrementally from their centroids. *Courtesy of the author.*

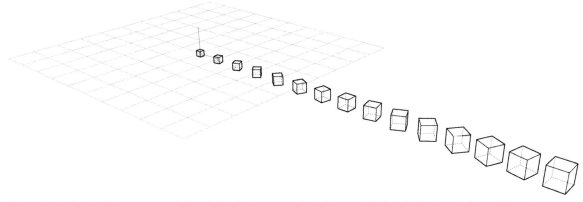

Figure 12.27. A series of boxes generated along the X axis that rotate and scale incrementally from their centroids. *Courtesy of the author.*

This algorithmic definition has multiple variable parameters that can be adjusted to generate various configurations of a linear row of transformed boxes. Additional components and parameters can be added and modified to this algorithmic definition to generate new patterns. For example, if the initial Series component output list is cross referenced to define the X and Y input parameters of the Construct Point component, a grid of boxes will be generated along the X and Y axes. The variable numeric values defined by the Number Sliders, such as the number of boxes in the series, the degrees of rotation, and scale factor, can easily be modified to yield different patterns. These various configurations can be viewed as two-dimensional patterns by switching to the Top viewport in the Rhino 3D model. (See Figure 12.28.)

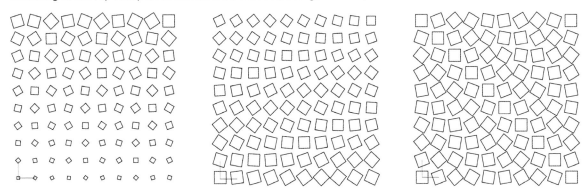

Figure 12.28. Drawings of different versions of a series of boxes parallel to the X and Y axis that rotate and scale incrementally from their centroids. *Courtesy of the author.*

Attractors

Modeling with Attractors is a technique for creating geometric elements that vary incrementally based on their proximity to a point or curve in space. Similar to a magnet, which attracts or repels other ferromagnetic materials, Attractors act as "virtual magnets" that can influence parameters based on their relationship to the attractor geometry.[11] "Attractor" is simply the nomenclature given to a geometric object or component, typically a point or curve that is used to influence the parameters of other geometry. This produces a variegated patterning effect that yields aesthetic qualities and geometric conditions that can influence the architectural performance of a building. In the design of the Sinosteel International Plaza, by MAD Architects, based in Beijing, China, various sizes of hexagonal windows flow across the building in an irregular pattern. (See Figures 12.29 and 12.30.) This provides an interesting visual aesthetic, changing the way the building looks from different perspectives, and also serves to enhance the building's performance. The pattern of the windows provides energy efficiency, and the windows are positioned according to solar and wind patterns on the site, in order to minimize heat loss in the winter and heat gain in the summer. The honeycomb pattern also provides a structural logic, allowing the skin to function as the primary structure of the building.[12]

Figure 12.29. MAD Architects, Sinosteel International Plaza (Tianjin), Beijing, China. Rendering of the facade. *Courtesy of MAD Architects.*

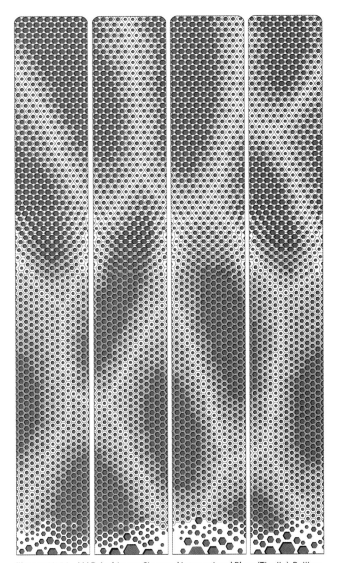

Figure 12.30. MAD Architects, Sinosteel International Plaza (Tianjin), Beijing, China. Elevation drawings. *Courtesy of MAD Architects.*

Point Attractors

In the following Grasshopper definition, a hexagonal pattern with incremental variation is produced using a single *point attractor*. (See Figure 12.31.) In this example, the point attractor is a point object that is modeled in the Rhino 3D modeling space and assigned as a Point parameter component in Grasshopper. This Rhino point object can be defined as a parameter in the Grasshopper workspace, by using a Point parameter component, which is located in the Params tab, Geometry panel. Place the Point parameter component in the canvas workspace, and right-click on the component. Choose Set one Point from the list of options, and select the point object in the Rhino 3D modeling space. This assigns and links the Rhino point object to the Grasshopper Point parameter component, which will be used in the definition as the point attractor. Create a hexagonal pattern using the Hexagonal component located in the Vector tab, Grid panel, and assign values to the input parameters. The output parameters of the Hexagonal component are cells (C) and points (P).

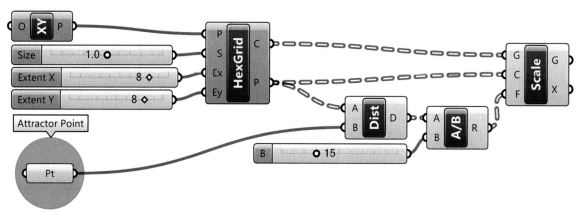

Figure 12.31. A Grasshopper definition for a hexagonal pattern that varies in scale based on a point attractor. *Courtesy of the author.*

In this definition a Scale component is used to reduce the size of the original hexagonal cells. The Hexagonal component's output cells (C) are the input parameters for the Scale component's base geometry (G), and the output points (P) are the input parameters for the Scale component's center of scaling (C). The scaling factor (F) is based on the distance from the point parameter component (the point attractor) to the hexagonal cell center points, which are the output points (P). In this example, the distance can be divided by a variable number to increase or decrease the scaling factor. The resulting pattern consists of hexagonal cells that each have a unique scaling factor based on their distance to the point attractor. When the Point object in Rhino is moved, the distances change, resulting in various patterns in which the scales of the hexagonal cells incrementally vary. (See Figure 12.32.)

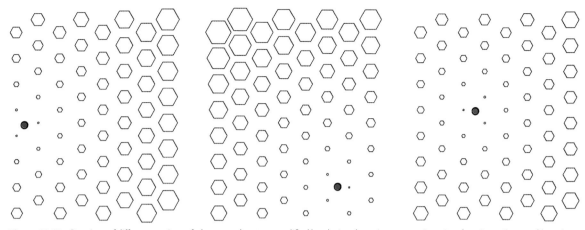

Figure 12.32. Drawings of different versions of a hexagonal pattern modified by placing the point attractor in various locations. *Courtesy of the author.*

Endnotes

1. Simon Bell, *Landscape: Pattern, Perception and Process* (New York: Routledge, 2012).
2. Patricia Rodeman, "Psychology and Perception of Patterns in Architecture," *AD: Patterns of Architecture,* ed. Mark Garcia. (December 2009): 101–107.
3. Branko Grunbaum and G.C. Shepard, *Tilings and Patterns* (2nd ed.) (Mineola, NY: Dover Publications, 1987).
4. Ibid.
5. Benjamin Aranda and Chris Lasch, *Pamphlet Architecture 27: Tooling* (New York: Princeton Architectural Press, 2006).
6. Kent Bloomer, *The Nature of Ornament: Rhythm and Metamorphosis in Architecture* (New York: W.W. Norton & Company, 2000).
7. Anastasia Globa, "Fibonacci Spiral," Algorithmic Design in Architecture (blog), May 2015, http://parametric-design.blogspot.com/2015/05/fibonacci-spiral.html.
8. Gil Akos and Ronnie Parsons, Mode Lab, "Intro to Grasshopper 08 | Phyllotaxis + Expressions," YouTube video, 21:08, filmed and posted August 2015, https://www.youtube.com/watch?v=hMx23t_3oMU.
9. Rodeman, "Psychology and Perception."
10. Mary Chamot, Dennis Farr, and Martin Butlin, *The Modern British Paintings, Drawings and Sculpture* (London: Oldbourne Press, 1964).
11. Gil Akos and Ronnie Parsons, *The Grasshopper Primer*: Foundations (3rd ed.), http://grasshopperprimer.com/en/index.html?index.html.
12. Rose Etherington, "Sinosteel International Plaza by MAD," *Dezeen,* July 30, 2008, https://www.dezeen.com/2008/07/30/sinosteel-international-plaza-by-mad/.

Chapter 13
Parametric Modeling

Chapter 13 introduces concepts and methods for working iteratively through parametric modeling processes that allow for the generation of multiple formal systems. By defining geometric parameters, constraints, and relationships, multiple versions of a formal system can be quickly generated and evaluated based on design criteria. These criteria are determined by the designer, who establishes the design parameters of a project. Using similar principles to those of evolution by natural selection, multiple iterations of a self-similar system can be tested and evaluated to determine the *optimal* solution to a design problem. Parametric modeling allows for the design of adaptive systems, continuous differentiation, and articulated complexity. This method of design has been characterized by Patrik Schumacher, architect and partner of Zaha Hadid Architects (ZHA), as *parametricism*, a new style in architecture in which new systematically connected design problems are being worked on competitively by design researchers, who share design ambitions and problems.[1]

13.1 Parametric Surfaces

The repetition of identical components to create architectural assemblies was streamlined during the Industrial Age and played a major role in the development of Modernist architecture. Modernism reflects the age of mass production, the manufacturing of identical parts that can be assembled to create architectural systems. Industrial processes continue today and reflect the majority of current design and manufacturing processes that make up our built environment. Over the last three decades, however, digital design and fabrication processes have demonstrated and continue to advance the possibility for designing systems that comprise a variation of self-similar components, as opposed to identical components. Digital design processes, rooted in digital animation techniques from the mid-1990s, along with advances in digital fabrication tools, such as 3D printers, laser cutters, CNC milling machines, and robotics, allow for the production of multiple objects and parts that can be uniquely customized, while maintaining competitive costs. This shift from the mass production processes of the industrial age to the mass customization process of the digital age continues to evolve and influence the design and fabrication of contemporary architecture.

Parametric models are 3D models that can be controlled through input *parameters* and geometric *constraints*. When input parameters are changed, these changes are automatically reflected in an updated 3D model. Additionally, geometric constraints establish geometric hierarchies and dependencies within the 3D model. The approach to creating a parametric model may vary depending on the overall goals and objectives of the model. There are often multiple methods and various techniques for generating parametric models that have the exact same outcome or that yield similar results, yet "behave" differently. Strategically designing the workflow in which the model is generated can have a big impact on its use in exploring possible design solutions and the ease and flexibility at which different versions can be produced. Parametric models can be generated through the use of 3D modeling and scripting processes. In Figure 13.1, two simple truncated cones are generated through two different workflows. The truncated cone on the left is generated entirely through an Grasshopper definition with variable parameters, while the one on the right uses 3D modeled curve objects from Rhino, which are referenced as geometric parameters in a Grasshopper definition. Both yield the same formal results: a truncated cone; however, the method in which the model can be transformed into various iterations by modifying its parameters is different. The form on the left, generated entirely through the algorithmic definition, is efficient for quickly producing multiple variations by editing the variable parameters, while the form on the right, generated through a combination of 3D modeling and an algorithmic definition, is efficient for exploring more complex formal outcomes by manipulating the curve objects and their control points within the 3D modeling space. (See Figures 13.2 and 13.3.) While this example simply demonstrates two parametric models that yield the same results yet "behave" differently based on the different workflows that are used to construct them, there are often multiple workflow possibilities for creating parametric models. It is often desirable to produce efficient parametric models and algorithmic definitions that are streamlined to address a design problem, and that are flexible to adapt to a wide range of design criteria.

 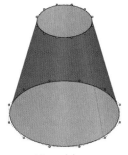

Figure 13.1. A preview of two similar parametric models generated with two different methods. The model on the left is generated entirely with a Grasshopper definition, while the model on the right is generated with a combination of 3D-modeled curve objects and a Grasshopper definition. *Courtesy of the author.*

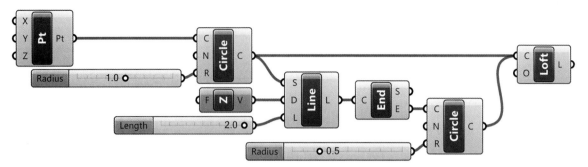

Figure 13.2. A Grasshopper definition with variable parameters used to generate a lofted surface of a truncated cone. *Courtesy of the author.*

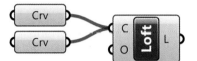

Figure 13.3. A Grasshopper definition with two curve parameters referenced from the Rhino 3D model used to generate a lofted surface of a truncated cone. *Courtesy of the author.*

13.2 Paneling Surfaces

Paneling Surfaces

As described in Section 7.3, two-dimensional patterns can be applied to surfaces in a 3D model. The plug-in PanelingTools for Rhino, developed by Rajaa Issa, is also available as an add-on for Grasshopper. This provides the same features that are available in Paneling Tools for Rhino, with the additional ability to control the panelization of the surface parametrically.[2] By modifying the numeric variable input parameters that create the point grid on the surface, multiple paneling options and scales can be quickly developed. This provides the ability for designers to produce more iterations of a project, to study and evaluate within a set amount of time. With Paneling Tools (pt), a point grid can be generated and modified to create various tessellated patterns such as rectangular, triangular, and diamond shaped. The Grasshopper definition illustrated in Figure 13.4, generates a diamond-shaped pattern that is applied to a truncated cone, which is lofted in Grasshopper using two curve parameters referenced from two curve objects (circles) in a Rhino 3D model. The Loft surface is used as the input surface (S) for a pt Surface Domain Number component, which creates a point grid that is defined by a specified number of U and V values (uN and vN inputs). This rectangular grid of points (Gd) is output and converted into a diamond pattern using the pt Convert to Diamond component. The surface is panelized into individual wires (lines), cells (cell points), and meshes using the pt Cellulate component. (See Figures 13.5.)

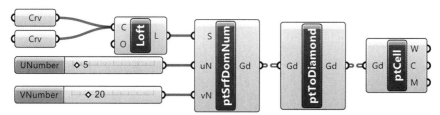

Figure 13.4. A Grasshopper definition for panelizing a surface into diamond-shaped cells. *Courtesy of the author.*

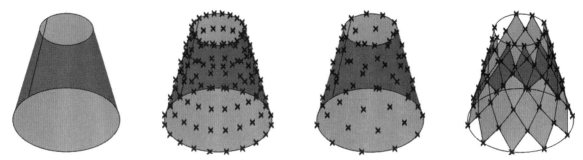

Figure 13.5. A preview of models that demonstrate the steps of panelizing a surface into diamond-shaped cells. *Courtesy of the author.*

The wires (lines), can be baked, to create the pattern as curve objects in the Rhino 3D model. Various orthographic projections can be generated from the parametric model and new drawings can be created. For example, the surface in Rhino can be unrolled to create a drawing that illustrates the unrolled surface with the pattern of the panels. By editing the parametric model and creating multiple versions, the line-work can be exported to create drawings that document the various iterations of the panelized surface. Additional reference lines can be added to illustrate the relationship between the various drawing elements. (See Figure 13.6.)

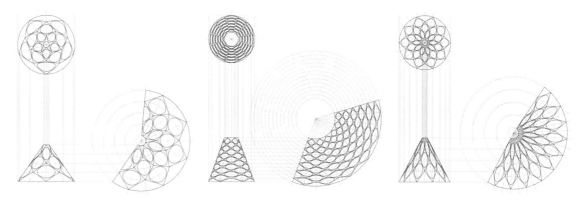

Figure 13.6. A drawing of the top, side, and unrolled surface views for three versions of a parametric, panelized truncated cone. Drawing by Esty Deutsch. Instructor, Frank Melendez. The Bernard and Anne Spitzer School of Architecture, City College of New York. *Courtesy of the author.*

The technique of drawing and modeling with Attractors as described in Section 12.3, can also be applied to panelized surfaces parametrically using attractor components that are available in the Paneling Tools tab, Grid Attractors panel. This allows for the generation of patterns that incrementally vary.

Mapping Patterns to Surfaces

Patterns that are generated within a two-dimensional plane can be applied to three-dimensional surfaces. The previous example in Chapter 7.3 describes this process of applying a two-dimensional pattern to a three-dimensional surface in Rhino using the Flow Along Surface command. A similar technique can be achieved parametrically in Grasshopper using the Map to Surface component. In both cases, the pattern is *mapped* by defining a bounding surface, in which the pattern lies, and a target NURBS surface, in which the pattern is mapped to. Both the bounding surface and target surface are defined with U and V values, which have a numerical domain from 0 to 1. This allows the two surfaces, which are different in shape and form, to remain topologically the same. This is a very useful feature of NURBS modeling, as it allows surfaces, whether flat or curved, to be defined within the same 2D space, UV coordinate system. Therefore, 2D patterns can be drawn on simpler planar surfaces and transferred to more complex curved surfaces.

The following example combines the techniques of mapping two-dimensional patterns to a three-dimensional surface using the Map to Surface component. (See Figure 13.7.) Two patterns are mapped to the surface, one regular hexagonal pattern and one hexagonal pattern that incrementally varies. The Map to Surface component requires three input parameters: the curves to map (C), the source (S) that is the base/reference surface, and the target surface (T). The Grasshopper definition begins with a two-dimensional hexagonal pattern component generated with numerical variables. The regular hexagonal pattern is incrementally varied through the point attractor technique, using a Scale component, with a scale factor (F) that is defined by the distance from the hex center points and the point attractor, which is a referenced point object from the Rhino 3D model. Both the hexagonal pattern and scaled (attracted) pattern are combined into one list using the Flatten component. This flattened list is used to define the Bounding Box of the pattern geometry, which is used as the source

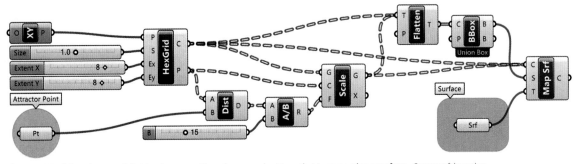

Figure 13.7. A Grasshopper definition for generating a hexagonal pattern that is mapped to a surface. *Courtesy of the author.*

(S) input on the Map to Surface component. The curves to map (C) are both the regular hexagonal pattern output (C) and the incrementally scaled hexagonal pattern output (G). The target surface (T) is a referenced surface object from the Rhino 3D model. (See Figures 13.8 and 13.9.)

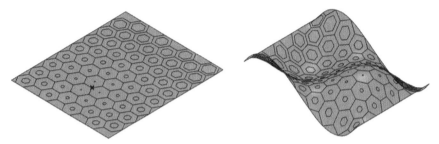

Figure 13.8. A preview of two surfaces with hexagonal patterns. The hexagonal patterns on the planar surface (left) are mapped to the curved surface (right). *Courtesy of the author.*

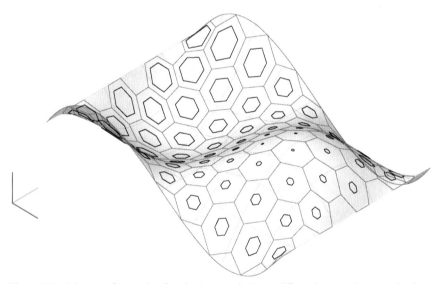

Figure 13.9. A drawing of a curved surface that is mapped with two different hexagonal patterns. One hexagonal pattern is uniform while the other is scaled incrementally with an attractor point. *Courtesy of the author.*

13.3 Modular Assemblies

Architectural systems often consist of assemblies of modular parts. These systems are based on part-to-whole relationships, meaning individual parts can be assembled in a variety of ways to create whole configurations and forms. Throughout most of our history, handcrafted manufactured methods were the only method available for fabricating artifacts, and they required a great amount of human energy. During the Industrial Revolution, production processes shifted from handcrafted methods to machine manufacturing methods. The dream of machine production was pursued by many of the leading architects of the twentieth century, with social and economic agendas that were merged with architecture and construction methods.[3] With these changes, design, manufacturing, and construction were separated, changing the historical role of architect as designer, craftsperson, and master builder.

Additionally, the modernist focus on utility and function in architectural design gained priority, while the traditional role of ornament in architecture diminished. With the rise of digital technologies, including advances in parametric modeling, BIM, and digital fabrication methods, the strict separation of labor in design and production has changed, by increasing collaboration and the sharing of information, and by expanding the design and manufacturing repertoire of the architect. With this change, architects and designers have a direct tie to making and manufacturing through the use of computer numerical control (CNC) machines. Parametric modeling and digital fabrication processes allow for the mass production of customized modules, as opposed to the replication of identical elements, to form architectural assemblies. This method of design to production has had a profound impact in the field of architecture, beginning in the early 1990s, with a resurgence toward craft, ornament, pattern, and effects, seen in the early digital fabrication experiments of Bernard Cache's "objectiles," where topological surface variations were produced with CNC milling technologies, allowing for the mass-customized production of unique objects.

The design of individual modules and the use of computational procedures of replicating and varying geometry provide opportunities for bottom-up approaches to the design of systems. As opposed to traditional top-down approaches to design, where a project is designed from a holistic point of view and the individual elements and parts of the project are designed secondary to the whole, bottom-up approaches to design begin with the design of an individual unit and explore the multiple methods in which the unit can be replicated and assembled to form a larger system. Bottom-up approaches to design allow for emergent formations and patterns that are based on the input of parameters and constraints, and more aligned with processes found in natural systems.[4] This has led to an architectural discourse based on the optimization and performance of formal systems. These methods of design have continued to evolve along with advances in computational processes and digital manufacturing tools, including robotic fabrication.

Modularity in Architectural Assemblies

Modernist methods of creating assemblies typically involve the repetition of identical elements. Until the recent technological advances associated with digital fabrication tools such as 3D printers, CNC milling machines, and industrial robotic arms, the ability to create sinuous, sculptural forms continued to rely on traditional, labor intensive, hand-making techniques. The beautiful and intricate architectural screens designed and fabricated by the sculptor Erwin Hauer exemplify this process, where complex geometries are sculpted and cast in a traditional mold-making process, and repeated to cast multiple identical components that are stacked and arranged to form light-filtering architectural walls. These assemblies consist of volumetric modules that are made of gypsum cement, and arranged to allow for surface continuity and porosity. (See Figures 13.10 and 13.11.)

Figure 13.10. Erwin Hauer Studios, Design 1, 1950. Architectural screen, Showroom of Knoll Internacional de Mexico, Mexico City. *Courtesy of Erwin Hauer Studios.*

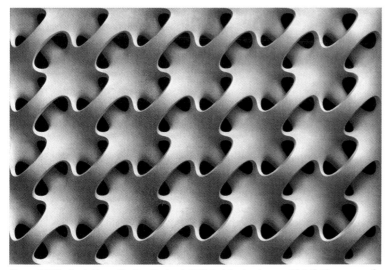

Figure 13.11. Erwin Hauer Studios, Design 1, *1950*. Architectural screen (detail), Showroom of Knoll Internacional de Mexico, Mexico City. *Courtesy of Erwin Hauer Studios.*

Digital technologies and fabrication processes have provided opportunities for architects and designers to advance the methods of designing, fabricating, and assembling modules to create architectural systems. Parametric and algorithmic modeling processes, coupled with advances in digital and robotic fabrication technologies, allow for the design and production of complex modular systems. Modular geometries can be designed as non-repeating elements that continuously vary across a larger field, and output directly to fabrication through the use of computer-aided manufacturing (CAM) technologies. *Pinch Wall*, an innovative project by the architect Jeremy Ficca at the Carnegie Mellon University School of Architecture, utilizes parametric and algorithmic design techniques to generate a pattern of hexagonally shaped cells that gradually change in shape and scale throughout the assembly. (See Figure 13.12.) The molds for the concrete components were fabricated from a parametric model with the use of an industrial robotic arm, which allowed for the use of undercuts in the milling process, in which material is subtracted, or carved, from a larger volume. Additionally, the robotic milling process allowed for the use of the edge of the bit to cut material, a method referred to as swarfing, in which the axis of the bit acts as a rule line that can be traced through the material to develop a ruled surface.[5] The Pinch Wall project demonstrates the opportunities for merging computation and fabrication processes in the design and manufacturing of architectural systems. These processes are based on the mass customization of unique modules that continuously differentiate to form architectural

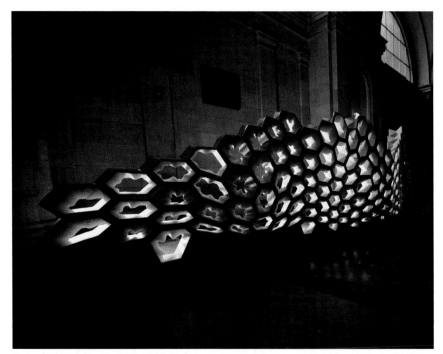

Figure 13.12. Jeremy Ficca, *Pinch Wall*. Photograph of the installation. *Courtesy of Jeremy Ficca, Carnegie Mellon University, School of Architecture; students: Nelly Dacic, Matthew Huber, Puga Patel, Craig Rosman, Giacomo Tenari.*

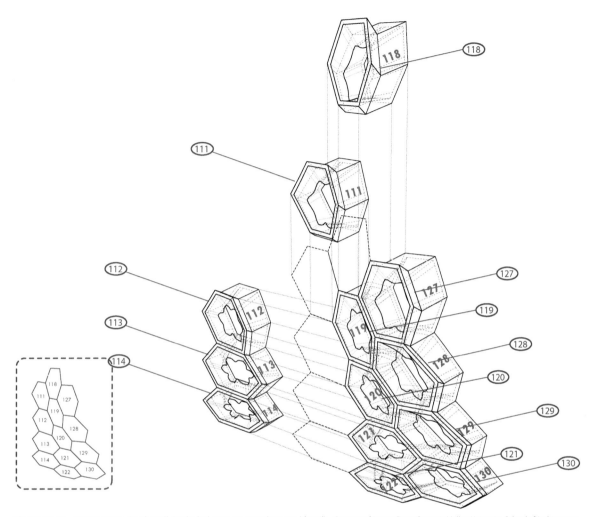

Figure 13.13. Jeremy Ficca, *Pinch Wall*. Exploded axonometric drawing (detail). *Courtesy of Jeremy Ficca, Carnegie Mellon University, School of Architecture; drawings by students: Nelly Dacic, Matthew Huber, Puja Patel, Craig Rosman, Giacomo Tenari.*

assemblies that convey "performative effects" of texture and pattern that "affect" our senses, perception, and experience of surfaces, forms, and spaces.[6] (See Figure 13.13.)

Replicating a Module across a Surface

There are many methods for replicating the geometry of a module across a surface. In the following definition, the geometry of a module is replicated along a conical surface that is created by lofting two curve objects (circles) from the Rhino 3D modeling space. (See Figure 13.14.) The two curve objects are referenced in the Grasshopper canvas with curve parameter components to create lofted surface with the Loft component. This surface is divided into segments in the U and V directions using the Divide Domain component locate in the Maths tab, Domain panel. This domain is converted into three-dimensional cells using the Surface Box component located in the Transform tab, Morph panel. The Surface Box requires three input parameters: the base surface (S), the surface domain (D), and the height of the surface box (H). The input parameter for the base surface (S) is the Loft surface output (L). The input parameter for the surface domain (D), is the Divide Domain output (S). The height of the boxes (H) is a variable numeric parameter that results in the thickness of the boxes, offset from the surface. The Box Morph component in Grasshopper morphs an object into a twisted box. The module in Figure 13.15 is a three-dimensional surface that is modeled in Rhino and referenced in Grasshopper using a Geometry parameter component from the Params tab, Geometry panel. The Box Morph component requires three input parameters, the base geometry (G), reference box (R), and the target box (T). The input parameter for the base geometry (G) and the reference box (R) are the Geometry parameter component, and the input parameter for the target box (T) is the Surface Box output of the twisted box (B). The resulting model generates modules that are replicated across the lofted surface. If the lofted surface dimensions are changed, the modules parametrically adapt to allow the specified number of modules with the U and V directions to fit within the updated surface. Additionally, the number of rows and columns of modules can be increased or decreased by changing the number of U and V divisions.

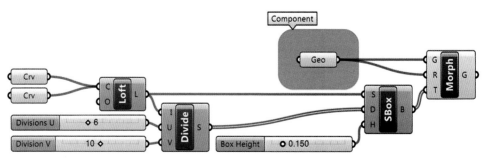

Figure 13.14. A Grasshopper definition for generating modular geometry on a surface with a Box Morph component. *Courtesy of the author.*

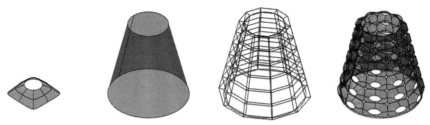

Figure 13.15. A preview of models that demonstrate the steps in replicating a modular geometry across a surface (left to right): the referenced modular geometry, the base surface, the Surface Box, and the Box Morph geometry. *Courtesy of the author.*

Blending Modules across a Surface

Multiple modules with different geometry can also be replicated across a surface in various ways. Two different modules can be replicated across a surface and remain as discrete geometries. They can also be replicated across a surface in a manner to blend their geometries from one form to another. In Figure 13.16, two different modules, one with a shallow taper inward (small aperture) and one with a steeper taper inward (large aperture), are used to generate a series of components that gradually transition from one form to the other.

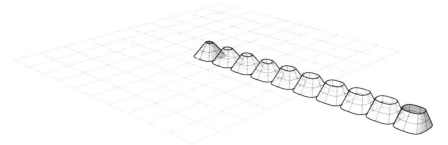

Figure 13.16. A blend between two different components. *Courtesy of the author.*

This method of blending modules is achieved using components within the Paneling Tools add-on for Grasshopper. In the Grasshopper definition in Figure 13.17, the geometry of two modules are replicated along a surface that is created by lofting two curve objects (line segments) from the Rhino 3D modeling space, and transition from one module to the other based on their proximity to curve attractor. The Loft surface is used to create a parametrically defined point grid using the Paneling Tools (pt) Surface Domain Number component. (See Figure 13.18.) This point grid (Gd) is offset in the direction of the Z axis using the pt Offset Grid component. These two grid (Gd) outputs are used as the input grid 1 (Gd1) and grid 2 (Gd2) input parameters of the pt Morph 3d Mean component. This establishes the cells that will be populated with the two modules that are modeled in the Rhino 3D modeling space as surfaces. These two modules are referenced in Grasshopper with Surface parameter components, which are input as the start object (SO) and end object (EO). The start and end objects are morphed based on their proximity to an curve attractor, which is a curve object in Rhino that is referenced in Grasshopper with a Curve parameter component that serves as the curve attractor (A) input in the pt Curve Attraction component. The grid input (Gd) for the pt Curve Attraction component is the grid output (Gd) of the pt Surface Domain Number component. The output weights (W) are the input weights (W) of the pt Morph 3d Mean component. The resulting geometrical pattern results in components that gradually vary from small apertures to larger apertures. (See Figures 13.19 and 13.20.) Variations of the pattern can be generated by modifying the curve attractor, loft curves, U and V division values, and the dimension of the offset grid. The regular grid geometry of the pattern can be changed to an irregular grid pattern by changing the initial line segments into sinuous curves by adding and editing the curve control points in the Rhino 3D model.

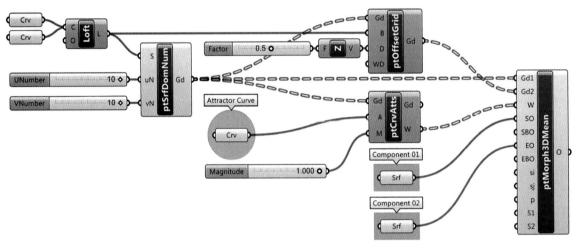

Figure 13.17. A Grasshopper definition with Paneling Tools, used to generate modules that blend across a surface based on their proximity to a curve attractor. *Courtesy of the author.*

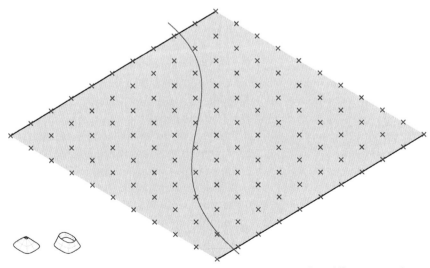

Figure 13.18. A lofted surface divided into grid points, a curve attractor, and two different geometric modules. *Courtesy of the author.*

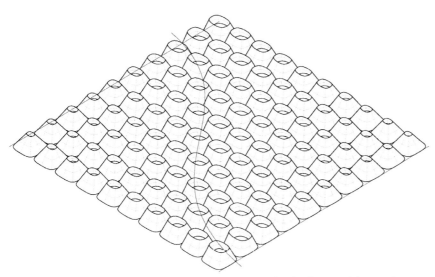

Figure 13.19. Axonometric drawing of a regular grid pattern populated with two module types that blend from one to the other based on their proximity to a curve attractor. *Courtesy of the author.*

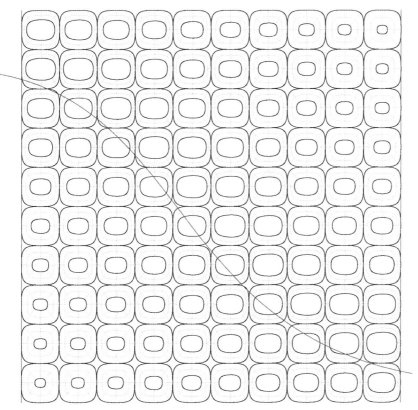

Figure 13.20. Plan drawing of a regular grid pattern populated with two module types that blend from one to the other based on their proximity to a curve attractor. *Courtesy of the author.*

Additional architectural and geometric effects can be produced through the variation of the grid pattern by using point attractors to distort the grid. Using the previous definition, a pt Point Attraction component is placed to create a grid (Gd) output that replaces the input grid (Gd) of the pt Offset Grid component and the input grid 1 (Gd1) of the pt Morph 3D Mean component. Two point objects modeled in the Rhino 3D modeling space are referenced into Grasshopper as point parameter components, which are used as the input parameters for the point attractors (A) on the pt Point Attraction component. The magnitude (M) input can be adjusted with a variable parameter to increase or decrease the strength of attraction. (See Figure 13.21.) The resulting distortion of the grid results in components that compress in scale based on their proximity to the attractor points and the magnitude of attraction numerical variable. (See Figures 13.22 and 13.23.)

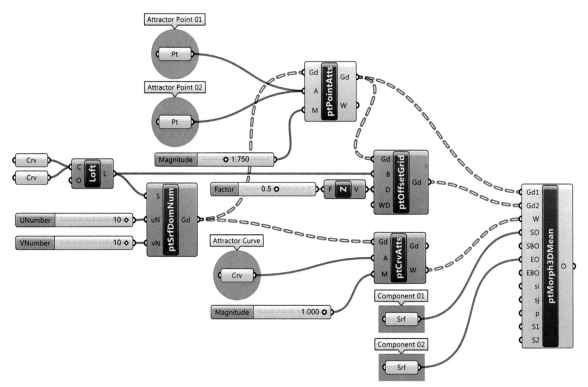

Figure 13.21. A Grasshopper definition with Paneling Tools, used to generate modules that blend across a surface based on their proximity to a curve attactor and point attractors. *Courtesy of the author.*

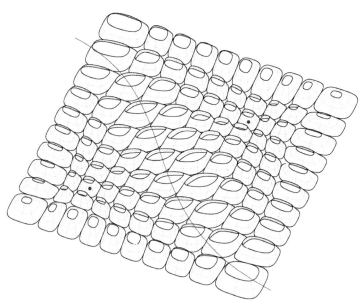

Figure 13.22. Axonometric drawing of a regular grid pattern populated with two module types that blend from one to the other based on their proximity to a curve attractor and point attractors. *Courtesy of the author.*

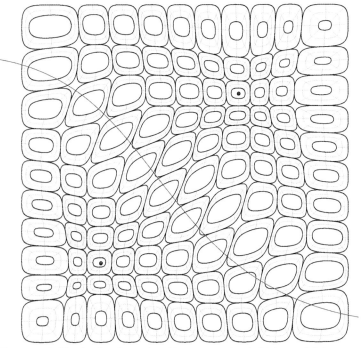

Figure 13.23. Plan drawing of a regular grid pattern populated with two module types that blend from one to the other based on their proximity to a curve attractor and point attractors. *Courtesy of the author.*

Endnotes

1. Patrik Schumacher, "Parametricism: A New Global Style for Architecture and Urban Design," *AD Architectural Design: Digital Cities* 79 (no. 4, July–August 2009), Neil Leach, guest ed.; Helen Castle, general ed.

2. PanelingTools for Grasshopper, developed by Rajaa Issa, Robert McNeel and Associates, Seattle, WA, https://wiki.mcneel.com/_media/labs/panelingtools4grasshopperprimer.pdf.

3. Stephen Kieren and James Timberlake, *Refabricating Architecture: How Manufacturing Methods Are Poised to Transform Building Construction* (New York: McGraw Hill Companies, 2004).

4. Richard Garber, "Alberti's Paradigm," *AD Architectural Design: Closing the Gap* 79 (no. 2, March–April 2009).

5. Jeremy Ficca, "Material Resistance," *Matter: Material Processes in Architectural Production,* Gail Peter Borden and Michael Meredith (eds.) (New York: Routledge, 2012), pp. 343–355.

6. Branko Kolarevic, *Architecture in the Digital Age: Design and Manufacturing* (New York and London: Routledge, Taylor & Francis, 2005).

Chapter 14
Simulations and Data Visualizations

Chapter 14 provides an overview of methods for creating and working with computational simulations. This section focuses on the use of simulations as computational methods that aid in the design process to inform design decisions. This includes environmental simulations that utilize data and represent phenomena such as sunlight and wind, as well as physics-based simulations that use particles to explore material properties or emergent behavior. These tools provide insights into forces and phenomena that are temporal and/or invisible. Simulations and data visualizations expand the scope of architectural drawing and provide new methods for the design and representation of form, forces, and data.

14.1 Simulations

Simulations are temporal imitations of real-world processes or systems. There are many different fields and applications in which simulations are utilized, such as medicine, economics, engineering, gaming, and education. Simulations can be used to re-create real-world scenarios or abstract information. For example, full flight simulators (FFS) are simulation environments that use vision and motion to train pilots how to fly aircraft by allowing for a safe and effective practice of particular procedures.[1] (See Figure 14.1.) A simulation is an artificial re-creation of an experience or condition in a manner that relates to reality. The effectiveness of a simulation is based on the reification of values based on performance, by achieving a particular result.[2] This provides opportunities for designs to be tested against specific criteria, evaluated, and adjusted to increase their performative quality. For example, the flows and velocities in which air currents move through a space can be simulated through computational fluid dynamics (CFD) software. (See Figure 14.2.) This CFD analysis can be used to gain insight on the relationship between the geometry of the design and its relationship to air flow. Changes to the geometry of the design impact the movement of air around the object, which can be used to inform design decisions and increase the performative aspects of the design. In this sense, simulation tools can be used for design optimization. In architectural design, computational simulations are often implemented to test the performance and achieve optimization in design. For example, simulations can be used to test the effectiveness of an architectural design in response to various external factors involving environmental conditions and various forces. Environmental simulations include testing a building's performance in relation to solar conditions, energy efficiency, and wind patterns. These models rely on climatic information and can be useful in designing buildings that are more energy efficient and sustainable. This is not only an issue that is related to architecture, but a global concern as we (humans) are confronted with increasing issues pertaining to climate change due to negative anthropogenic impacts on our environment. Physics-based simulations involve testing a building's performance in relation to forces such as gravity, wind loads, and material properties. These models provide opportunities to simulate material behavior and performance. In this context, simulations can be considered as different types of computational models; one is representational while the other is based on activity, or experimentation.[3]

Figure 14.1. The full flight simulator manufactured by Thales Training and Simulation.

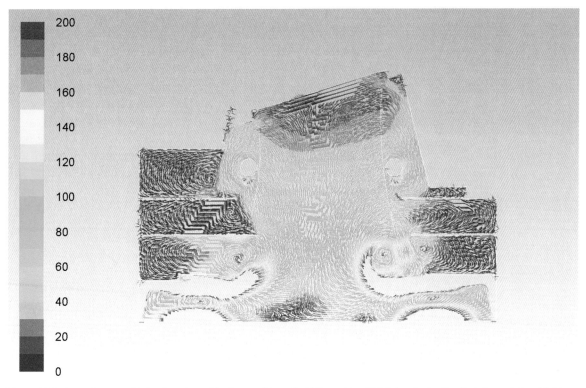

Figure 14.2. James Carpenter Design Associates, Grimshaw, and Arup, Sky Reflector Net, 2014, Fulton Center, New York. Computational fluid dynamic (CFD) simulation of air-flow velocity vectors colored by velocity magnitude (ft/min). *Courtesy of Arup.*

14.2 Environmental Simulations

In architecture, environmental simulations can be used in the architectural design process to visualize information and support design decisions. There are various visualization and simulation tools that provide data and information pertaining to solar conditions, temperature, wind, and so on. One resource that is useful for working with weather data is Ladybug Tools, which was started by Mostapha Sadeghipour Roudsari, and co-founded with Chris Mackey. Ladybug is a visual programming add-on for Grasshopper that allows data to be imported and utilized to create visualizations and simulations of environmental conditions. Ladybug imports EnergyPlus Weather Files (EPW) into the visual programming environments Grasshopper and Dynamo to produce interactive climate graphics, sunlight hours modeling, solar radiation studies, view analyses, and more.[4] EnergyPlus™ is an open-source, whole-building energy simulation program that architects, engineers, and researchers use to model energy and water consumption in buildings. EnergyPlus provides weather data in a text format for more than 2100 locations around the world. Ladybug provides a platform for importing this data into Grasshopper, which can be used as input parameters for visualizations and simulations.

Within the Grasshopper interface, Ladybug components appear under the Ladybug component tab, which contains various component panels that can be expanded to view the various Ladybug components. (See Figure 14.3.)

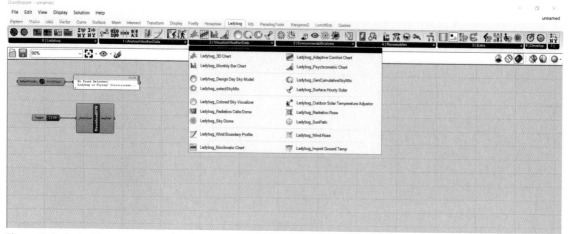

Figure 14.3. The Ladybug component tab and expanded component panel. *Courtesy of the author.*

To import the weather data of a specific location in the world into Ladybug, begin by placing a Ladybug_Ladybug component, located in the Ladybug panel, onto the Grasshopper canvas. The Ladybug_Ladybug component contains code that runs other components in Ladybug. Connect a panel component to the component's output to confirm that there are no errors, which is indicated by the "Ladybug is Flying!" message. (See Figure 14.4.)

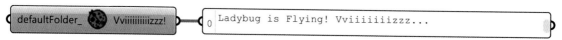

Figure 14.4. The Ladybug component and attached panel component. *Courtesy of the author.*

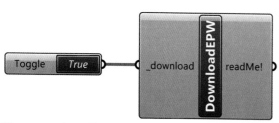

Figure 14.5. The Ladybug download EPW component and Boolean toggle used to activate the EPW map. *Courtesy of the author.*

Place a Ladybug_download EPW Weather File component onto the canvas. Place and connect a Grasshopper Boolean Toggle component, located in the Grasshopper Params tab, Input panel. Double-click on the toggle to "True" and the *Ladybug Tools EPW map* will open up in an Internet Explorer web browser. (See Figures 14.5 and 14.6.) The EPW map is an interactive map of the world that can be zoomed into to select the weather data for a specific location. Zoom into the desired location on the map and click the location dot and a pop-up window will appear. Click on "Copy link to clipboard". (See Figure 14.7.)

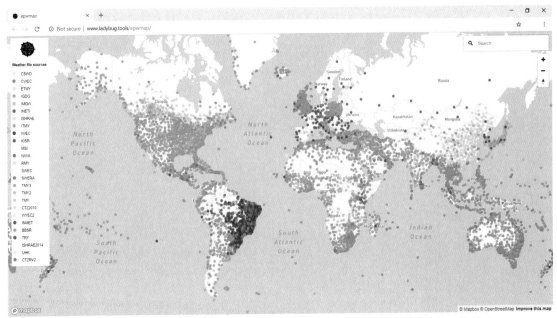

Figure 14.6. EPW map, Ladybug tools. Interface for accessing free EPW weather files. *Courtesy of Mostapha Sadeghipour Roudsari.*

Figure 14.7. EPW map pop-up window with download and URL link. *Courtesy of the author.*

Paste the copied link into a Grasshopper Panel component. This text will be used to link to the URL. Place a Ladybug_Open EPW and Stat Weather Files component into the canvas. Connect the Panel component output to the weatherFileURL input. This imports the weather file into Grasshopper, which can be parsed to display the various categories of weather data, such as temperature, humidity, wind speeds, radiation, etc. This is achieved by placing and using the Ladybug_importEPW component in the canvas. Connect the output epwFile of the Ladybug_Open EPW and Stat Weather File component to the input parameter of the Ladybug_importEPW component. When a panel component is connected to any of the Ladbug_importEPW component outputs, the data related to each category will be displayed as a list of text and numerical information. For example, connecting a panel to the dryBulbTemperature output will provide the name of the location, the type of data (Temperature), the scale of measurement (Celsius), and the unit of measurement (Hourly), followed by a list of numerical values that convey the average hourly temperature, throughout the year. (See Figure 14.8.)

257

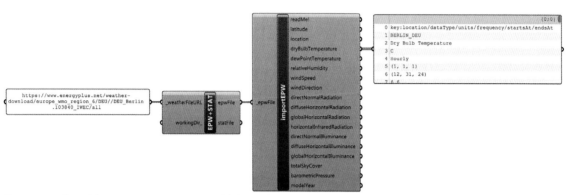

Figure 14.8. The Ladybug Import EPW component and definition for accessing the weather data. *Courtesy of the author.*

Ladybug provides tools to create visualizations of this data. To create a visualization of the dry bulb temperature, place a Ladybug_3D Chart component in the canvas. Connect the dryBulbTemperature output into the inputData input parameter. (See Figure 14.9.) The chart will appear as a three-dimensional colored graph, within the Rhino viewports. (See Figure 14.10.) This visualization consists of pixels, each pixel representing the temperature of each hour within the year. The number of hours in a day are represented as columns and the number of days/months are represented as rows. By default, the graph contains a range of values from low to high, with the low values (temperatures) colored blue and high values (temperatures) colored red. Additionally, the vertical displacement of the graph relates to the low and high values. This graph can be modified in various ways by specifying input parameter values to change the graphics and colors. For example, the scale and proportions of the chart can by modified by specifying an xScale input parameter. Additionally, the chart graphics can be modified. For example, the graphCurves color can be specified with a Grasshopper Preview Custom Color component. Additional components in Ladybug can be used to parse the data in various ways. This allows specific data to be visualized. For example, visualizations can be created that display only the dry bulb temperatures that range between 10 and 20 degrees Celsius.

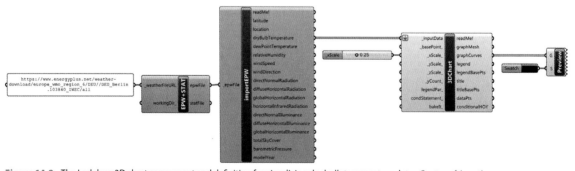

Figure 14.9. The Ladybug 3D chart component and definition for visualizing dry bulb temperature data. *Courtesy of the author.*

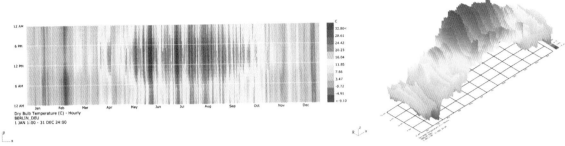

Figure 14.10. Ladybug 3D chart data visualization of annual dry bulb temperature (C), Berlin, Germany. *Courtesy of the author.*

Ladybug tools can also be used to create visualizations and simulations based on solar conditions. This is useful for visualizing the angles of the sun in relation to the earth's rotation and orbit, within a 3D model. This information is paramount when considering and designing the relationship between a building and the amount of direct sunlight it receives throughout the day and year, as well as the shade and shadows that it creates. The location or coordinates (latitude and longitude) of a location can be specified to visualize the solar conditions of a specific place in the world. The design of a building or architectural system in a hot, dry climate will require a different approach to the design than the design of a building or architectural system in a cold, wet climate, in order to maintain comfort. Therefore, the ability to visualize solar conditions and simulate daylighting is very useful in the design process for making informed design decisions based on accurate solar information.

The Ladybug_Sun Path component, found under the Ladybug Visualize Weather Data panel, can be used to visualize the sun path in relation to a specific location in the world, and to create shadow studies. Continuing with the previous Ladybug definition example, connect the "location" output from the Ladybug_importEPW component into the "location" input parameter of the Ladybug_Sun Path component. (See Figure 14.11.)

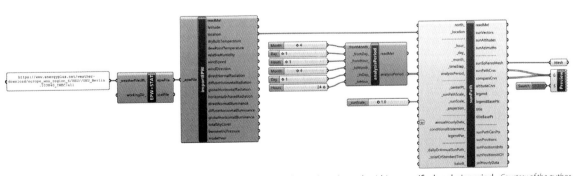

Figure 14.11. The Ladybug_Sun Path component and definition for visualizing the solar path within a specified analysis period. *Courtesy of the author.*

The Ladybug_Analysis Period component allows for the specification of the number of hours, days, and months, to define the "analysisPeriod" input parameter on the Ladybug_Sun Path component. To analyze the solar path for a 24-hour period, specify the "from" input month, day, hour, and the "to" input month, day, hour, for example, from month 8, day 1, hour 1, to month 8, day 1, hour 24. This will result in a visualization of the sun on August 1, and its relationship to the specified location at hourly intervals. (See Figure 14.12.)

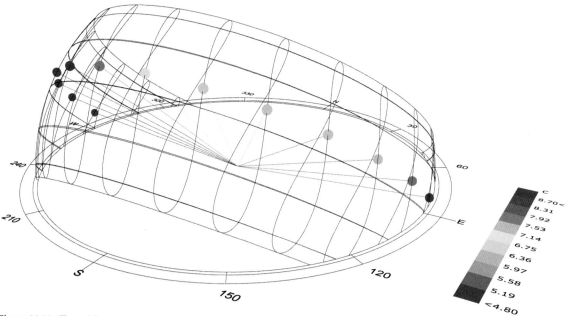

Figure 14.12. The Ladybug Sun Path visualization and simulation for a specified analysis period. *Courtesy of the author.*

Continuing with the previous sun path definition, the Ladybug_Sunlight Hours Analysis component can be used to simulate and visualize shadows. (See Figure 14.13.) The surface geometry of the 3D model (e.g. the building) in Rhino can be imported and specified as the input geometry in the Ladybug_Sunlight Hours Analysis component. The grid size input parameter specifies the pixel size of the raster image that is created, which in this example, is set to 1. The Ladybug_Legend Parameters component establishes the visual graphics of the simulation. To run the simulation, attach a Boolean Toggle component to the "run it" input parameter, and double-click this toggle to "True." The resulting simulation will generate the shadows for the specified analysis period. (See Figure 14.14.)

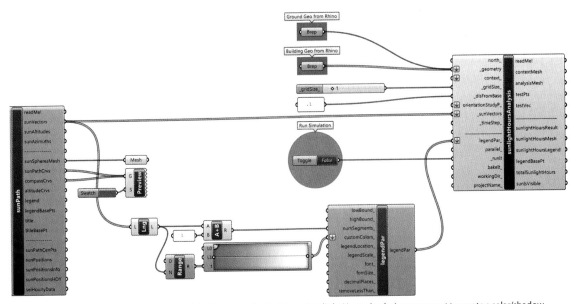

Figure 14.13. Continuation of the Sun Path definition using the Ladybug_Sunlight Hours Analysis component to create a solar/shadow simulation. *Courtesy of the author.*

Figure 14.14. A solar/shadow visualization and simulation used to study the massing of a building design in Berlin, Germany. Simulation drawings by Lars Anders Hakan Westergren and Christy Lau. Instructor, Frank Melendez. The Bernard and Anne Spitzer School of Architecture, City College of New York. *Courtesy of the author.*

14.3 Physics Simulations

The field of physics includes the study of motion and forces. In addition to being exposed to environmental phenomena such as sunlight, buildings must be designed to sustain various forces, such as gravity, and lateral loads caused by wind pressure. Various simulation platforms are available for testing the performance of a structure or building under various stresses and forces through the use of 3D models. These tools are used by engineers and architects to test the performance of a buildings structure, impact within a site, and response to various loads. (See Figure 14.15.)

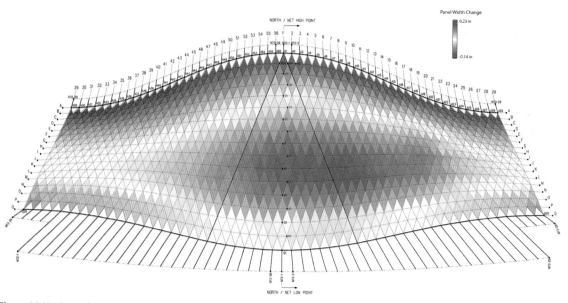

Figure 14.15. James Carpenter Design Associates, Grimshaw, and Arup, Sky Reflector Net, 2014, Fulton Center, New York. Simulation of panel width change due to imposed forces. *Courtesy of Arup.*

In addition to testing and optimizing performance, computational simulation tools can be used by architects and designers to explore and experiment with novel processes for generating geometry and form. Analog form-finding techniques, such as the performance models of Antoni Gaudi and Frei Otto, can now be explored through digital means using particle-spring systems, which simulate the physical behavior of deformable bodies.[5] Particle-spring systems discretize continuous models into particles that are connected by springs, allowing architects and designers to explore the impact of forces and variable parameters on models in real-time.[6] Their main components include particles, springs, forces, and anchor points. The work of SOFTlab, based in New York, explores these technologies and their possibilities for designing and fabricating complex architectural surfaces and structures. These projects, such as Ventricle, a hanging structure made of aluminum and solar mirror film, in the Southbank

Centre, London, combine simulation, computation, and fabrication processes to generate and realize minimal surface structures with complex curvature. (See Figure 14.16.)

Figure 14.16. SOFTlab, Ventricle, Southbank Centre, London. Photo by Alan Tansey. *Courtesy of SOFTlab.*

The Grasshopper add-on, Kangaroo, developed by Daniel Piker, is a live physics engine for 3D modeling. Kangaroo provides tools for simulating the effects of forces upon geometry within 3D models, and can be used for physics-based form finding of lightweight and tensile structures such as cable nets and fabrics.[7] During the simulation, particles are moved from their initial position until reaching a state of equilibrium based on the geometry, forces, spring properties, and anchor points.[8] This allows polylines and mesh surfaces to be "relaxed", which is useful for exploring catenary curves and minimal surface geometry within virtual environments, in a similar manner to the way architects such as Antoni Gaudi and Frei Otto used hanging chains and soap film, respectively, to explore geometry through analog physical models. The "Form, Force, Matter" workshops led by Mode Lab, based in Portland, OR, demonstrate methods and results of working with mesh relaxation tools and the impact of forces. By changing various parameters within the simulation, a matrix of design iterations was produced to visualize the impact that various forces and variables have on the mesh geometry. (See Figure 14.17.)

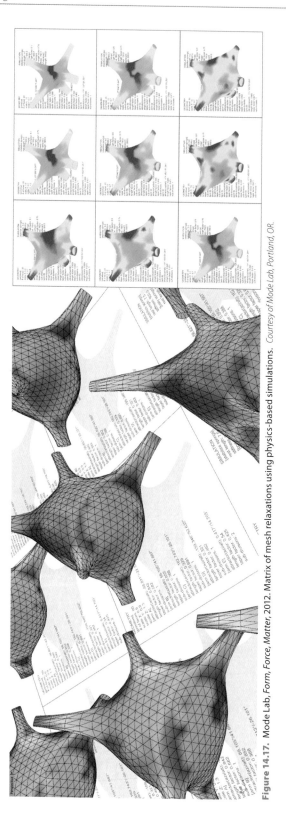

Figure 14.17. Mode Lab, *Form, Force, Matter,* 2012. Matrix of mesh relaxations using physics-based simulations. *Courtesy of Mode Lab, Portland, OR.*

The Kangaroo definition seen in Figure 14.18 can be used to "relax" a surface through the simulation of spring behavior. When running the simulation, the anchor points of the model will remain stationary, while the remaining surface deforms based on the amount of force that is parametrically defined. (See Figure 14.19.)

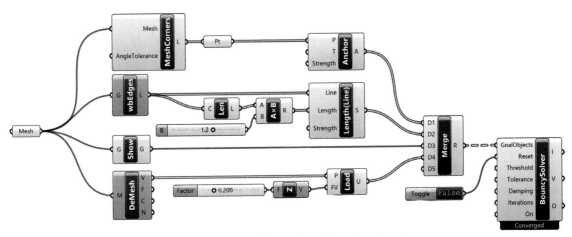

Figure 14.18. A Grasshopper and Kangaroo definition for simulating a relaxed surface. *Courtesy of the author.*

Figure 14.19. Iterations of a relaxed surface simulated with Kangaroo. *Courtesy of the author.*

Additional simulation tools that utilize forces are those that simulate "swarm" and "flocking" behavior. These agent-based simulations provide methods for defining particle (point) movements and trajectories. These particles can be programmed to respond to agents that attract, repel, and steer the particles. These behaviors are based on the work of Craig Reynolds, who developed boid models that consist of rules for simulating swarm behavior. These rules include collision avoidance (avoiding collision with nearby flockmates), velocity matching (matching velocity with nearby flockmates), and flock centering (attempting to stay close to nearby flockmates).[9] These three behaviors provided a means for steering the boids, and simulating the behavior of flocks. Additional parameters can be applied and implemented, such as obstacle avoidance, allowing the flocks to steer around objects. Within the Rhino 3D modeling environment, Quelia, an agent-based design plug-in for Grasshopper, developed by Alex Fischer, provides a visual-programming interface for simulating swarm behavior. This interface provides components and tools for creating forces, containing agents within defined boundaries, and specifying behaviors.[10] This agent-based simulation software can be utilized to explore emergent forms and patterns, simulate water flow, simulate crowd behavior, and other innovative uses. This aids in the design process by providing a better understanding of temporal and dynamic information at specific sites or within specific environments. (See Figure 14.20.)

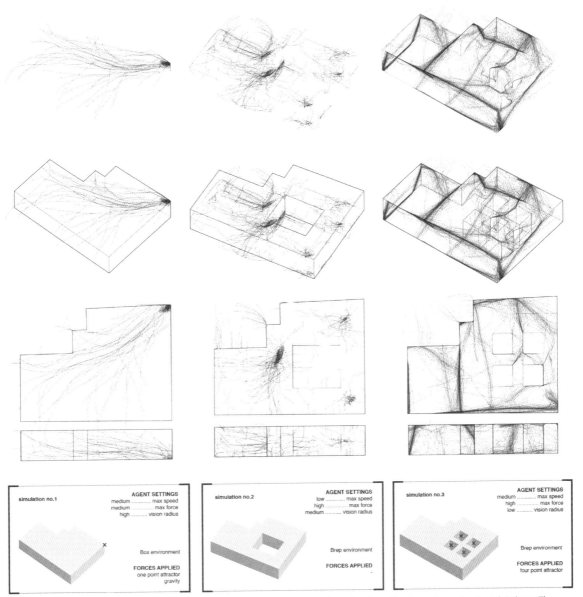

Figure 14.20. Swarm simulation within a specified boundary. Drawing and simulation by Miguel Escribano. Instructor, Patrick Delorey. The Bernard and Anne Spitzer School of Architecture, City College of New York. *Courtesy of the author.*

Endnotes

1. Marcel Bernard, "Real Learning Through Flight Simulation," FAA Safety Briefing, July/August 2012, https://www.faa.gov/news/safety_briefing/2012/media/SepOct2012ATD.pdf.
2. David Ross Scheer, *The Death of Drawing: Architecture in the Age of Simulation* (New York: Routledge, 2014).
3. Eric Winsberg, *Science in the Age of Computer Simulation* (Chicago: University of Chicago Press, 2010).
4. http://www.ladybug.tools/ladybug.html.
5. Arturo Tedeschi, *AAD_Algorithms-Aided Design: Parametric Strategies Using Grasshopper* (Brienza, Italy: Le Penseur, 2014).
6. Ibid.
7. Daniel Piker, "Project Kangaroo: Live 3D Physics for Rhino/Grasshopper, Update," Space Symmetry Structure: Journeys in the Apeiron (blog), January 21, 2010, https://spacesymmetrystructure.wordpress.com/2010/01/21/kangaroo/.
8. Tedeschi, *AAD_Algorithms-Aided Design*.
9. Craig Reynolds, "Flocks, Herds, and Schools: A Distributed Behavioral Model," SIGGRAPH '87 Proceedings of the 14th Annual Conference on Computer Graphics and Interactive Techniques, Maureen C. Stone, ed. (New York: ACM, 1987).
10. http://quelea.alexjfischer.com/.

Chapter 15
Robotics and Physical Computing

Chapter 15 describes current uses of robotics and physical computing technologies in architectural design, visual representation, and manufacturing. Industrial robots, autonomous robots, microcontrollers, sensors, and actuators provide novel methods for the fabrication and assembly of modular architectural systems, sensing data, and creating visualizations. These tools also open up opportunities to design kinetic systems that are responsive and interactive, creating a shift from static to dynamic environments. Through the use of robotics and physical computing, experimental drawings that are based in automation are emerging as methods for creating geometric patterns and formal and spatial representations, by conflating the use of traditional drawing instruments with mechanical devices that are computationally controlled.

15.1 Robotics

In 1948, the American mathematician Norbert Weiner coined the term cybernetics, from the Greek word *kybernetes,* meaning "governor." Cybernetics was also defined in the title of his book *Cybernetics, or Control and Communication in the Animal and the Machine.* Cybernetics stems from the field of psychology, and shifted from traditional studies of the brain as an organ of knowledge (memories, images, and representations) to an understanding of the brain as an organ of performance (tied to the body's ability to survive and adapt).[1] In his book, *The Cybernetic Brain: Sketches of Another Future,* Andrew Pickering provides a preliminary definition of cybernetics as a postwar science of the adaptive brain. The study of cybernetics was approached through making electromechanical devices that were adaptive and could be understood as models for the brain.[2]

Although cybernetics emerged from psychology, it has influenced many other fields, including robotics, politics, engineering, architecture, music, and more. One of the earliest examples of robotics came from one of the pioneers in cybernetics, Grey Walters, who developed a series of small, autonomous electro-mechanical robots, which he titled *Machina speculatrix,* and which he called tortoises due to their shape and slow movement. They had three wheels that were powered by electric motors, and they could react to obstacles and light. The robots served as models to demonstrate how simple connections in the brain could create complex behaviors. They were influential to the current field of robotics, the branch of engineering that deals with the design of robots, mechanical machines that are programmed by a computer that can carry out tasks automatically.

Industrial Robots

Industrial robots are automated, programmable robotic systems that are used primarily for manufacturing. The first industrial robot, called the Unimate, was developed in 1958 by Joseph Engelberger, an American engineer and entrepreneur. The Unimate robot was a hydraulically powered, big, strong arm that could go through a series of motions, moving from place to place, to carry out actions repeatedly.[3] Engelberger convinced automotive manufacturers in Detroit that these robots would be more cost efficient, and after this proved to be true, hydraulically controlled robots used in the automotive industry flourished in the United States, Japan, and Europe.[4] Approximately 20 years later, electrically powered robotic arms were developed that contained multiple axes designed to simulate the movement of a human arm. These robotic arms developed into the electronic industrial robots of today, which are used as a standard means of production in the automotive industry. (See Figure 15.1.) They can be

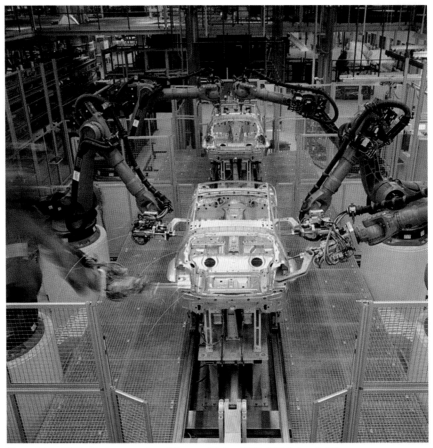

Figure 15.1. KUKA robots on an automobile assembly line, 2013. *KUKA Systems GmbH.*

programmed to repeat tasks such as gripping and assembling parts, welding, spraying, and other tasks with extreme precision. They can also be arranged to work in tandem with one another in an assembly line for mass production purposes. Unlike human labor, industrial robots can perform these tasks over and over without getting tired, and can operate with materials and under conditions that are typically hazardous for humans, such as rooms that have airborne toxic chemicals.

Although industrial robots have been utilized in the automotive industry for many decades, it wasn't until more recently that they were implemented into architectural design and construction processes. Even today, their use is primarily within academic and research settings and is just beginning to play a role in the process of fabricating buildings, as new possibilities continue to develop. Beginning in the 2000s, architectural research in academic institutions began to utilize industrial robots for the fabrication of building systems. At the ETH Zürich, Gramazio Kohler Research focuses on additive methods for fabricating nonstandard architectural assemblies. In 2005, they began to use robotic technologies to assemble brick structures. This propagated an interest in academia and industry to study robotically driven procedures that dealt with both standard and nonstandard approaches toward assemblies. A research project that demonstrates this approach to robotic fabrication is the Hestnes Column, designed and fabricated at the Digital Fabrication Laboratory (DFL), at the Faculty of Architecture of the University of Porto (FAUP). In this project, robotic technologies are explored as a method for rethinking traditional methods of designing brick structures.[5] The arrangement and stacking of the bricks are influenced by the work of the Portuguese architect Raúl Hestnes Ferreira, who designed structures in which the tectonic arrangements of the bricks are intertwined, using traditional hand-laying brick construction techniques. The Hestnes Column project is based on a computational model and incorporates robotic fabrication processes through the use of a KUKA industrial robot and a KUKA vacuum gripper, which picks up and places EPS bricks in the form of a twisted column with variable openings. (See Figures 15.1, 15.2, and 15.3.) The robotic motions are controlled using the KUKA|prc plug-in for Grasshopper, which converts the movements and speeds necessary for the geometric configuration into the language of the robot.

Figure 15.2. José Pedro Sousa, Hestnes Column, 2015. Digital Fabrication Laboratory (DFL), CEAU/FAUP. Kuka industrial robot programmed to assemble bricks; detail of the gripping mechanism. *Courtesy of DFL.*

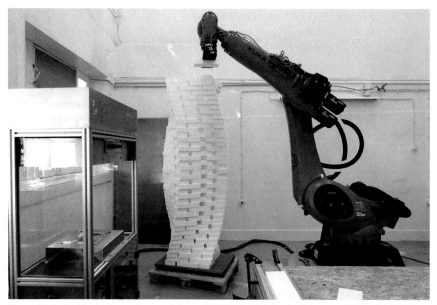

Figure 15.3. José Pedro Sousa, Hestnes Column, 2015. Digital Fabrication Laboratory (DFL), CEAU/FAUP. Kuka industrial robot programmed to assemble bricks to form a twisted column. *Courtesy of DFL.*

Figure 15.4. José Pedro Sousa, Hestnes Column, 2015. Digital Fabrication Laboratory (DFL), CEAU/FAUP. Curvature of the robotically assembled brick column. *Courtesy of DFL.*

Industrial robots are also being used to explore new methods for creating visual representations. Novel processes for producing drawings, paintings, and imagery are being explored through experiments that conflate traditional mediums with robotic technologies—for example, attaching representational tools such as cameras, pens, extruders, lights, paintbrushes, and other instruments and end effectors to the robotic arm. The artist group robotlab, based in Germany, is one example of artists who are testing the possibilities for combining traditional methods of drawing with computation, robotics, computer vision, and other technologies. In their installation "profiler" (2004), a wall of light serves as a background for people to stand in front of and pose. (See Figure 15.5.) The robot moves into position to capture an image of the person with its "video eye" (camera). The computer processes the image and translates it into a set of lines that are drawn by the robot with a marker on a drawing board. (See Figure 15.6.) The drawing produced by this systematic process results in unforeseeable formations and compositions of single, grouped, and overlapping silhouettes.

Figure 15.5. robotlab, "profiler," 2004. Collage of human silhouettes captured with the robot's video eye and drawn by the robot. *Courtesy of robotlab.*

These methods for using robots as tools for exploring topics of animation, projection, sensing, time-lapse capture, luminosity, and more are evolving the possibilities for drawing, pattern making, mapping, imagery, visual thinking, and new ways of seeing. For example, the Robot House at SCI-Arc (Southern California Institute of Architecture) is exploring real-time imaging and projection mapping to generate visualizations, using the robot as an image-inducing apparatus.[6] At the Consortium for Research and Robotics, Pratt Institute, both fabrication and representational methods are being explored in various ways. The "4DRLD-Object-1" (robotic light drawing) produced by the artist Mark Parsons, visualizes the movement of the industrial robot by illuminating the end of the arm to trace digital tool paths in a long exposure image. (See Figure 15.7.)

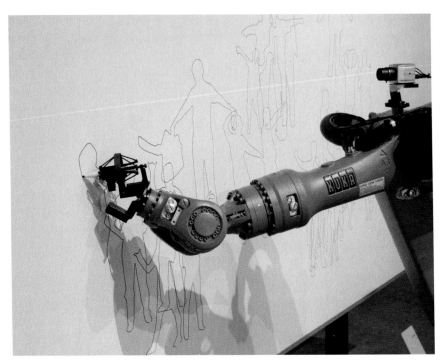

Figure 15.6. robotlab, "profiler," 2004. Collage of human silhouettes drawn by the robot (detail). *Courtesy of robotlab.*

Figure 15.7. Artist Mark Parsons @ Consortium for Research and Robotics, Pratt Institute, *4DRLD-Object-1*, 2015. Robotic light drawings using the IRB 6700 and the IRB 1600 with illuminated end-of-arm tools to trace digital tool paths through long-exposure images. *Courtesy of the Consortium for Research and Robotics.*

Autonomous Robots

In his book *Vehicles: Experiments in Synthetic Psychology,* Valentino Braitenberg, the Italian neuroscientist and cyberneticist, describes thought experiments through detailed explanations and diagrams of hypothetical analog "vehicles" that move around autonomously based on the input of sensors.[7] These mobile mechanical devices, known as Braitenberg vehicles, use sensors to measure analog values (such as temperature and light) that actuate mechanical elements (such as motors that control spinning wheels). The vehicles can be goal directed (for example, moving toward the light source), or directed away from the light source. In environments with multiple stimuli, the movement of the vehicles becomes complex, which results in the vehicles appearing to have behaviors and intelligence, such as aggression, knowledge, and memory.

These psychological experiments provide insight into concepts related to our perception and understanding of intelligence, empathy, feelings, and their relationship to machines. Among other things, the Braitenberg vehicles have been influential in current research in robotics and the design of autonomous machines, their abilities to perform tasks, and the development of artificial intelligence (AI).

The uses of autonomous robots in architectural design are being explored in various ways, and opening up new possibilities for design and fabrication. For example, a semi-autonomous robotic system, developed at the Institute for Computational Design (ICD), University of Stuttgart, is exploring the potential for mobile construction machines capable of operating on-site to expand the capabilities of on-site fiber composite fabrication.[8] In this scenario, wall climbing, semi-autonomous robots are used to weave a doubly curved, hollow fiber structure. At the California College of the Arts (CCA), Jason Kelly Johnson of Future Cities Lab is exploring the potentials of autonomous robotic fabrication through projects such as *Geoweaver,* a mobile 3D printing robot that eliminates the dimensional constraints of typical 3D printing beds, through the use of a thermoplastic printing walking robot. (See Figure 15.8.) In his design studio, Creative Architecture Machines, co-taught with Michale Shiloh, students explored the use of autonomous robots to fabricate three-dimensional constructs. This includes the work of Alan Cation and Clayton Muhleman, whose project Swarmscapers proposes to use multiple autonomous robots to construct structures. In this speculative project, the use of multiple, on-site, mobile, autonomous robots are used to 3D print large-scale structures out of composite materials over various terrains. (See Figures 15.9 and 15.10.)

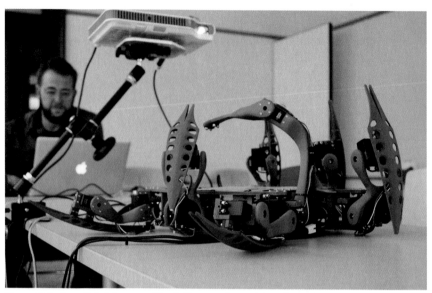

Figure 15.8. Jason Kelly Johnson and Nataly Gattegno, Future Cities Lab, Metabot Zoo, 2014. One of the *Metabot Zoo* creative architecture machines, exhibited at the *Eliciting Environments | Actuating Response* symposium and exhibition, Carnegie Mellon University, School of Architecture. *Courtesy of Future Cities Lab.*

Figure 15.9. Alan Cation and Clayton Muhleman, Swarmscapers, 2014. Autonomous robot prototype, Creative Architecture Machines studio, Instructors, Jason Kelly Johnson and Michael Shiloh, California College of the Arts, Architecture Division. *Courtesy of Alan Cation.*

Figure 15.10. Alan Cation and Clayton Muhleman, Swarmscapers, 2014. Autonomous robot 3D-printed structure, Creative Architecture Machines studio, Instructors, Jason Kelly Johnson and Michael Shiloh, California College of the Arts, Architecture Division. *Courtesy of Alan Cation.*

15.2 Physical Computing

Physical computing platforms provide a means of connecting physical and digital worlds. In architectural design, physical computing technologies can be used to create interactive and responsive objects, devices, and environments, through the use of microcontrollers, sensors, and actuators. *Microcontroller* boards are small computers that have programmable input and output peripherals. *Sensors* are devices that detect changes in the environment, such as light, sound, temperature, or movement, which are sent to the microcontroller as input data. *Actuators* are mechanisms that are used to operate a physical device, such as a servo, LED light, motor, or valve, and are controlled by the microcontroller through output data. This ability to input (sense) information and output (actuate) a response creates opportunities for the design of feedback loops and self-regulating systems. (See Figure 15.11.) This concept stems from cybernetics, which is the science of control

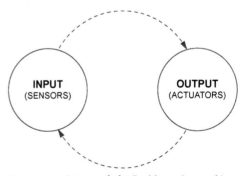

Figure 15.11. Diagram of a feedback loop. *Courtesy of the author.*

277

and communication within humans, animals, and machines. In the late 1960s, author, inventor, and theorist Gordon Pask made significant contributions to cybernetics. In his article "The Architectural Relevance of Cybernetics," Pask describes how buildings are not simply isolated structures but part of a larger system, which includes human occupants and "interacts with its inhabitants," creating a "mutualism" between structures and societies.[9] Therefore, architecture, as a built structure has an effect upon its occupants and environment and is part of a larger cybernetic system. This requires architects to design architectural systems as dynamic rather than static entities.[10]

Figure 15.12. Philip Beesley, Living Architecture Systems Group, *Hylozoic Ground*, 2010, Canadian Pavilion, Venice Biennale, Venice, Italy. Photograph of the responsive architectural environment. *Courtesy of Philip Beesley Architect Inc.*

Through the development of current physical computing platforms and other nascent digital technologies, architects and designers are continuing to explore and advance the opportunities for designing dynamic and responsive architectural systems. This includes exploring the use of microcontrollers, sensors, and actuators and their integration with traditional and contemporary materials. This shift from architecture that is static to architecture that is dynamic prompts a whole range of questions and establishes new territories for investigating "living" architectural systems and their impact and relationships to humans, nature, environments, cities, landscapes, ecologies, and more.

The work of the architect and artist Philip Beesley explores the possibility for environments that create chains of reflexive responses to inhabitants of the space. In the project *Hylozoic Ground*, designed as the Canadian Pavilion at the Venice Biennale in 2010, visitors move freely among hundreds of kinetic devices within an interactive environment.[11] (See Figure 15.12.) The work of the architect Behnaz Farahi explores the interface between sensing, interactive media, and architecture to design architectures that are responsive to user feedback, movements, and emotions.

Figure 15.13. Behnaz Farahi, *Alloplastic Architecture,* 2012. Adaptive tensegrity structure that responds to human movement. *Courtesy of Behnaz Farahi.*

In her research project *Alloplastic Architecture,* a tensegrity structure is designed to respond to the movement of a dancer. The dancer's gestures are tracked by a Kinect motion-sensing device that recognizes bodily movements and depth, and also has the ability to learn from the users over time.[12] (See Figure 15.13.) Her project *Caress of the Gaze* is a 3D-printed wearable device that serves as an interface using facial recognition technologies to capture facial expressions of others. This input information is used to actuate various responses through subtle movements in the garment that reflects different emotions. (See Figure 15.14.)

Figure 15.14. Behnaz Farahi, *Caress of the Gaze,* 2015. Interactive 3D-printed gaze-actuated wearable. *Courtesy of Behnaz Farahi.*

In the project *pneuSENSE,* a responsive architectural installation developed for the IaaC Global Summer School, New York, the geometry for a pneumatic structure was developed through the use of various urban data that was acquired with sensors while walking around New York City. This included biometric and environmental data collected from sensors that measured phenomena such as heart rate, sound, light, CO_2 levels, and more. A GPS tracking device allowed for the collected data to be matched to its specific location within the city. The pneumatic device served as a visualization of this data, while additional real-time r incorporated through biometric sensors. Users could "plug in" to the installation to measure their heart rate, or breathe out to measure carbon dioxide levels, which would actuate various responses through LED lighting effects and sounds. (See Figure 15.15.)

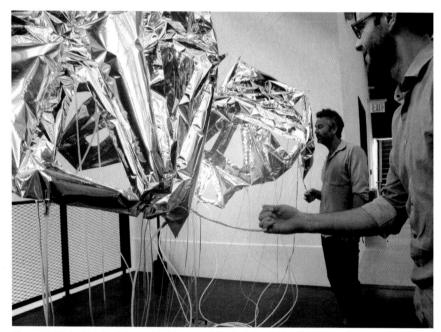

Figure 15.15. Institute for Advanced Architecture of Catalonia (IaaC), Global Summer School, NYC, *pneuSENSE,* 2016. Interactive pneumatic architectural intervention that is responsive to biometric data. *Courtesy of the author.*

The *Interactive Artifacts* research project by Nancy Diniz of Augmented Architectures explores the use of physical computing platforms to design responsive architectural devices that operate at multiple scales, ranging from the scale of a wearable device on the body to the scale of a component on a building facade. The prototypes integrate sensing and actuation technologies to open and close modular units based on the user's proximity to the building facade, allowing for changes in light levels and ventilation in relation to their location within the building. (See Figure 15.16.)

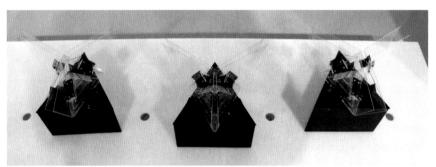

Figure 15.16. Nancy Diniz, *Interactive Artifacts,* 2014. Exhibited at *Design and Research: Shared Territories,* curated by the Design Research Institute, XJTLU, October 28–November 11, 2014, Suzhou China. *Courtesy of Nancy Diniz.*

The research project *Soft Robotic Architectures,* by Nancy Diniz and Frank Melendez of Augmented Architectures, explores the use of soft robotic systems in architectural design. Unlike mechanical robots that are made out of hard materials such as metal, these robotic systems utilize soft materials such as silicone that promote human interaction and tactile experiences. Rather than using mechanical devices for actuation, such as servos, the project generates soft actuations, through the use of fluids, such as air and water, to create bending movements. These movements act more like muscles that expand and contract. The prototype demonstrates how these muscle-like movements can be used to create dynamic, corporeal, architectural envelopes that bend, expand, contract, open and close, based on input from sensors. This allows for the control of airflow and light levels and mediation between interior and exterior spaces. (See Figure 15.17.)

Figure 15.17. Nancy Diniz and Frank Melendez, Augmented Architectures, *Soft Robotic Architectures,* 2017. Prototype for a soft robotic architectural wall system that uses computationally controlled pneumatic actuation to bend, expand, contract, open, and close. *Courtesy of © Augmented Architectures.*

15.3 Arduino Hardware and Software

One popular and commonly used platform for getting started with robotics and physical computing is Arduino. The Arduino platform is an open-source computer hardware and software that consists of two major parts: the Arduino microcontroller board and the Arduino IDE (Integrated Development Environment). The Arduino microcontroller board is the hardware, consisting of a processor, memory, and input/output (I/O) pins that can be used to connect sensors and actuators. (See Figure 15.18.) The Arduino IDE is the software that provides an interface for creating sketches ("little computer programs"), debugging, and uploading sketches to the board.[13] (See Figure 15.19.)

Figure 15.18. The Arduino Uno microcontroller. *Courtesy of the author.*

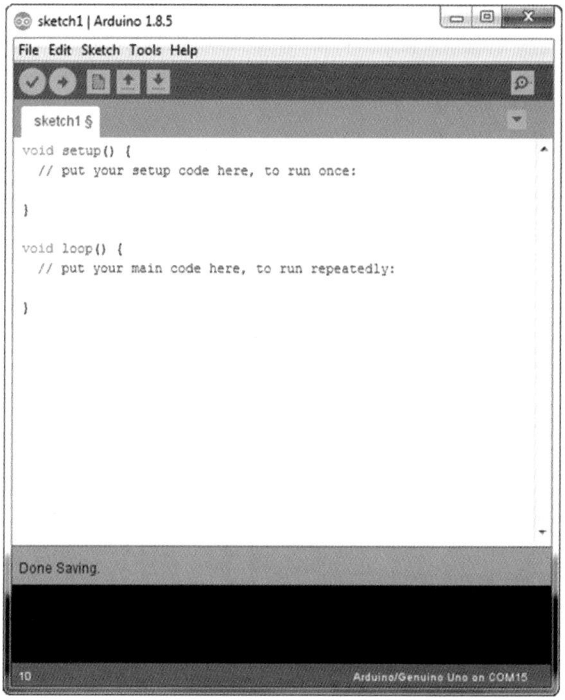

Figure 15.19. The Arduino IDE.

Hardware

There are various versions of Arduino boards. The Arduino Uno is one of the most commonly used microcontrollers for getting started with physical computing. The Arduino Uno microcontroller board consists of various elements that primarily fall within the categories of power, analog pins, digital pins, power pins, ground pins, a reset button, and the microcontroller. (See Figure 15.20.)

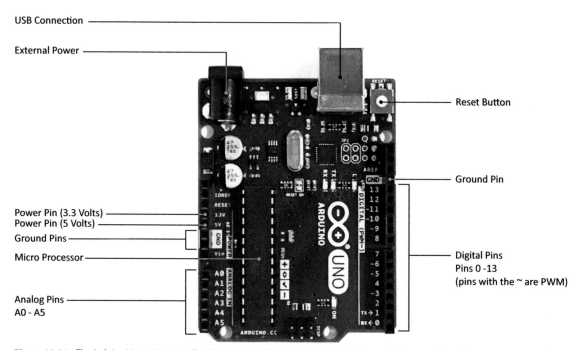

USB Connection

External Power

Reset Button

Ground Pin

Power Pin (3.3 Volts)
Power Pin (5 Volts)
Ground Pins
Micro Processor

Digital Pins
Pins 0 -13
(pins with the ~ are PWM)

Analog Pins
A0 - A5

Figure 15.20. The Arduino Uno microcontroller. Organization of the various parts and elements. *Courtesy of the author.*

Figure 15.21. Example of environmental sensors: photo cell sensors. *Courtesy of the author.*

There are two ways to power the Arduino Uno microcontroller board. The USB connection provides power to the board from your computer, and is also used to upload Arduino code from the Arduino IDE to the microcontroller board. There is also an external power connection that allows for powering the board through an external power source, such as a battery or wall socket. (Please note that working with power from wall sockets is very dangerous and should not be done without proper knowledge and experience of working with electrical power supplies.) The rows of pins that run along either side of the board allow for input, output, power, and ground. The analog pins provide inputs for analog information, which is information that has a continuous range of possible states.[14] This includes data captured from analog sensors, such as environmental and biometric sensors. Environmental sensors include photo cell sensors (for detecting changes in lighting levels), temperature sensors, humidity sensors, sound sensors, and many others. (See Figure 15.21.) Biometric sensors can be used to sense information from our bodies, such as heart rate sensors, dermal activity sensors, and many others. This "sensed" analog information can be captured and converted and output into digital information, which is information that is expressed as two possible outcomes, through the "digital" pins on the microcontroller board. These pins can be used to output data in a digital format to drive and control actuators. Actuators include mechanical devices such as light emitting diodes (LEDs), servos, motors, and many other mechanical devices. (See Figures 15.22 and 15.23.) The microprocessor is the "brains" of the Arduino Uno, which converts analog values into digital values. This information, along with power, can be used to control electronic devices. The Arduino Uno provides two power pins for outputting power as 5 volts or 3.3 volts, and three ground pins for grounding the circuit. Through the use of input and output data, physical computing workflows allow for prototyping systems that connect physical and digital worlds, providing new opportunities for designing responsive architectural systems.

Figure 15.22. Example of actuator: light-emitting diodes (LEDs). *Courtesy of the author.*

The Arduino IDE

The Arduino IDE provides a platform for writing, evaluating, and uploading code to the microcontroller board. The IDE interface consists of main menus, toolbars, file tabs, the workspace, and the sketch compiler. (See Figure 15.24.) New files can be created from the Main Menus, File menu. Arduino provides many example files that are useful for getting started, also accessible from the Main Menus, File menu, expanded Examples heading. (See Figure 15.25.) Additional resources are available and can be found on the Arduino website (www.arduino.cc). The Toolbar provides icons and tools for creating new files (New), opening files (Open), saving files (Save), as well as tools for verifying the code to check for errors (Verify), and uploading the code to the microcontroller board (Upload). (See Figure 15.26.)

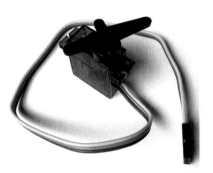

Figure 15.23. Example of actuator: micro servo. *Courtesy of the author.*

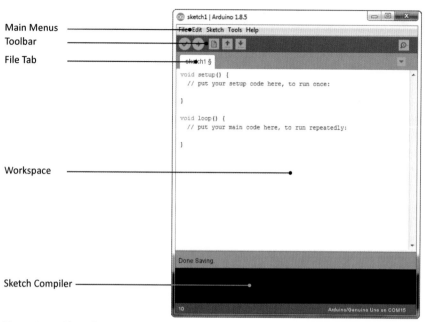

Main Menus

Toolbar

File Tab

Workspace

Sketch Compiler

Figure 15.24. The Arduino IDE Interface. *Courtesy of the author.*

Figure 15.25. The Arduino IDE File menu accessed to open example files. *Courtesy of the author.*

Figure 15.26. The Arduino IDE Toolbar (from left to right): Verify, Upload, New, Open, and Save.

The microcontroller board can be powered by physically connecting the Arduino Uno microcontroller board with a standard A-B USB cable to the computer's USB port. Connection between the IDE and microcontroller board is established by selecting the Arduino Uno board from the Main Menus, Tools menu, and also selecting the correct Port, also under the Main Menus, Tools menu. (See Figure 15.27.) The Arduino IDE is written in the programming language Java, and is based on the Processing language and IDE. The structure and syntax of Arduino text-based code consists of two parts: void setup and void loop. The "void setup" function provides the block of code that instructs the board and runs once, while the "void loop" function provides the block of code for instructions that repeat over and over until prompted to stop.

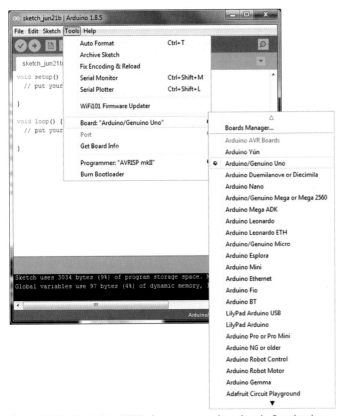

Figure 15.27. The Arduino IDE Tools menu accessed to select the Board and the Port. *Courtesy of the author.*

Blinking an LED

To blink an LED light using Arduino, begin by opening the Arduino IDE. Open the sketch for blinking an LED, which can be found in the example files, by navigating to File, Examples, 01.Basics, Blink. A slightly different version of this sketch, shown below, lists the microcontroller's pin 13 as the OUTPUT parameter under the "void setup ()" function. The "void loop()" function is used to define the blinking pattern of the LED by using two constants, HIGH and LOW. When the pin is set to OUTPUT, the HIGH value is 3.3 or 5.0 volts, which turns the LED on, and the LOW value is 0 volts, which turns the LED off. Each statement in the Arduino programming language ends with a semicolon.

```
void setup(){
    pinMode(13, OUTPUT);
}

void loop(){
    digitalWrite(13, HIGH);
    delay(100);
    digitalWrite(13, LOW);
    delay(100);
}
```

Connect an LED to the microcontroller board. LEDs have two "legs" that are different lengths, one short and one long. These are designed this way to identify the anode and cathode of the diode, in order to define the flow of current. The long leg is the anode, which is positive, and the short leg is the cathode, which is negative. Place the anode leg into pin 13 and the cathode leg into the adjacent ground pin.

Connect your Arduino microcontroller to your computer's USB port. Click on the Upload button in the Arduino IDE toolbars to upload the sketch to the microcontroller board. The LED should begin to blink, by turning on and off. The parameter of the delay function is the value of time, in milliseconds (1000 milliseconds equals one second), used to turn the LED on or off. By changing this parameter, and uploading the sketch to the board, the LED will begin to blink (turn on and off) at a different speed.

Prototyping

Connecting sensors and actuators directly to the Arduino is very limiting, and in most cases not possible. In order to quickly prototype various sensors and actuators, the use of solderless breadboards, jumper wires, and resistors allows for quickly connecting, completing, and testing circuits and controlling the flow of electrical currents. (See Figure 15.28.) Breadboards contain rows of holes that are connected by rows of metal strips. These holes are used to fit wires and pins of various sensors and actuators so they can be pushed in or out quickly to complete circuits without having to solder. (See Figure 15.29.)

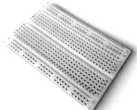

Figure 15.29. A standard bread-board. *Courtesy of the author.*

Figure 15.28. An example of using breadboards and jumper wires for prototyping. *Courtesy of the author.*

Wires are typically insulated and available in two varieties: solid core and stranded core. Solid core wires are stiffer and useful for prototyping because they fit easily into the breadboard; however, they are less flexible. Stranded core has fine strands of wire that are softer, requiring a header to insert into the breadboard, however, many presized stranded wires with headers are available and are typically included in starter kits.[15] (See Figure 15.30.) Resistors are used to control the flow of power in a circuit by converting electrical energy into heat. (See Figure 15.31.) This prevents the undesirable condition of creating a short circuit, by providing resistance in the circuit.[16] Resistance is measured in *ohms*, and the amount of resistance in a circuit varies depending on the amount of input and output power required to actuate electronic devices. The amount of resistance necessary in a circuit can be calculated using Ohm's law, which is $I = V/R$, where I is the current, measured in amps; V is the voltage, measured in volts; and R is the resistance, measured in ohms. Many different resistors are available to control varying amounts of current, and the amount of resistance of resistors can be identified using the color-coding system, which includes the use of a resistance chart and the bands of colors on the resistor.

Figure 15.30. Jumper wires. *Courtesy of the author.*

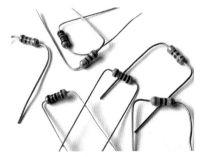

Figure 15.31. Resistors. *Courtesy of the author.*

Rotating a Micro Servo

To rotate a micro servo using Arduino, begin by opening the Arduino IDE. Open the sketch for rotating a servo, which can be found in the example files, by navigating to File, Examples, Servo, Sweep. The code (listed below) begins by calling servo from a library. The Arduino IDE comes with pre-installed libraries, which provide sketches with extra functionality. Additionally, libraries can also be installed and created. The "#include" statement is used to call the library, in this case, the Servo.h library. The rotational position of the servo is based on a variable which is declared as an integer, "int pos = 0;". In the "void setup()" function, pin 9 is declared as the output pin. The "void loop" function is used to define the parameters of the servo's rotation, which is set to rotate within a range of 0 to 180 degrees in increments of 1, and pausing for 10 milliseconds (delay), in between each incremental rotation. This is repeated continuously in a loop until the servo reaches 180 degrees, at which point it reverses back to 0 degrees, back to 180, and so on.

```
#include <Servo.h>

Servo myservo;

int pos = 0;

void setup(){
   myservo.attach(9);
}

void loop(){
   for (pos = 0; pos <= 180; pos += 1){
      myservo.write(pos);
      delay(10);
   }
   for (pos = 180; pos >= 0; pos -= 1){
      myservo.write(pos);
      delay(10);
   }
}
```

Connect the micro servo to digital pin 9, the ground pin, and the 5V power pin, using a breadboard and jumper wires, based on the wiring diagram. (See Figure 15.32.)

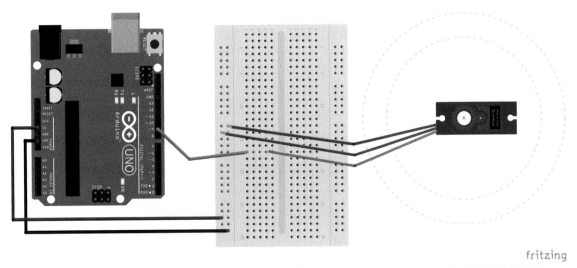

fritzing

Figure 15.32. Wiring diagram: connecting a micro-servo to an Arduino Uno microcontroller through the use of a breadboard. Diagram created with Fritzing. *Courtesy of author.*

Connect your Arduino microcontroller to your computer's USB port. Click on the Upload button in the Arduino IDE toolbars to upload the sketch to the microcontroller board. The micro servo should begin to rotate from 0 to 180 degrees, back and forth, in a continuous sweeping motion. The parameters in the sketch can be modified to change the speed of rotation and the angle range.

Drawing Machines

Through the use of physical computing tools, various simple machines and devices can be constructed to perform automated tasks. Constructing such devices is useful for gaining a better understanding of the basics of robotic and physical computing technologies and their potential for designing architecture, landscape, and urban systems through the implementation of kinetics, automation, and fabrication processes. One useful method for achieving this involves creating experimental drawings through the use of automated drawing machines. By attaching pens and pencils to mechanical devices that are kinetic and automated, designers and artists can explore emergent patterns, linework, and geometry, which are produced through the device's computationally controlled movements. One example of a drawing machine is a scissor bot, which can create fluid, swaying mechanical motions through linear elements that are hinged together at their connections, to create a scissor-like structure. The end of the scissor structure can be connected to servos or motors, that are programmed to rotate with and Arduino Uno microcontroller and code, allowing the elements to move in a fluid, swaying motion. The opposite ends of the structure are connected to a drawing instrument, such as a pen or pencil. By adjusting the code's parameters to rotate the servos or motors at different speeds and/or different directions, a range of movements can be produced, resulting in various drawing patterns that are a visual recording of the movement of the tip of the pen. (See Figure 15.33.)

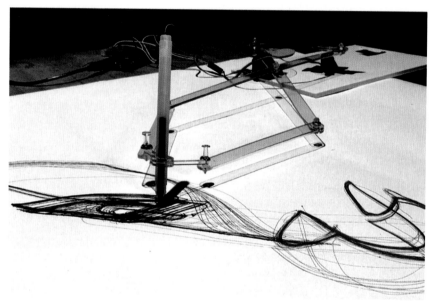

Figure 15.33. Hannah Deegan and Zara Tamton, scissor bot drawing machine. Instructor, Frank Melendez. The Bernard and Anne Spitzer School of Architecture, City College of New York. *Courtesy of the author.*

Another example of a drawing machine is a bristle bot, which creates a forward crawling motion. A bristle bot can be created with a few simple parts: an Arduino Uno microcontroller, angled bristles (e.g., toothbrush bristles), a platform (to create a flat plane, e.g., foam core), two vibrating motors, pens and/or pencils, and a 9-volt battery. Through the use of an offset weight, a motor will vibrate when it spins at a high speed. By supporting a platform with angled bristles, attaching two motors on one end of the platform, and drawing instruments, such as pens or pencils, to the opposite end of the platform, various crawling motions can be created by the vibrating effects of the motors. The Arduino Uno microcontroller and motors can be powered with a 9-volt battery, allowing the bot to move autonomously. The Arduino code can be modified to change the parameters of the motor rotation speed and duration, yielding different movements of the bot and tracings of this motion, resulting in various line weights, line types, patterns, and drawings. (See Figures 15.34 and 15.35.)

Figure 15.34. Nancy Diniz and Frank Melendez, Augmented Architectures. *Bristle bot drawings.* Courtesy of © Augmented Architectures.

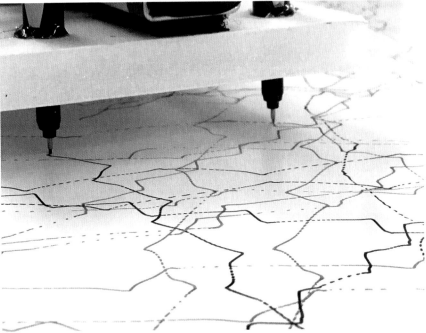

Figure 15.35. Nancy Diniz and Frank Melendez, Augmented Architectures. *Bristle bot drawings.* Linework detail. Courtesy of © Augmented Architectures.

Firefly

In addition to writing text-based code within the Arduino IDE, the Arduino micro-controller can be programmed through the software Firefly, a visual programming add-on for Grasshopper developed by Jason Kelly Johnson of Future Cities Lab and Andrew Payne of LIFT Architects. Firefly allows for near real-time data flow between the Grasshopper environment and the Arduino microcontroller.[17] This provides a plat-form for controlling 3D models in Rhino that are responsive to real-time data that is captured through sensors. (See Figure 15.36.)

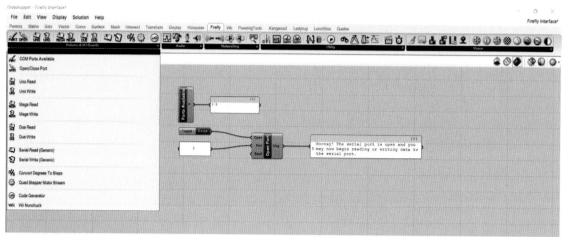

Figure 15.36. The Firefly tab, panels, and components. *Courtesy of the author.*

The Arduino Uno can be connected to the Grasshopper interface through the visual-programming components available in Firefly. Connect the Arduino Uno microcontroller to a USB port on the computer. The Ports Available component is used to check the value of the Port number. The Open Port component can be used to open the Port using a Grasshopper Boolean Toggle component and setting it to "True." Once opened, this port can be connected to the Firefly Uno Read compo-nent. A Grasshopper Timer component can be connected to the Uno Read compo-nent. Right-clicking on the timer will allow access to various time interval settings, which set the duration rate for updating the model. Setting the interval to 20 ms (milliseconds) updates the data values in near real-time. When Panel components are connected to the analog and digital pin outputs of the Uno Read component, this numerical data can be read and used as input parameters. (See Figure 15.37.)

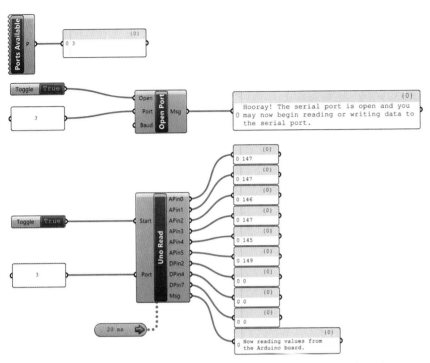

Figure 15.37. Firefly components: Ports Available, Open Port, and Uno Read. *Courtesy of the author.*

Through the use of sensors, these values can be read using Firefly, and input as parameters to drive digital, parametric models. For example, an environmental sensor, such as a photo cell sensor, can be connected to the Arduino Uno microcontroller board. The analog values that are captured with the sensor can be "remapped" and calibrated as digital values that can define and control variable parameters, resulting in a responsive and interactive parametric model. (See Figure 15.38.)

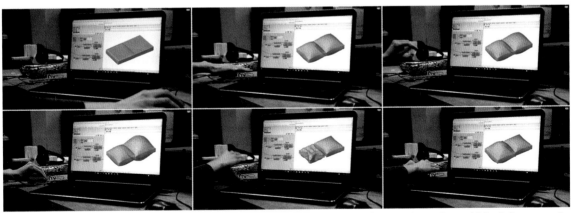

Figure 15.38. Frank Melendez and Nancy Diniz, Augmented Architectures, *Liquid Actuated Elastomers.* Interactive model simulating pneumatic behavior using Arduino, Firefly, and Kangaroo. *Courtesy of © Augmented Architectures.*

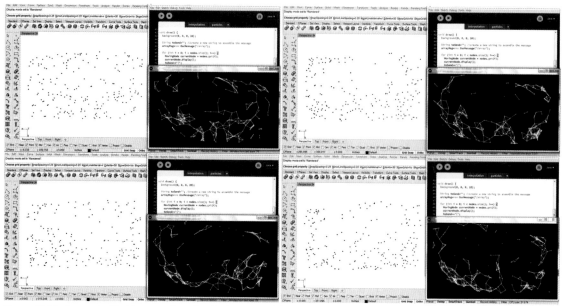

Figure 15.39. Augmented Architectures. Data visualizations created through the use of sensors, physical computing technologies, visual programming, text-based programming, and 3D modeling. *Courtesy of © Augmented Architectures.*

The ability to work with sensors, actuators, and physical computing technologies, has opened up new possibilities for architectural representation and design. Invisible, intangible, and temporal phenomena can be captured as data, and visualized through visual programming, text-based programming, and 3D modeling environments. (See Figures 15.39 and 15.40.) These computational frameworks provide architects and designers with opportunities to expand upon historical and traditional methods of representing architectural form, by simulating spatial and atmospheric phenomena through data visualizations and experimental drawings. This evolves the role of architectural drawing as a communicative instrument and design tool, allowing for novel modes of visualizing contemporary architectures that are based in computation, simulation, robotics, and physical computing technologies

Figure 15.40. Institute for Advanced Architecture of Catalonia (IaaC), Global Summer School, NYC, *pneuSENSE*, 2016. Data collection device with biometric and environmental sensors. *Courtesy of the author.*

Endnotes

1. Andrew Pickering, *The Cybernetic Brain: Sketches of Another Future* (Chicago: University of Chicago Press, 2010).
2. Ibid.
3. Rodney Brooks, *Flesh and Machines: How Robots Will Change Us* (New York: Vintage Books, 2001).
4. Ibid.
5. Rui Oliviera and Jose Pedro Sousa, "Building Traditions with Digital Research: Reviewing the Brick Architecture of Raúl Hestnes Ferreira through Robotic Fabrication," *eCAADe 2016: Complexity and Simplicity, Proceedings of the 34th International Conference on Education and Research in Computer Aided Architectural Design in Europe,* Aulikki Herneoja, Toni Österlund, and Pia Markkanen, eds.
6. Peter Testa, *Robot House: Instrumentation, Representation, Fabrication* (New York: Thames & Hudson, 2017).
7. Valentino Braitenberg, *Vehicles: Experiments in Synthetic Psychology* (Cambridge, MA: MIT Press, 1984).
8. Maria Yablonina, Marshall Prado, Ehsan Baharlou, and Tobias Schwinn. "Mobile Robotic Fabrication System for Filament Structures." In *Fabricate 2017*, by Achim Menges, Bob Sheil, Ruairi Glynn, and Marilena Skavara, 202–209. London: UCL Press, 2017, http://www.jstor.org/stable/j.ctt1n7qkg7.32.
9. Gordon Pask, "The Architectural Relevance of Cybernetics," *AD Reader: Computational Design Thinking,* Achim Menges and Sean Alquist, eds. (Chichester, UK: John Wiley & Sons, Ltd. 2011) 68–76.
10. Ibid.
11. Rob Gorbert, "Revealing the Hylozoic Ground Interaction Layer," *Hylozoic Ground: Liminal Responsive Architecture* Philip Beesley (Toronto: Riverside Architectural Press, 2010).
12. Behnaz Farahi, "Alloplastic Architecture," *Arch 2o,* https://www.arch2o.com/alloplastic-architecture-behnaz-farahi/.
13. Massimo Banzi, *Make: Projects, Getting Started with Arduino* (2nd ed.) (Sebastopol, CA: O'Reilly Media, 2011).
14. Dan O'Sullivan and Tom Igo, *Physical Computing: Sensing and Controlling the Physical World with Computers* (Mason, OH: Course Technology, CENGAGE Learning, 2004).
15. Ibid.
16. Ibid.
17. Jason Kelly Johnson and Andrew Payne, *Firefly Primer,* 2011, www.scribd.com/document/101073066/Firefly-Primer-1006.

Appendix: Design Drawing and Modeling Exercises

The following section contains a series of drawing, modeling, and visual programming exercises that are aimed toward providing a better understanding of the concepts, tools, and techniques described in this book. The exercises are chronological, covering a range of workflows required to create digital two-dimensional drawings, digital 3D models, digitally fabricated models, computational patterns, and mechanical devices controlled through the use of physical computing technologies. Analog methods are also used in various exercises, merging traditional and contemporary design drawing and modeling processes. The exercises are intended to establish a pedagogical framework for learning and teaching various methods for creating architectural drawings.

Drawing Exercises

Exercise 1: Drawing an Unrolled Truncated Cone

The purpose of this exercise is to gain a better understanding of descriptive geometry, projection techniques, and developable surfaces, while learning and developing two-dimensional digital drafting tools and skills.

This drawing composition consists of five projections of a truncated cone: a top view (plan), front view (elevation), side view (elevation), a view of the unrolled (developable) surface of the cone, and an auxiliary view ("true" elevation) of the truncated surface of the cone.

To complete this drawing, use Rhino 3D modeling tools to create points, lines, polylines, circles, and curves; replication tools, such as copy, ArrayPolar, and mirror; editing tools, such as trim and extend; and transformation tools, such as move and rotate. Use modeling aids to control the snap and ortho settings. Draft the linework at a 1:1 scale and constrained to the XY CPlane in the Top viewport.

To begin the drawing, set the units in the 3D model to inches, maximize the Top viewport, and draw the boundaries for a 24" (width) x 18" (height) sheet. Draw a circle to establish the radius of the cone's base, project side elevations, and establish the cone's height, and an elevation line to establish the starting edge of the unrolled surface. (See Exercise 1.1.)

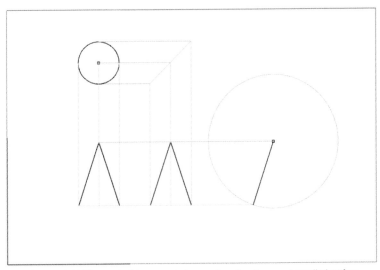

Exercise 1.1. Initial linework of the truncated cone plan, elevations, and unrolled surface area. *Courtesy of the author.*

Draw a diagonal line in the front view (elevation), to establish the angle at which the cone is sliced (truncated). Divide the circle into twelve equally spaced segments. Draw lines to project the division points onto the base of the cone in the elevations, and draw lines that connect these new points to the top of the cones to represent the cone segments in elevation. (See Exercise 1.2.)

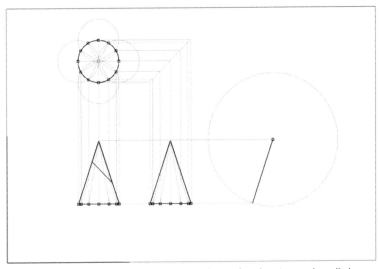

Exercise 1.2. Developed linework of the truncated cone plan, elevations, and unrolled surface area. *Courtesy of the author.*

Continue with descriptive geometry and projection techniques to draft the unrolled (developable) surface of the cone and the "true" elevation of the truncated shape that defines the top of the cone. Organize and format the drawing on a single sheet as a multi-view drawing that contains the five projections of the truncated cone. Export the linework to Adobe Illustrator to set up the sheet and assign various line weights and line types to emphasize the differences between construction lines, primary geometry, secondary geometry, and cut lines. (See Exercise 1.3.)

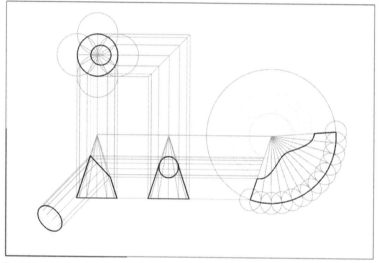

Exercise 1.3. Final drawing of the truncated cone plan, elevations, unrolled surface, and auxiliary elevation of the truncated surface. *Courtesy of the author.*

Create a physical model of the truncated cone using a plotted drawing that is scaled 2:1 so that the physical model is twice as big as the measurement of the digital drawing. To construct the model, adhere the drawing to a one-ply sheet of museum board using spray adhesive and cut out the following three shapes from the plotted drawing: the original circle (bottom of the cone), the unrolled shape (side of the cone), and the "true" elevation of the truncated shape (top of the cone). Inscribe the cone segment lines onto the surfaces that will be used as guidelines during the assembly process. Assemble the three pieces with glue and transparent tape, focusing on precision and craft while fabricating the model. (See Figure Exercise 1.4.)

Exercise 1.4. Final physical model of the truncated cone. *Courtesy of the author.*

Exercise 2: Drawing Axonometric Projections

This exercise continues with a focus on descriptive geometry and projection techniques and developing digital drafting skills, through the drawing of an axonometric (trimetric) projection, which is generated from a plan and using "fold" lines. Refer to the axonometric projection process diagram to understand the proportions, measurements, and geometrical relationships that describe the process for constructing the drawing. (See Exercise 2.1.) Create the drawing at a 1:1 scale and constrained to the XY CPlane in the Top viewport.

Begin the drawing in a new Rhino 3D model by maximizing the Top viewport, drafting an orthogonal, equally spaced grid, and placing three to four rectangular shapes (representing box forms) that are defined by the grid intersections. Draw a horizontal line, which will be the first "fold" line, and below this line, draw the front elevation of the box forms. Draw a second "fold" line that is rotated–30 degrees from the first "fold" line, and below this, project the box corner points using the A, B, distances in the plan. Connect these points with lines to create the first auxiliary view. Draw a third "fold" line that is rotated 60 degrees (in the opposite direction) from the second "floor" line and project the box corner points using the C, D, E, F distances from the elevation. Connect these points to create the second auxiliary view (the final axonometric projection) of the box forms.

Draft lines that visualize the projections of points, "construction" lines, to represent the geometrical relationships and construction process. Export the linework to Adobe Illustrator and assign various line weights and line types to represent the rectangular forms (heavy, continuous line type) and hidden geometry (medium weight, dashed line type), "fold" lines (medium weight, center line type), and "construction" lines (light weight, continuous line type). Add text to communicate elements and the various views that make up the drawing. (See Exercise 2.2.)

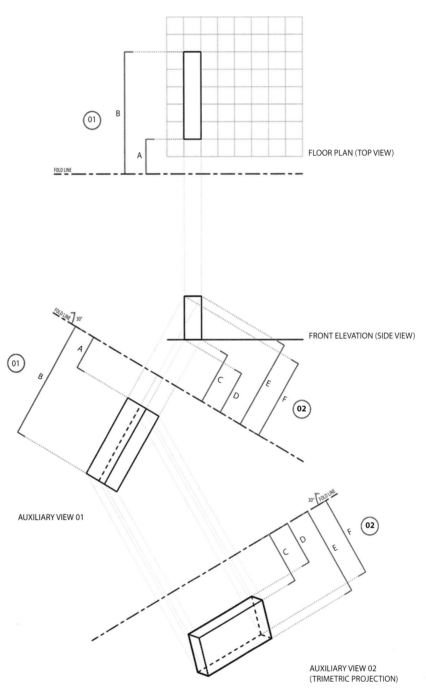

FLOOR PLAN (TOP VIEW)

FOLD LINE

FRONT ELEVATION (SIDE VIEW)

AUXILIARY VIEW 01

AUXILIARY VIEW 02
(TRIMETRIC PROJECTION)

Exercise 2.1. Diagram illustrating the steps for creating an axonometric projection using a plan, elevation, and "fold" lines. *Courtesy of the author.*

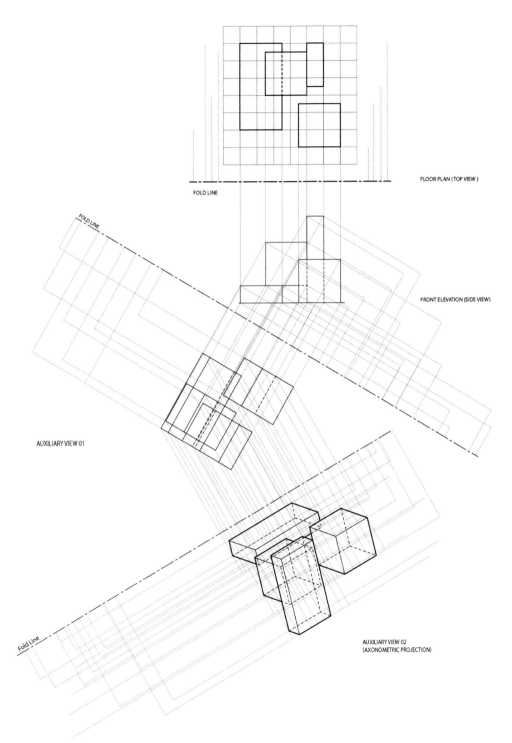

FLOOR PLAN (TOP VIEW)

FOLD LINE

FOLD LINE

FRONT ELEVATION (SIDE VIEW)

AUXILIARY VIEW 01

Fold Line

AUXILIARY VIEW 02
(AXONOMETRIC PROJECTION)

Exercise 2.2. Final drawing of an axonometric projection of box forms using a plan, elevation, and "fold" lines.
Courtesy of the author.

Exercise 3: Drawing a Section

This exercise focuses on developing an understanding of section drawings through the creation of a hybrid drawing that combines the use of digital drafting and hand-rendering techniques.

Begin the drawing by importing a raster image of a case study section drawing that has been saved in a JPEG or TIFF file format. Import and scale this image in Rhino's Top viewport using the Picture and Scale commands. Place the image on a "locked" layer and use the image as a guide to begin to trace over the image with line segments, polylines, and curves using 3D modeling tools and techniques. Create and use layers to organize the linework of the drawing. Import the linework into Adobe Illustrator to assign line weights and line types to the drawing, and print or plot the drawing out on a sheet of paper. (See Exercise 3.1.)

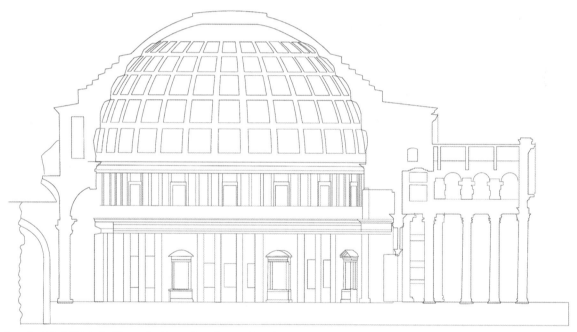

Exercise 3.1. Initial drafted linework of the section. *Courtesy of the author.*

The hand-rendering portion of this assignment is intended to introduce methods for shading a drawing with tones to represent light, shade, shadow, and material textures. Using a range of pencils (various B, HB, H lead weights), begin to add tone to the section drawing, to replicate the shading techniques of the original image. Create a wide range of tonal values, from dark to light, and replicate smooth transitions (gradients) where necessary (for example, round columns), to emphasize three-dimensional forms and add depth to the drawing. Additional linework and details can be "sketched" to create the illusion of intricate details and material textures. (See Exercise 3.2.) Through the use of digital and analog techniques, architectural drawings can be generated quickly and enhanced with tone to create depth, lighting effects, and material properties.

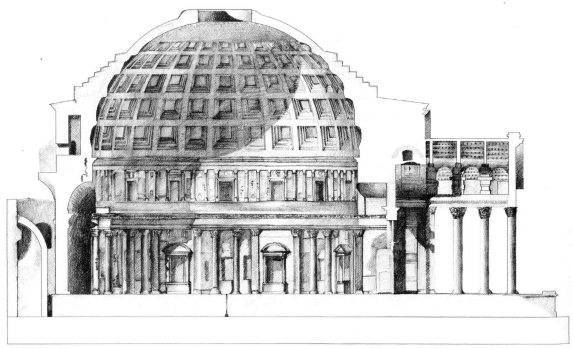

Exercise 3.2. Final hybrid (digital and analog) drawing of the digitally drafted, hand-rendered architectural section. Drawing by Ngawang Tenzin. Instructor, Frank Melendez. The Bernard and Anne Spitzer School of Architecture, City College of New York. *Courtesy of the author.*

3D Modeling Exercises

Exercise 4: 3D Modeling and Generating Axonometric Projections

In this exercise, a 3D model is created and used to generate a series of axonometric (isometric) projection drawings that represent the "void" space of an architectural massing model. This process introduces basic 3D modeling and projection tools, techniques, and workflows. The intent of this exercise is to develop the ability to understand solid-void relationships through the use of 3D models and axonometric drawings.

Begin the drawing in the Top viewport by creating an orthogonal grid, with equally spaced lines, parallel to the X and Y axes. Use various viewports to model a composition of three-dimensional cuboid forms (boxes) that are positioned and defined by the grid spacings, divisions, and intersections and extruded to various heights, and positions, in the positive Z axis. (See Exercise 4.1.)

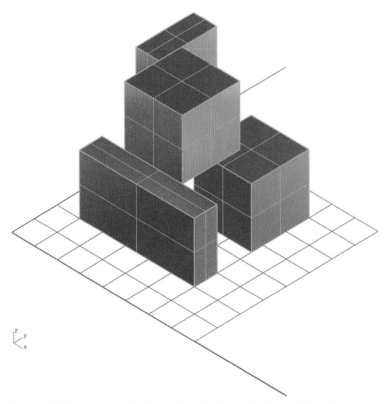

Exercise 4.1. Composition cuboid forms (boxes) in a 3D model. *Courtesy of the author.*

Create a bounding box in which all of the cuboid forms are contained. Create an inversion of the original model using the bounding box and original boxes, using the Boolean difference command. This results in a three-dimensional form and massing of the "void" spaces that are in between the composition of the original boxes. Use the preset NE, NW, SE, SW Isometric View options to establish the four different iso-metric views of the void geometry, and the Make 2D command to generate the axo-nometric projections. Export the linework to Adobe Illustrator and edit the linework of the drawing with line weights and line types to represent the massing of the forms (heavy, continuous line type), hidden massing geometry (medium weight, dashed line type), and grid lines (lightweight, continuous line type). Add text to communicate the various views that make up the drawing. (See Exercise 4.2.)

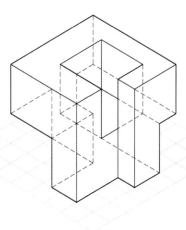

ISOMETRIC VIEW NW

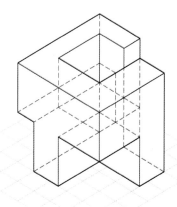

ISOMETRIC VIEW NE

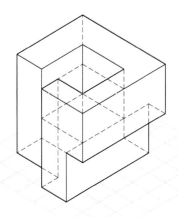

ISOMETRIC VIEW SW

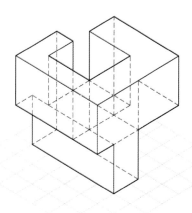

ISOMETRIC VIEW SE

Exercise 4.2. Final drawing of four axonometric projections of the box composition "void" space. *Courtesy of the author.*

Exercise 5: 3D Modeling and Fabrication

In this exercise, a cuboid form (box) is intersected with conical forms to create a stereotomic model with void spaces. This process continues to build and expand upon 3D modeling skills, and aids in developing an understanding of solid-void relationships. The exercise introduces digital fabrication workflows for creating physical models from models, using planar and developable surface geometry.

Begin by creating a 3D model of a solid cuboid (box) form. Model solid, tapered conical forms that intersect the cuboid form. Create a solid, tapered conical form by drawing and lofting two circles that are positioned on opposite planar surfaces of the box forms, capping the open faces of the lofted surface closed, and joining the loft and capped surfaces to make a polysurface. (See Exercise 5.1.)

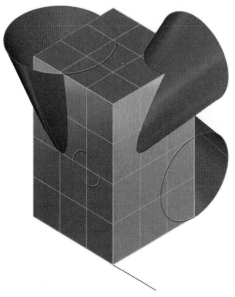

Exercise 5.1. A solid cuboid form with intersecting conical surfaces. *Courtesy of the author.*

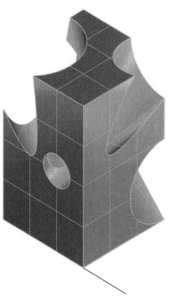

Use the Boolean Difference tool to subtract the solid, tapered conical forms from the cuboid form. This process will join all of the surfaces together as a single polysurface. Explode the polysurface in order to separate the model into discrete surfaces. (See Exercise 5.2.)

Create a two-dimensional, flattened representation of the shapes that form that 3D digital model by using tools such as the Unroll (for the conical, developable surfaces) and Rotate3D (for the box, planar surfaces) commands. Position all of the surfaces so that they are spaced out from each other and lay flat on the XY CPlane, Top viewport. (See Exercise 5.3.) Extract the curve boundaries of the surfaces to generate curves of the shapes. These curve objects will be used as the toolpaths for the laser-cut file.

Exercise 5.2. A final solid cuboid form with conical shaped voids. *Courtesy of the author.*

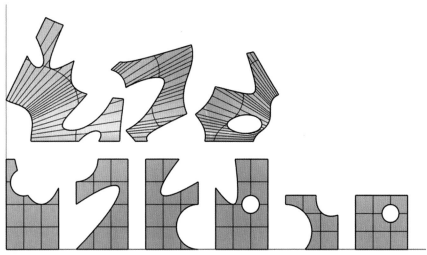

Exercise 5.3. Planar templates: faces and unrolled surfaces of the 3D model. *Courtesy of the author.*

Export the linework to AutoCAD or Adobe Illustrator to digitally fabricate the parts for the physical model, by using a laser cutter to cut the shapes out of two-ply chipboard or museum board. (Alternatively, plot or print out the drawing and adhere the plot or print to chipboard to cut out the parts of the model by hand.) Assemble the two-ply chipboard shapes to create the physical model of the stereotomic form, using a hot glue gun, and leave one face of the physical model removed. The physical model will be used as a mold for a plaster cast. Leave the open face of the physical model positioned so that it is facing upward. Line the mold with a release agent, such as diluted oil soap, and mix and pour plaster, Hydrocal, into the mold, until filled to the top of the mold. Once the plaster cures, tear and remove the chipboard surfaces from the plaster cast. (See Exercise 5.4.)

Exercise 5.4. Plaster casts of stereotomic forms that were fabricated from various 3D model templates. Models produced by first-year undergraduate architecture students. Instructor, Frank Melendez. The Bernard and Anne Spitzer School of Architecture, City College of New York. *Courtesy of the author.*

Exercise 6: 3D Modeling and Drawing Auxiliary View Projections

This exercise builds off of Exercises 2 and 4 and focuses on creating an axonometric drawing that illustrates the process of creating auxiliary views from a 3D model. The intent is to build and expand on 3D modeling skills and methods of creating projections based on the use of "fold" lines.

Continuing with the 3D model of solid cuboid forms from Exercise 4, select and move the model so that it is positioned below the XY Cplane. Create the first projection using the Make2D tool to project a plan view onto the XY CPlane. (See Exercise 6.1.)

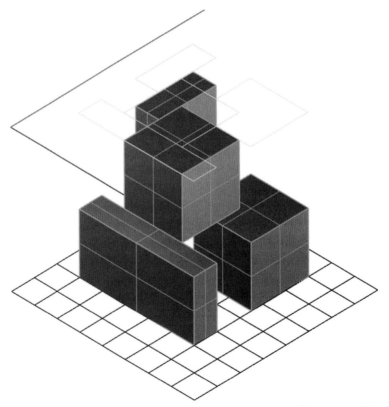

Exercise 6.1. 3D model of cuboid forms (boxes) projected onto the XY CPlane. *Courtesy of the author.*

Create a line segment that runs parallel to the X axis and that is positioned in the negative Y direction. This will be used as the first "fold" line, which will serve as an axis around which to 3D rotate a copy of the cuboid forms 90 degrees, below the XY CPlane. This copy will be used to create the second projection (the front elevation), onto the XY CPlane using the Make2D command. (See Exercise 6.2.)

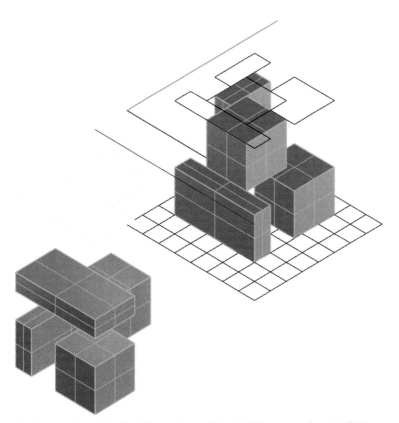

Exercise 6.2. 3D model with a 3D rotated copy of the cuboid forms around an axis ("fold" line) and projected onto the XY CPlane. *Courtesy of the author.*

Create another line segment that is rotated -30 degrees from the X axis. This line segment will be used as a second "fold" line, the axis around which to 3D rotate a copy of the previously rotated cuboid forms. This copy will be used to create the third projection onto the XY CPlane using the Make2D command. (See Exercise 6.3.)

Continue to create additional fold lines, which will serve as the axes to create additional 3D rotated copies of the cuboid forms, and 2D projections. Draw additional line segments, "fold" lines, at various angles, to show the relationships between the digital models and their corresponding projections, as well as the relationships between the various 2D projections. After all of the geometry is modeled, switch to an isometric view viewport to create a single axonometric drawing that illustrates the projection process that includes all of the geometry in the 3D model. Create an axonometric projection of this compilation of models, fold lines, and projections, using the Make2D command. Connect the various geometries with line segments to illustrate the projection of the points onto the XY CPlane as "construction" lines. Export the linework to Adobe Illustrator to set up the sheet and assign line weights and line types to represent the projected geometries, rectangular forms, hidden geometries, "fold" lines, and "construction" lines. Add text to communicate elements and the various views that make up the drawing. Plot or print the final drawing. (See Exercise 6.4.)

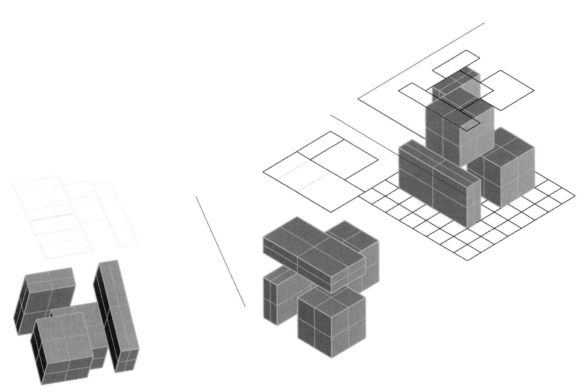

Exercise 6.3. 3D model with a third 3D rotated copy of the previously rotated cuboid forms around a second axis ("fold" line) and projected onto the XY CPlane. *Courtesy of the author.*

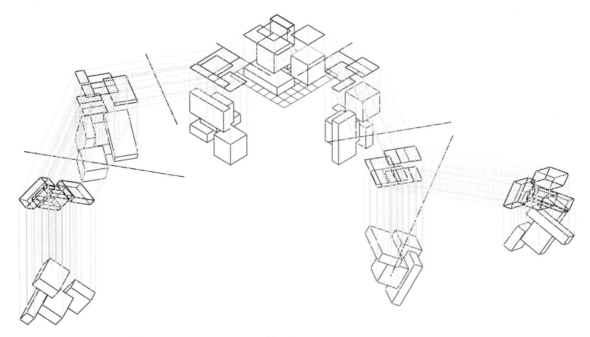

Exercise 6.4. Final drawing of the projection process. *Courtesy of the author.*

Computational Design Exercises
Exercise 7: Drawing 2D Parametric and Algorithmic Patterns

This exercise is intended to develop parametric and algorithmic design skills and digital fabrication workflows through the design and fabrication of architectural patterns and modules. These patterns can be modified to create three-dimensional pattern geometries, which can be output using rapid prototyping technologies, and used as molds to cast other materials. In this example, a two-dimensional pattern is generated using paneling techniques, modified to create three-dimensional geometry, 3D-printed to create a mold, and used to cast a flexible material, silicone. This exercise provides a visual-programming , Grasshopper definition, that is used to generate the pattern.

Begin by creating a new Rhino 3D model and modeling a planar surface on the XY CPlane in the Top viewport. Place a single point on the surface, which will be used as an "attractor" point to create incremental variation within the two-dimensional pattern. Using Grasshopper and Paneling Tools components, recreate the algorithmic definition illustrated below in Exercise 7.1, to create a triangular grid pattern on the surface that is distorted through the use of an attractor point. (See Exercise 7.2.)

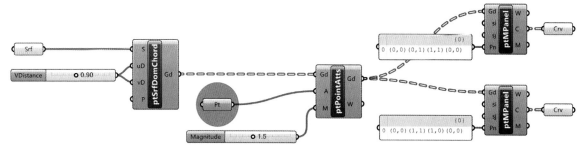

Exercise 7.1. Grasshopper definition used to create a non-uniform triangular grid pattern using Paneling Tools. *Courtesy of the author.*

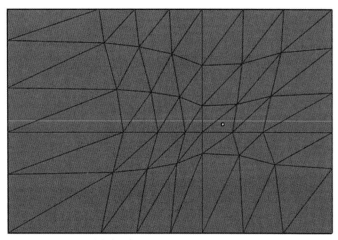

Exercise 7.2. 3D modeled surface with a parametric and algorithmically defined triangular grid. *Courtesy of the author.*

Use the triangulated pattern to create a second pattern that is offset inward. Use the Grasshopper Cull component to remove a defined or random selection of triangulated panels and the Grasshopper Offset component to offset the curves inward. (See Exercise 7.3.) The resulting pattern will be reflected in the preview model. (See Exercise 7.4.)

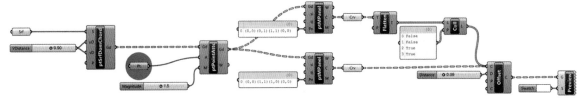

Exercise 7.3. Grasshopper definition used to create a nonuniform triangular grid and offset culled pattern using Paneling Tools. *Courtesy of the author.*

Exercise 7.4. 3D modeled surface with a triangular grid and culled set of curves offset inward. *Courtesy of the author.*

Bake the patterns to bring the previewed objects into the Rhino modeling space, and use 3D digital modeling techniques, such as translating, lofting, extruding, and so on, to create three-dimensional geometry and forms. Add additional side walls that are higher than the pattern geometry in order to create a 3D model that can be used as a mold. (See Exercise 7.5.) Export the digital model as an .stl file, which will create a mesh model. Use the .stl file to 3D-print the model out of ABS plastic. (See Exercise 7.5.) Create a cast from the 3D-printed ABS plastic mold using flexible and robust materials that can be released from the mold. In this example, Ecoflex 30 silicone, from the company Smooth-On, was mixed and poured into the mold to create a cast out of an elastomer material. (See Exercise 7.6.)

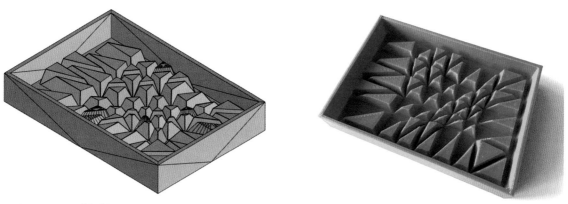

Exercise 7.5. 3D model of the pattern mold and the final 3D printed ABS plastic mold. *Courtesy of the author.*

Exercise 7.6. Silicone casts of the patterned module. *Courtesy of the author.*

Exercise 8: Drawing 3D Parametric and Algorithmic Patterns

This exercise builds off of the concepts and techniques presented in Exercise 1. In this process, a series of conical, developable surfaces are unrolled and patterned, and printed as templates for creating plastic structures fabricated with a 3Doodler pen and filament. This exercise utilizes parametric modeling techniques to develop three versions of a truncated cone, each with a unique geometric pattern that is generated through algorithmic design processes. This exercise advances one's ability to generate multiple versions of models using parametric modeling and fabrication techniques.

Begin by creating a parametric model of a cone that has a parametric pattern on the surface through the use of Grasshopper and Paneling Tools. (Refer to Chapter 13, Sections 13.1 and 13.2.) Unroll the surface and pattern, and draft additional linework to create a drawing that reflects similar techniques utilized in Exercise 1.3. This drawing will include multiple versions of truncated cones and patterns, and includes plans, elevations, and unrolled surfaces of the different versions. (See Exercise 8.1.) Plot the sheet and fabricate one version of the truncated cone out of one-ply museum or chipboard, with the plotted pattern adhered to the surface.

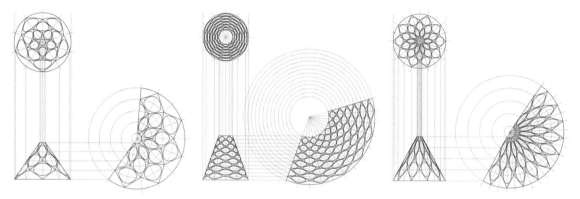

Exercise 8.1. A drawing of the top, side, and unrolled surface views for three versions of a parametric, panelized truncated cone. Drawing by Esty Deutsch. Instructor, Frank Melendez. The Bernard and Anne Spitzer School of Architecture, City College of New York. *Courtesy of the author.*

Similar to 3D printers, 3Doodler pens can be used to extrude ABS or PLA plastic filament through a heated nozzle. (See Exercise 8.2.) However, 3Doodler pens are analog hand-held instruments, similar to a regular pen or pencil, with the advantage of being able to "draw" in 3D with plastic.

Exercise 8.2. A 3Doodler pen.

Using a 3Doodler pen, trace over the pattern on the physical model, in order to extrude ABS plastic filament and fabricate the pattern as a physical, plastic print model. Plastic models can be created using the same or different color combinations of plastic filament. Once the pattern is completely drawn onto the template model, remove the plastic model from the template to view the pattern as a physical structure. (See Exercise 8.3.)

Exercise 8.3. Parametric Patterns, Plastic 3D Drawings, 2017, Plastic 3D drawings created by first-year undergraduate architecture students using 3Doodler pens to create structural patterns. Instructor, Frank Melendez. The Bernard and Anne Spitzer School of Architecture, City College of New York. *Courtesy of the author.*

Exercise 9: Environmental Simulation Drawings

This exercise introduces environmental simulation tools to evaluate the effects of daylighting on three-dimensional forms. Continuing with the stereotomic model created in Exercise 5, this process will use the visual-programming environmental simulation software Ladybug (for Grasshopper) to create a solar simulation and shadow analysis of the solid model. (Refer to Chapter 14, Section 14.2.)

Use various views of the stereotomic model and Ladybug components to visualize the solar paths, and the resulting shadows that are cast over a specified time period throughout the day, month, or year. These visualizations can be exported as raster images to create a composition of drawings. Additional linework and the solar path information can be exported and used to enhance the visualizations and drawings. (See Exercise 9.1.)

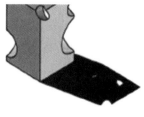

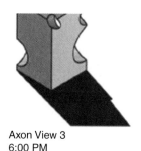

Axon View 1
12:00 PM

Axon View 2
3:00 PM

Axon View 3
6:00 PM

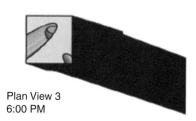

Plan View 1
12:00 PM

Plan View 2
3:00 PM

Plan View 3
6:00 PM

Exercise 9.1. Visualizations of the effects of daylighting on a 3D model using environmental simulation tools in Ladybug. Simulations produced by first-year undergraduate architecture students. Instructor, Frank Melendez. The Bernard and Anne Spitzer School of Architecture, City College of New York. *Courtesy of the author.*

Exercise 10: Drawing Machines

This exercise is intended to introduce concepts related to physical computing and robotics, by creating a computationally controlled drawing machine: a scissor-bot. The process of creating the drawing machine involves digital drafting, digital fabrication (laser cutting), text-based coding, and the use of physical computing technologies. This requires the use of an Arduino Uno microcontroller and two micro-servos to control the movements of the scissor mechanism.

Begin by connecting an Arduino Uno microcontroller to the USB port on a computer. (Refer to Chapter 15, Section 15.3.) Using a breadboard, connect the servo to the microcontroller using jumper wires. (See Exercise 10.1.) Open the Arduino IDE and open the code for controlling one servo. This can be found in the Arduino IDE drop-down menu: File > Examples > Servo > Sweep. This code controls the servo so that it rotates back and forth in a sweeping motion from 0 to 180 degrees. Upload the code to the Arduino microcontroller and verify that the servo is moving back and forth. Repeat this process using two servos and modifying the code to rotate both servos at different speeds.

318

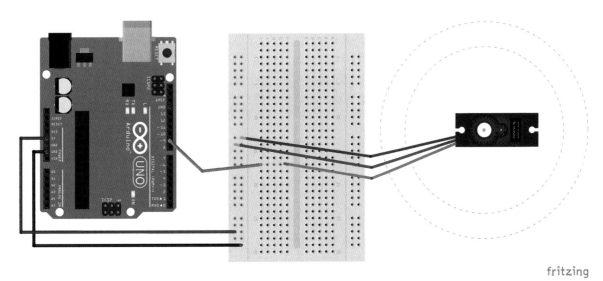

fritzing

Exercise 10.1. Wiring diagram: connecting a micro-servo to an Arduino Uno microcontroller through the use of a breadboard. Diagram created with Fritzing. *Courtesy of the author.*

Create a two-dimensional drawing of the parts necessary to create the scissor mechanism. This includes two disks (different sizes), two rings (equal in size), and four linear elements with small holes for screws to pass through and connect these pieces together. (See Exercise 10.2.) Draft the geometry in the Top viewport, constrained to the XY CPlane. Import the drawing into Adobe Illustrator and modify the line work to complete the drawing. This linework will be used for the toolpaths of the laser-cut file.

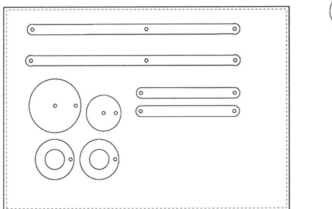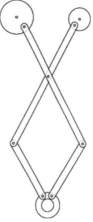

Exercise 10.2. Drawing of the separated scissor mechanism parts (left) and plan view of the assembled scissor mechanism. Students, Hannah Deegan and Zara Tampton. Instructor, Frank Melendez. The City College of New York, Bernard and Anne Spitzer School of Architecture. *Courtesy of the author.*

Laser-cut the pieces out of ⅛" acrylic and assemble them to create the scissor mechanism, with the each of the circular disks connected to each of the servos, and the two rings aligned at the end of the scissor mechanism. Place a pencil or pen through and attached to the rings. Space the servos apart from each other. Place a sheet of paper under the area where the pencil or pen is located. Connect the servos to the Arduino Uno microcontroller using a breadboard, and upload the code from the Arduino IDE to the microcontroller. When the servos are rotating, the scissor mechanism moves in a swaying motion, drawing a pattern on the paper. (See Exercise 10.3.) By changing the parameters in the code (for example, the angles of rotation and speed of rotation), different movements can be created, resulting in various type of patterns and drawings.

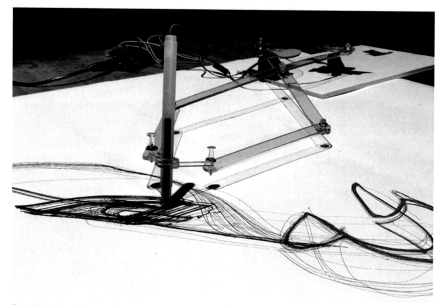

Exercise 10.3. Scissor bot drawing machine. Students, Hannah Deegan and Zara Tampton. Instructor, Frank Melendez. The Bernard and Anne Spitzer School of Architecture, City College of New York. *Courtesy of the author.*

Selected Bibliography

Akos, Gil, and Ronnie Parsons. *Foundations: Grasshopper Primer,* 3rd ed., http://grasshopperprimer.com/en/index.html?index.html.

Akos, Gil, and Ronnie Parsons. Mode Lab. "Intro to Grasshopper 08 | Phyllotaxis + Expressions." YouTube video, 21:08, filmed and posted August 2015. www.youtube.com/watch?v=hMx23t_3oMU.

Albers, Joseph. *Interaction of Color.* New Haven: Yale University Press, 1963.

Alberti, Leon Battista. *On Painting* (trans. John Spencer). New Haven: Yale University Press, 1966.

Aranda, Benjamin, and Chris Lasch. *Pamphlet Architecture 27: Tooling.* New York: Princeton Architectural Press, 2006.

Aukstakalnis, Steve. *Practical Augmented Reality: A Guide to the Technologies, Applications, and Human Factors for AR and VR.* New York: Pearson Education, Addison-Wesley, 2017.

Banzi, Massimo. *Make: Projects, Getting Started with Arduino,* 2nd ed. Sebastopol, CA: O'Reilly Media, 2011.

Bell, Simon. *Landscape: Pattern, Perception and Process.* New York: Routledge, 2012.

Bloomer, Kent. *The Nature of Ornament: Rhythm and Metamorphosis in Architecture.* New York: W.W. Norton & Company, 2000.

Bozdoc, Marian. "CAD Chronology: 1970–1989." *iMB: Resources and Information for Professional Designers.* http://mbinfo.mbdesign.net/CAD1970.htm.

Braitenberg, Valentino. *Vehicles: Experiments in Synthetic Psychology.* Cambridge, MA: MIT Press, 1984.

Brooks, Rodney. *Flesh and Machines: How Robots Will Change Us.* New York: Vintage Books, 2001.

Carpo, Mario. *The Alphabet and the Algorithm.* Cambridge, MA: MIT Press, 2011.

Carpo, Mario. "The Art of Drawing." *AD: Drawing Architecture,* Neil Spiller, guest ed.; Helen Castle, general ed. London: John Wiley & Sons, May 2013.

Chamot, Mary, Dennis Farr, and Martin Butlin. *The Modern British Paintings, Drawings and Sculpture.* London: Tate Gallery, 1964.

Ching, Francis D.K., and Steven P. Juroszek. *Design Drawing,* 2nd ed. Hoboken, NJ: John Wiley and Sons, 2010.

Christensson, Per. "Bit Definition." *TechTerms,* April 20, 2013, accessed Nov 15, 2017. https://techterms.com/definition/bit.

Christensson, Per. "Byte Definition." *TechTerms,* November 30, 2011, accessed Nov 15, 2017. https://techterms.com/definition/byte.

Christev, Daniel. "Grasshopper 10: Sine Functions." YouTube video, 10:11, filmed and posted January 2016. www.youtube.com/watch?time_continue=4&v=PKuZQhJhbbE.

Cook, Peter. *Drawing: The Motive Force of Architecture,* 2nd ed. West Sussex, UK: John Wiley & Sons, 2014.

Eastman, Chuck, Paul Teicholz, Rafael Sacks, and Kathleen Liston. *BIM Handbook: A Guide to Building Information Modeling for Owners, Managers, Designers, Engineers, and Contractors,* 2nd ed. Hoboken, NJ: John Wiley & Sons, 2011.

Emberton, Nathan. "Boolean." Computerhope.com, June 16, 2017, www.computerhope.com/jargon/b/boolean.htm.

Etherington, Rose. "Sinosteel International Plaza by MAD." *Dezeen,* July 30, 2008. www.dezeen.com/2008/07/30/sinosteel-international-plaza-by-mad/.

Farahi, Behnaz. "Aloplastic Architecture." *Arch 20,* www.arch2o.com/alloplastic-architecture-behnaz-farahi/.

Farin, Gerald, Josef Hoschek, and Myung-Soo Kim. *Handbook of Computer Aided Geometric Design.* Amsterdam: Elsevier Science B.V., 2002.

Ficca, Jeremy. "Material Resistance." *Matter: Material Processes in Architectural Production.* Gail Peter Borden and Michael Meredith, eds. New York: Routledge, 2012, pp. 343–355.

Frearson, Amy. "Lebbeus Woods: Early Drawings." *Deezen,* November, 2012. www.dezeen.com/2012/11/08/lebbeus-woods-early-drawings/.

Garber, Richard, guest ed. *Architecture Design: Closing the Gap-Information Models in Contemporary Design Practice.* London: John Wiley & Sons, March–April 2009.

Globa, Anastasia. "Fibonacci Spiral." Algorithmic Design in Architecture (blog), May 2015. http://parametric-design.blogspot.com/2015/05/fibonacci-spiral.html.

Gorbet, Rob. "Revealing the Hylozoic Ground Interaction Layer." *Hylozoic Ground: Liminal Responsive Architecture by Philip Beesley.* China: Riverside Architectural Press, 2010.

Imperiale, Alicia. *New Flatness: Surface Tension in Digital Architecture.* Basel, Boston, Berlin: Birkhäuser, 2000.

Issa, Rajaa. *Paneling Tools for Grasshopper.* Seattle: Robert McNeel & Associates, 2013.

Johnson, Jason Kelly, and Andrew Payne. *Firefly Primer.* 2011. www.scribd.com/document/101073066/Firefly-Primer-1006.

Iwamoto, Lisa. *Digital Fabrications: Architectural and Material Techniques.* New York: Princeton Architectural Press, 2009.

Kalay, Yehuda E. *Architecture's New Media: Principles, Theories, and Methods of Computer-Aided Design.* Cambridge, MA: MIT Press. 2004.

Kieren, Stephen, and James Timberlake. *Refabricating Architecture: How Manufacturing Methods Are Poised to Transform Building Construction.* New York: MacGraw Hill Companies, 2004.

Kolarevic, Branko. *Architecture in the Digital Age: Design and Manufacturing.* New York and London: Routledge, Taylor & Francis, 2005.

Krassenstein, Brian. "G3DP Project: Mediated Matter & MIT Glass Lab Develop Advanced Glass 3D Printer." 3DPrint.com, August 20, 2015. https://3dprint.com/90748/g3dp-glass-3d-print/.

Leach, Neil, guest ed. "Swarm Urbanism," *AD: Digital Cities* 79 (no. 4, July–August 2009), Helen Castle, general ed.

Lynn, Greg. *Animate Form.* New York: Princeton Architectural Press, 1999.

Langdon, David. "AD Classics: Yokohama International Passenger Terminal." ArchDaily.com, October 7, 2014. www.archdaily.com/554132/ad-classics-yokohama-international-passenger-terminal-foreign-office-architects-foa.

Libeskind, Daniel. *Daniel Libeskind: Countersign.* New York: Rizzoli International Publications, 1992.

Ma, Yidong, and Wieguo Xu. "Physarealm: A Bio-inspired Stigmergic Algorithm Tool for Form-Finding." In *Protocols, Flows and Glitches: Proceedings of the 22nd International Conference of the Association for Computer-Aided Design Research in Asia (CAADRIA) 2017,* Hong Kong, P. Janssen, P. Loh, A. Raonic, and M.A. Schnabel, eds., 499–509.

Mitchell, William J., and Malcolm McCullough. *Digital Design Media.* New York: Van Nostrand Reinhold, 1995.

Nettelbladt, Marten. The Geometry of Bending. http://thegeometryofbending.blogspot.com/.

Oliviera, Rui, and Jose Pedro Sousa. "Building Traditions with Digital Research: Reviewing the Brick Architecture of Raúl Hestnes Ferreira through Robotic Fabrication." *eCAADe 2016: Complexity and Simplicity: Proceedings of the 34th International Conference on Education and Research in Computer Aided Architectural Design in Europe,* Aulikki Herneoja, Toni Österlund, and Pia Markkanen, eds.

O'Sullivan, Dan, and Tom Igoe. *Physical Computing: Sensing and Controlling the Physical World with Computers.* Mason, OH: Course Technology, CENGAGE Learning, 2004.

Payne, Andrew. Grasshopper Primer, http://grasshopperprimer.com/en/index.html?index.html.

Pask, Gordon. "The Architectural Relevance of Cybernetics," *AD Reader: Computational Design Thinking,* Achim Menges and Sean Alquist, eds. London: John Wiley & Sons, 2011.

Peiffer, Jeanne. "Constructing perspective in sixteenth-century Nuremberg," *Perspectives, Projections, and Design: Technologies of Architectural Representation,* Mario Carpo and Frederique Lemerle, eds. New York and London: Routledge, Taylor and Francis Group, 2008.

Pickering, Andrew. *The Cybernetic Brain: Sketches of Another Future.* Chicago: University of Chicago Press, 2010.

Reas, Casey, and Ben Frye. "Environment IDE." Processing.org, accessed October 15, 2017. https://processing.org/reference/environment/.

Reas, Casey, and Ben Frye. "Integers Floats." Processing.org, accessed October 15, 2017. https://processing.org/examples/integersfloats.html.

Reas, Casey, and Chandler McWilliams. *Form + Code: In Design, Art, and Architecture.* New York: Princeton Architectural Press, 2010.

Rodeman, Patricia. "Psychology and Perception of Patterns in Architecture." *AD: Patterns of Architecture,* ed. Mark Garcia. (December 2009): 101–107.

Roncato, Sergio. "Piranesi and the Infinite Prisons." *Spatial Visions* 21 (no. 1–2): 3–18, Koninklijke, Brill, NV, Leiden.

Scheer, David Ross. *The Death of Drawing: Architecture in the Age of Simulation.* New York: Routledge, 2014.

Schubert, Howard. "Embryological House. *Origins of the Digital, Article 4, Canadian Center for Architecture.* www.cca.qc.ca/en/issues/4/origins-of-the-digital/5/embryological-house.

Schumacher, Patrik. "Parametricism: A New Global Style for Architecture and Urban Design." *AD: Digital Cities* 79 (no. 4, July–August 2009), Neil Leach, guest ed.; Helen Castle, general ed.

Sheldon, Dennis. "Information Modelling as a Paradigm Shift." *AD: Closing the Gap: Information Models in Contemporary Design Practice,* Richard Garber, guest ed. London: John Wiley & Sons, March–April 2009.

Shene, Ching-Kuang. "Finding a Point on a Bezier Curve: De Casteljau's Algorithm." Introduction to *Computing with Geometry Notes, Unit 5: Bezier Curves.* Houghton: Michigan Technological University, 1997–2014. http://pages.mtu.edu/~shene/COURSES/cs3621/NOTES/spline/Bezier/de-casteljau.html.

Stavric, Milena, Predrag Sidanin, and Bojan Tepavcevic. *Architectural Scale Models in the Digital Age: Design, Representation, and Manufacturing.* New York: Springer Wien, 2013.

Stern, Robert A.M., with Raymond W. Gastil. *Modern Classicism.* New York: Rizzoli International Publications, 1988.

Testa, Peter. *Robot House: Instrumentation, Representation, Fabrication.* New York: Thames & Hudson, 2017.

Townsend, Alastair. "On the Spline." In Jonathon Anderson and Meg Jackson, *International Journal of Interior Architecture + Spatial Design: Applied Geometries.* Houston: University of Houston, September 16, 2014.

Vitruvius Pollio. Marcus. *De architectura.* (*The Ten Books on Architecture,* trans. Morris Hickey Morgan). Chapter XVI, "Measures of Defence." Cambridge: Harvard University Press, 1914.

Wood, Lebbeus. "Libeskind's Machines." November 24, 2009. https://lebbeuswoods.wordpress.com/2009/11/24/libeskinds-machines/.

Young, Michael. "Essay: Drawing, Painting, Photography." *Economy* 14: All Visual. http://theeconomymagazine.com/ISSUE-14-MICHAEL-YOUNG-ESSAY-DRAWING-PAINTING-PHOTOGRAPHY-SYMMETRY.

INDEX